INTERPRETING ACROSS BOUNDARIES

INTERPRETING ACROSS BOUNDARIES

New Essays in Comparative Philosophy

EDITED BY
GERALD JAMES LARSON AND
ELIOT DEUTSCH

PRINCETON UNIVERSITY PRESS

Published by Princeton University Press, 41 William Street,
Princeton, New Jersey 08540
In the United Kingdom: Princeton University Press,
Guildford, Surrey

Library of Congress Cataloging in Publication Data will be
found on the last printed page of this book

ISBN 0-691-07319-8

Publication of this book has been aided by a grant from
the Paul Mellon Fund of Princeton University Press

This book has been composed in Linotron Bembo

Clothbound editions of Princeton University Press books
are printed on acid-free paper, and binding materials are
chosen for strength and durability. Paperbacks, although
satisfactory for personal collections, are not usually
suitable for library rebinding

Printed in the United States of America by
Princeton University Press,
Princeton, New Jersey

CONTENTS

PREFACE

In the summer of 1984 the Society for Asian and Comparative Philosophy (SACP) sponsored an international research conference for Asian and comparative philosophy in Honolulu, Hawaii, with the general theme "Interpreting Across Boundaries." The conference was funded by grants from the National Endowment for the Humanities, The Robert Maynard Hutchins Center for the Study of Democratic Institutions, The Rowny Foundation, the University of California at Santa Barbara, the University of Hawaii at Manoa, The East–West Center and the Institute for Philosophy and Religion (Boston). The conference was attended by 165 philosophers from some fourteen countries, including Australia, Austria, England, India, Israel, Japan, the People's Republic of China, and the United States. A narrative account of that conference together with abstracts from the proceedings have been published in the journal *Philosophy East and West* (volume 36, no. 2, April 1986).

The purpose of the conference was to examine critically the "state of the art" in comparative philosophy and to fashion some new research agendas for the future. In the twentieth century comparative philosophy developed in its present form, so it seemed appropriate to have an international research conference that, on one level, would assess where the field has been to date but, on another level, would project where it should be going as we approach the end of the century. Moreover, we were aware that it was still possible to include a number of senior philosophers who had been involved in the field throughout much of the century (for example, Wing-tsit Chan, Hajime Nakamura, and Charles Hartshorne, to name but a few).

Choosing a theme for the conference was something of a risk. We wanted to avoid focusing on any particular problem, tradition, figure, or method, any one of which would have prematurely foreclosed the sort of broad "state of the art" deliberations that we wanted to evoke. At the same time, we dreaded the "general call for papers" so typical of academic gatherings in the humanities, which allows participants to withdraw into their own eccentric (and frequently boring) specializations. In the final analysis, we decided to focus on the notion of "limit" but to do so in a metaphorical way: hence, the metaphor "boundary" and the general theme "Interpreting Across Boundaries." Use of such a metaphorical theme left open both the definition of "boundary" (whether cultural, religious, linguistic, epistemological, historical, disciplinary, or whatever) and the matter of "interpreting" or, in other words, the issue of "understanding" (hermeneutics). To change the metaphor, we endeavored to "let a hundred flowers bloom," the problems of weeds, birds, and crabgrass notwithstanding.

In any case, the risk appears to have been worth it, for the conference produced a variety of significant philosophical analyses and research proposals, most of which have been carefully summarized and reported in the number of *Philosophy East and West* cited before. Beyond that, however, there emerged a specific group of essays, derived directly or indirectly from the conference, that provide some intriguing insights into the future directions of comparative philosophy as a field and which we are characterizing in this volume as "new essays in comparative philosophy." These essays are sufficiently interesting and sufficiently indicative of new directions for comparative philosophy to deserve publication in their entirety as a collection. Not only are they the work of some of the leading comparativists of the century (and thus of historical interest) but also they represent an array of analytic and programmatic approaches to comparative philosophy that are symptomatic of a much more mature, sophisticated grasp of the comparative enterprise. Wilhelm Halbfass comments, in the January 1985 issue of *Philosophy East and West*, that " 'comparative philosophy' as an open-minded, methodically rigorous, hermeneutically alert, and yet existentially committed comparative study of human orientations is still in a nascent stage" (p. 14). This observation is surely reasonable and one to which all of us who "do" comparative philosophy would subscribe, and it is our hope that this volume will contribute significant insights by way of identifying those areas of productive growth which comparative philosophy should nurture.

Gerald James Larson
Eliot Deutsch

INTERPRETING ACROSS BOUNDARIES

GERALD JAMES LARSON

Introduction: The "Age-Old Distinction Between the Same and the Other"

I DRAW the title for my introductory remarks to this volume from the opening passage of Michel Foucault's *The Order of Things*. Says Foucault,

> This book first arose out of a passage in Borges, out of the laughter that shattered, as I read the passage, all the familiar landmarks of my thought—*our* thought, the thought that bears the stamp of our age and our geography—breaking up all the ordered surfaces and all the planes with which we are accustomed to tame the wild profusion of existing things, and continuing long afterwards to disturb and threaten with collapse our age-old distinction between the Same and the Other. This passage quotes "a certain Chinese encyclopaedia" in which it is written that "animals are divided into: (a) belonging to the Emperor, (b) embalmed, (c) tame, (d) sucking pigs, (e) sirens, (f) fabulous, (g) stray dogs, (h) included in the present classification, (i) frenzied, (j) innumerable, (k) drawn with a very fine camelhair brush, (l) *etcetera*, (m) having just broken the water pitcher, (n) that from a long way off look like flies." In the wonderment of this taxonomy, the thing we apprehend in one great leap, the thing that, by means of the fable, is demonstrated as the exotic charm of another system of thought, is the limitation of our own, the stark impossibility of thinking *that*.[1]

The passage is diagnostically interesting for comparative philosophy as a field for several reasons. First, the passage describes an encounter between a modern French intellectual and

[1] Michel Foucault, *The Order of Things: An Archaeology of the Human Sciences*, a translation of *Les Mots et les choses* (New York: Pantheon, 1971), p. xv.

an apparently old "Chinese encyclopaedia" that contains a taxonomy of "animals" that is, to say the least, somewhat unusual. Such encounters are routine in comparative philosophy as a field, and Foucault's reactions to the encounter are not unlike those of the comparative philosopher. Initially Foucault laughs at the taxonomy, but it is clear enough that he is also disturbed and threatened when he realizes that the taxonomy presents him with "the stark impossibility of thinking *that*." Second, the passage is interesting in the manner in which it presents us with an intriguing set of transmissions not unlike the sets of transmissions to which comparative philosophy must continually attend. Foucault found the taxonomy cited in the writings of José Luis Borges, an Argentinian poet, who writes in the medium of Spanish. The "Chinese" taxonomy, then, has been mediated through Spanish into French and finally appears in the English translation quoted above. One wonders what has happened in the process of transmission, a process not only involving translation into several languages but also mediated through divergent disciplinary perspectives (a poet, an intellectual historian, and so forth). That remarkable changes can occur in such a process is evidenced in the very English title of the book in which the passage occurs, namely *The Order of Things*, which is the English version of the French *Les Mots et les choses*! Third, and most interesting, however, the passage is finally *not* what it appears to be. There is, of course, no such "Chinese encyclopaedia." The passage is an invention, a fiction, a "fable" of a certain Latin American poet, Borges. To be sure, there are taxonomies in ancient Chinese and Japanese texts that organize, classify, and categorize items in the world in remarkably different ways from traditional or modern western taxonomies, but this particular taxonomy cited by Foucault is not one of them. One is dealing here with a poetic projection by a Latin American writer, who expresses his own doubts about notions of rational order in the guise of a "certain Chinese encyclopaedia." For the literalists and the fundamentalists among us, there is perhaps a tendency to dismiss the passage as a kind of hoax or at best a bad joke. Only if a "certain Chinese encyclopaedia" actually exists is there a comparative problem worth addressing. In many ways, however, the passage is even more powerful, even more threatening and disturbing, precisely because its referent is not what we initially thought it was. What appears as Other turns out to be an imaginary projection of what any one of us could have imagined—in other words, the Other becomes the Same. What appears as foreign turns out to be nothing more than what we think and imagine the foreign to be. But most disturbing, the content of the cited taxonomy, whether it be Other or the Same, whether it be "imagined" or "real," whether it be foreign or familiar, whether it be Spanish, French, English (or Chinese?), presents us with "the stark impossibility of thinking *that*." But what, finally, is "*that*"? Says Foucault, "the animals '(i) frenzied, (j) innumerable . . .'—where could they ever meet, except in the immaterial sound of the voice pronouncing their enumeration, or on the page transcribing it? Where else could they be juxtaposed except in the non-place of language?"[2]

Let me now juxtapose this passage from Foucault to the opening lines of Wing-tsit Chan's essay in the present volume:

> Let me begin by recalling the first East–West philosophers conference in 1939. It was a very small beginning. There were only five of us: Charles A. Moore, the organizer, and Filmore S. C. Northrop from Yale representing the West, George P. Conger of Minnesota representing India, Takakusu Junjirō, the eminent Buddhist scholar, representing Japan, and I, representing China. We dealt in generalities and superficialities and lumped Brahman, Tao, and Buddhist Thusness together. We hardly went beyond Spinoza in western philosophy and confined Chinese thought largely to the pre-Christian era. We saw the world as two halves, East and West.

On one level, one reacts to this passage with laughter not unlike the laughter of Foucault at reading the "Chinese" taxon-

[2] Ibid., pp. xvi–xvii.

omy. On another level, however, one is disturbed and threatened by "the stark impossibility of thinking *that*." The reference to 1939 leaps off the page as does the following sentence: "It was a very small beginning." Wing-tsit Chan, of course, is referring to the first East-West philosophers conference; but we are aware that on September 1, 1939 Hitler unleashed his Blitzkrieg into Poland, Japan had become a militarist state that was devouring China, and the British viceroy without consulting the Indian National Congress had declared India a participant in the incipient war. We are aware, furthermore, that two years later there was to be a devastating bombing attack on the very venue of the first East–West philosophers conference in which it had been decided that Brahman, Tao, and Buddhist Thusness could be "lumped together." Two kinds of East–West encounter were clearly occurring, and one can only marvel at their divergence, at "the stark impossibility of thinking *that*." One wishes that the first East–West philosophers conference in 1939 belonged to the same set as Foucault's "Chinese encyclopaedia," namely the null set of a poet's imagination, but the tragedy of our century is that it does not. That conference did take place, and more than that, it was one of the formative events for the beginning of comparative philosophy as a field. Indeed, we are the progeny of that conference.

From the perspective of intellectual history, comparative philosophy as a field has many more antecedents than the 1939 conference. Those antecedents reach as far back as the rationalism of the Enlightenment in the eighteenth century and its encounter with things oriental, but it is perhaps the Romanticist speculations of nineteenth-century European thought together with progress in nineteenth-century science that represent the most important antecedents of comparative philosophy. One thinks, for example, of comparative mythology, comparative religion, and comparative linguistics, many of which enterprises paralleled and applied the models of nineteenth-century natural science, especially the biological sciences.[3] There is also the progress in orientalism, which had begun already in the eighteenth century, and the emergence of modern historiography, intellectual pursuits of the nineteenth century that sought to make sense of the spread of European political and economic institutions throughout the world.[4] Furthermore, there is the remarkable work in the nascent fields of anthropology, ethnology, ethnography, and sociology. Interestingly, the most prominent names for the antecedents of serious comparative work are primarily from the sciences and social sciences, including Comte, Darwin, Marx, Müller, Tylor, Dilthey, Frazer, Freud, Jung, Durkheim, Weber, and the like.

A somewhat embarrassing lacuna among the antecedents of comparative philosophy in the nineteenth century is, ironically enough, philosophy itself. Apart from the work of Hegel and Schopenhauer, there is hardly anything worth mentioning, and alas, even the work of Hegel and Schopenhauer is hardly worth mentioning. The latter's exuberant affirmation

[3] For recent discussions of the European intellectual background of comparative philosophy, see Wilhelm Halbfass, *Indien und Europa* (Basel and Stuttgart: Schwabe, 1981), especially pp. 70–188, and a shorter summary treatment of the same material in Wilhelm Halbfass, "India and the Comparative Method," *Philosophy East and West* 35.1 (1985): 3–15. Halbfass only deals with material pertinent to the encounter with India, and there is an emphasis overall on orientalism and philosophical hermeneutics. For useful discussions of the European background in terms of the social sciences and such areas as comparative religion, comparative mythology, and comparative linguistics, see Eric Sharpe, *Comparative Religion: A History* (London: Duckworth, 1975), pp. 27–250; Gerald J. Larson, "The Study of Mythology and Comparative Mythology," in *Myth in Indo-European Antiquity*, ed. Gerald J. Larson (Berkeley: University of California Press, 1974), pp. 1–16; and Jan de Vries, *The Study of Religion, a Historical Approach*, trans. Kees W. Bolle (New York: Harcourt, Brace and World, 1967), pp. 61–188.

[4] For useful discussions of orientalism and the history of historical writing, see Edward Said, *Orientalism* (New York: Random House, 1979), passim; David Kopf, *British Orientalism and the Bengal Renaissance* (Berkeley: University of California Press, 1969), pp. 127ff.; H. E. Barnes, *A History of Historical Writing*, 2d ed. (repr. New York: Dover, 1962), passim; and, of course, R. G. Collingwood, *The Idea of History* (New York: Oxford University Press, 1959; first English ed. 1946), pp. 86–133.

of matters non-European is clearly a case for the psychoanalyst, and the former's exuberant rejection of matters non-European is symptomatic of the tragedy of the modern West that continues to act itself out even now as we approach the end of the twentieth century. That tragedy is one of naïveté posing as sophistication, the sad specter of the intellectual who seriously believes that the cultures, languages, and traditions of the non-European world have been or could be "assimilated" (*aufgehoben*) or surpassed—or both—through the historical experience of the modern West. We are back with a vengeance to "the stark impossibility of thinking *that*"; and yet, strange as it may seem, many still believe the Hegelian myth or one of its many Anglo-Saxon variants. Philosophy as a field still harbors many, possibly a majority, who think that serious philosophizing has occurred only in the West, and who dismiss non-European modes of thinking along with most of the western metaphysical tradition prior to Kant as abstract nonsense, or to use the contemptuous idiom of Hegel, as "the night in which . . . all cows are black."[5] One is tempted to respond in kind and comment that the Hegelian legacy, at least in its handling of non-European traditions, has turned out to be little more than "the day in which all cows became Prussian," and that the sunset of that day has yet to occur in Europe or North America. One can only hope that when the Owl of Minerva spreads her wings on the evening of that day, a truly sophisticated and mature philosophizing will emerge for the century that is to come.

In any case, whether one looks to the first East–West philosophers conference of 1939 or to the intellectual achievements of nineteenth-century European thought for the antecedents

[5] The fuller passage in Hegel is as follows: "To pit this single assertion, that 'in the Absolute all is One,' against the organized and whole of determinate and complete knowledge, or of knowledge which at least aims at and demands complete development—to give out its Absolute as the night in which, as we say, all cows are black—that is the very *naïveté* of emptiness of knowledge." See G.W.F. Hegel, *The Phenomenology of Mind*, trans. J. B. Baillie (London: Allen & Unwin, 1910), p. 79.

of comparative philosophy, the picture that emerges is hardly a happy one. With the former, there is utter, albeit well-meant naïveté. With the latter, there is disguised, and hence much more dangerous, naïveté. With regard to both, there is hardly any point in regretting the history of comparative philosophy. One takes solace, if solace be needed, in the words of Wittgenstein. What he said about any "system of communication" can surely be said about the history of comparative philosophy:

> It is not based on grounds.
> It is not reasonable (or unreasonable).
> It is there like our life.[6]

The title of this collection of essays is *Interpreting Across Boundaries: New Essays in Comparative Philosophy*. The use of the adjective "new" is important, for what comes through in all of the essays in this volume is that the metaphor of "boundary" is being construed by the contributors in a variety of new ways. Put somewhat differently, there appears to be a discernible break in these essays with some older conventional notions of what comparative philosophy represents. If one reads, for example, back issues of the journal *Philosophy East and West* or the various volumes that have emerged from the East–West philosophers conferences, there are certain presuppositions, or perhaps biases, that are clearly evident, five of which are especially notable: a tendency to favor disciplinary boundaries that separate philosophy from religion, art, literature, law, science, and other cognitive pursuits; a tendency to favor philosophical boundaries of European thought since Descartes for identifying conceptual problems in general; a tendency to favor large, holistic boundaries of language, culture, and history; a tendency to treat conceptual systems as "entities" or "things" that can be externally compared; and a tendency to favor similarities in comparative work while ignoring or glossing over differences. Each of these tendencies is seriously

[6] Ludwig Wittgenstein, *On Certainty*, trans. D. Paul and G.E.M. Anscombe (New York: J. and J. Harper, 1969), p. 73.

called into question in the essays collected in this volume, and a useful way of introducing these new essays is to exhibit the manner in which these presuppositions or biases are now being challenged.

A tendency to favor disciplinary boundaries that separate philosophy from religion, art, literature, law, science, and other cognitive pursuits: Because of the history of the modern university's heuristic and academic divisions from which comparative philosophy (and philosophy) derives, it is surely no accident that comparative work takes its point of departure by way of looking for counterparts or comparable cognitive undertakings in other contexts. Moreover, in view of European dominance over the cultures of Asia, Africa, and the Americas since the middle of the eighteenth century, it is likewise no accident that non-European intellectuals begin to absorb or assimilate European categories, taxonomies, and divisions, and more than that, to retroject these same categories, taxonomies, and divisions into their own indigenous traditions. *Mirabile visu*, there emerges an Indian "philosophy," a Chinese "philosophy," a Japanese "philosophy," and so forth. *Mirabile dictu*, non-European intellectuals begin the apologetic we-have-philosophy-too refrain, and a dialogue of sorts commences, replete with a European hermeneutic of historical-critical research, isms, scholarly translations, and elaborate morphologies, and a non-European hermeneutic of perennial wisdom, detachment, harmony with nature, and the sanctity of the guru or the *chün-tzu*. As Ninian Smart wryly points out in his essay, however, there is a "messy lack of fit" in our modern academic distinctions, and furthermore, "if the categorization of Indian philosophy is traditionally a bit of a mess, so is it in western philosophy." The seemingly clean divisions that isolate philosophy in European traditions from other cognitive domains in the modern academy are, in fact, murky, ambiguous, and frequently little more than political. In non-European contexts—other than those which self-consciously imitate the confusions of the European tradition—such divisions do not exist; or, put somewhat less polemically, cognitive pursuits are divided in interestingly different ways. Overall there has been a tendency to assume that the European notion of philosophy as a distinct cognitive pursuit has some sort of universal validity and to overlook or ignore the largely historical origins of philosophy in European traditions. As a result, the search for "philosophy" in non-European traditions has been a distortion from the beginning. Hajime Nakamura's essay in the present collection addresses this issue, and he argues that the notions of "philosophy" and "religion" need to be carefully reexamined and reinterpreted from the perspective of what he calls "a broadly based cross-cultural cognitive anthropology." Similarly, Daya Krishna in his contribution argues for a comparative enterprise that takes seriously the differences in "alternative conceptual structures," a comparative philosophizing that focuses on "problems perceived and solutions attempted" even if the problems and solutions range far beyond the limits of "philosophy" as construed in the European heritage. The point here is not only that we distort non-European traditions in our search for some sort of universal "philosophy" but, more than that, we distort the European heritage itself. Again in Smart's words, there is a "messy lack of fit" in our attempts to separate "philosophy" from other cognitive pursuits, and an important agenda item for the future is a critical appraisal of this separation.

A tendency to favor philosophical boundaries of European thought since Descartes for identifying conceptual problems in general: This tendency is, clearly, a corollary of the first presupposition or bias, but it refers more to comparative philosophy's content than to its form. In other words, the comparative enterprise has not only been loaded from the beginning by the disciplinary separation of "philosophy" from other cognitive pursuits, it has also been loaded by the selection of conceptual problems for comparative analysis. Agenda items for comparative philosophizing have been selected from ethics, epistemology, philosophy of language, and so forth, and the framework for discussions has been built from "concept clusters" that make sense in one speech environment but may miss the mark in others. Karl H. Potter in his essay, for example, points out that the notion of Karma in a South Asian context depends on a specific metaphor of "making," and that, therefore, problems in the philosophy of mind in a South Asian environment are dramatically different from those in a western environment. He proposes a research program for identifying key metaphors within conceptual schemes and for determining "principles of individuation for conceptual schemes" both within and between cultures. He argues that "boundaries" between languages and cultures may not be as important or as difficult as the "boundaries" between metaphors among and within speech environments. Says Potter: "The question becomes: what are the boundaries we should be interested in, and what are the related categories or kinds, instances of which are going to be compared and contrasted?" Henry Rosemont in his contribution likewise speaks about "conceptual frameworks" or "concept clusters" and the need for careful articulation of "alternative conceptual frameworks." Both Potter and Rosemont reject the bias of a philosophical agenda that emphasizes "universals," but at the same time, it should be noted, they also reject the conceptual and ontological relativism of a Quine. Rosemont in his essay "Against Relativism" quarrels vigorously with radical conceptual relativism and proposes, instead, a research program for identifying what he calls "homoversals" (in contrast to "universals") in such cognitive areas as grammar, aesthetics, and others.

Other essays in the collection echo similar concerns for reworking the agenda of comparative philosophy to move away from the manner in which problems have been construed in modern western philosophy since the time of Descartes. Raimundo Panikkar, for example, calls for an "imparative philosophy," from the Latin *imparare*, in the sense of "learning" in an environment of "pluralism." Frits Staal in his essay "Is There Philosophy in Asia?" suggests a philosophical agenda derived from ritual and grammar à la much South Asian thought.

A tendency to favor large, holistic boundaries of language, culture, and history: What is meant by this presupposition or bias is the inclination in comparative philosophy toward what might be called premature totalization, or in other words, glossing over myriad differences for the sake of attaining a single form. Books have been written, for example, about the "Chinese mind," the "Indian mind," and so forth. Broad comparisons have been drawn between the Chinese language and Sanskrit, or Greek, or Latin, or modern European languages. The dichotomy of "ancient" versus "modern" and the dichotomy of "tradition" versus "modernity" are common in the field. Moreover, there is a notable bias in favor of the great or "classical" wholes: China, Japan, India, western Europe, and so forth. But if one refers to the "Indian mind," for example, what precisely is the referent: Vedic ritualism, the classical *darśanas*, *bhakti* spirituality, Sanskrit poetry, Indian vernacular literature, Gandhi, Subhās Chandra Bose, a ricksha wallah in Varanasi? As one begins to specify that about which one is speaking, such large, holistic characterizations begin to disappear.

According to Foucault in *The Archaeology of Knowledge*, the primary reason for premature totalization is that it provides "a privileged shelter for the sovereignty of consciousness."[7] Says Foucault,

> Continuous history is the indispensable correlative of the founding function of the subject: the guarantee that everything that has eluded him may be restored to him; the certainty that time will disperse nothing without restoring it in a reconstituted unity; the promise that one day the subject—in the form of historical consciousness—will once again be able to appropriate, to bring back under his sway, all those things that are kept at a distance by difference, and find in them what might be called his abode. . . .
>
> In various forms, this theme has played a constant role since the nineteenth century: to preserve, against all decen-

[7] Michel Foucault, *The Archaeology of Knowledge*, trans. A. M. Sheridan Smith (New York: Harper & Row, 1972), p. 12.

> terings, the sovereignty of the subject, and the twin figures of anthropology and humanism.[8]

Quite apart from whether one wishes to go as far as Foucault and the poststructuralists in the direction of "difference," there is a valid issue here for comparative philosophy. In Potter's idiom referred to earlier, "what are the boundaries we should be interested in?" Is there not a need to draw away from large, holistic boundaries and to focus attention on important differences within "concept clusters" or "conceptual frameworks"? Many of the essays gathered here do precisely this. Eliot Deutsch, Frits Staal, Ninian Smart, and Sengaku Mayeda focus this attention primarily on important differences that manifest themselves in a South Asian environment. Deutsch examines the distinctive "tradition-text" complex that operates in Indian thought. Staal analyzes the details of ritual in South Asia and the relation between ritual and grammatical analysis. Smart calls attention to the polarity of "horizontal contextuality" versus "vertical contextuality" in the Indian *darśana*s. Mayeda examines the process of "vedantinization" and the manner in which the low-caste movement of Nārāyaṇa Guru appropriates high-caste Vedanta. In a similar fashion the essays of Wing-tsit Chan, Roger Ames, A. S. Cua, and Wm. Theodore de Bary do much the same sort of specifying within an East Asian environment. Wing-tsit Chan outlines the remarkable progress in Chu Hsi studies in recent years and the manner in which comparative philosophy is getting a much firmer grasp of the substance of Neoconfucian thought. Roger Ames does much the same thing in terms of Chinese ontology. A. S. Cua focuses on the distinction between "moral tradition" and "moral theory" in the Chinese environment. Wm. Theodore de Bary examines the dichotomy of "traditional" and "modern" in a Chinese Neoconfucian environment and concludes with the interesting observation that "The real problem today is not parochialism. It is the lack of any parochialism, the lack of any loyalty or sense of responsibility to a particular com-

[8] Ibid.

munity, which has created the severe problems of dissociation in our times. What we need is not new worlds to conquer, star wars, and all that, but a *new parochialism of the earth*." To some extent, to be sure, the focus in these essays on the specifics within a tradition is not as much philosophically motivated as it is symptomatic of the remarkable progress in knowledge that has been occurring over the past several decades with regard to non-European traditions. There is no question, however, but that the large, holistic boundaries of earlier comparative philosophy are gradually being set aside. At the same time, moreover, this volume also contains the intriguing essay of Ben-Ami Scharfstein entitled "The Contextual Fallacy," warning that "an extreme emphasis on context can be unreasonable" and that more attention needs to be paid to the processes of "contextualization," "decontextualization," and "recontextualization." In any case, it is clear enough from the volume as a whole that there is a healthy discussion unfolding within comparative philosophy about the "boundaries we should be interested in" and how we go about formulating boundaries.

A tendency to treat conceptual boundaries as "entities" or "things" that can be externally compared: This presupposition or bias, more so than the others already mentioned, is clearly a result of the intellectual immaturity and the historical naïveté of comparative philosophizing in its early ventures. We have all been implicated in its temptations, and in spite of its limitations, there have been at least some heuristic benefits. I am referring, of course, to the endless articles and books in our field of the type "Śaṅkara and Bradley," "Kant and Nāgārjuna," "Aquinas and Chu Hsi," ad nauseam, wherein a conceptual system is treated as a spatialized "thing" and set down alongside another conceptual system so that the two may be compared and contrasted. As already indicated, there is some heuristic benefit from time to time in such an exercise by way of identifying some interesting problems; but overall the exercise is mechanical, one-dimensional, forced, anachronistic, and worst of all, tedious. The present collection of essays is a refreshing departure from such old-style comparative philosophizing. To be sure, Frederick Streng's essay in the present volume appears on the surface to be such an external comparison, but it becomes apparent immediately that Streng is precisely calling the technique into question. He argues, instead, that an external comparison between Jung and the Perfection of Wisdom tradition misses what is really important in the two traditions within their respective contexts, namely, remarkably divergent notions of egoity and intentionality.

A tendency to favor similarities in comparative work while ignoring or glossing over differences: This presupposition or bias, like the former one, is largely a product of the field's immaturity, but perhaps more than that, also a product of what might be called a misplaced civility. Regarding the latter point, it is not uncommon, for example, at gatherings of comparative philosophers for there to be a remarkable cordiality across cultural lines (among, say, the Chinese, Japanese, Indian, and European or American participants) and an equally remarkable animosity within a national group (for example, among the Chinese participants, among the Indian participants, or among the American participants). It is as if polemic or invective were reserved for one's own kind, while an irenic accentuation of positive similarities is asserted cross-culturally. Such a posture is of course, as we all are aware, the mirror reversal of the manner in which our various traditions have interacted with one another historically, and one can only wonder why in the context of intellectual exchange a kind of psychological repression of what one really thinks and feels is allowed to operate. One would imagine that the arena of comparative philosophy would be what Habermas has called "an ideal speech situation" in which the genuine differences between us could be honestly expressed. The forces of power, domination, resentment, racism, inferiority, prejudice, and a host of other human characteristics are very much a part of our world views, ideologies, philosophies, and conceptual frameworks, but they receive almost no attention whatever. The point here is not to assert that comparative philosophy should become a shouting match between opposing conceptual systems but simply to suggest that the premature assertion of similarity may be an insidious form of self-deception and the glossing over of important differences in the name of civility may, in fact, be the worst kind of uncivilized behavior. Hegel in one of his better moments called attention to the "dark" side of history, and we would perhaps do well as comparative philosophers to look a bit more honestly at the "dark" side of philosophizing, at the fundamental differences that divide us, at the resentments that fester because of inequities in economic circumstance, political domination, and historical accident. There is more than enough shame to go around on all sides, but there is also, I suspect, a tremendous reservoir of goodwill and courage to tap should we finally begin to deal with our differences in an honest way.

In the present volume there are some hints here and there along the lines of dealing with serious differences. Charles Hartshorne, for example, takes issue with the "fallacy of misplaced symmetry" in much of classical Asian philosophizing and the tendency toward "spatialized time" in Śaṅkara, Nāgārjuna, and Fa Tsang; and he expresses his general dissatisfaction with the "negative way," whether in European or Asian philosophical reflection. Daya Krishna from a quite different perspective takes issue with philosophizing that takes its standards from the West, that caricatures Indian thought as simply the quest for *mokṣa*, that deals with non-European traditions as "objects" and neglects to notice that much of its agenda grows out of the vicissitudes of political and economic power. The volume as a whole, indeed the field of comparative philosophy, would be much stronger if differences such as these could be pursued in a more vigorous and polemical manner. Overall, however, it is perhaps fair to say that the field is approaching the threshold of such exchanges and in that sense it is correct to characterize the contributions of this volume as *new* essays in comparative philosophy.

FINALLY, some comments about the order of the essays in this collection and about the structure of the volume as a whole. For reasons I have already mentioned, we have deliberately avoided some of the conventional "boundaries" or subdivisions that one might expect in a volume on comparative philosophy—for example, regional subdivisions such as India, China, Japan, and so forth, or western-style thematic subdivisions such as epistemology, ontology, ethics, and so forth. Instead, we have established a somewhat looser framework along the lines of "theory"and "praxis." The essays in the first half of the volume—those of Potter, Rosemont, Krishna, Scharfstein, Hartshorne, Panikkar, Nakamura, and Streng—take up general, theoretical issues having to do with comparative philosophy as an intellectual enterprise in search of new and more sophisticated perspectives. Among these more purely theoretical discussions, those of Potter and Rosemont are especially innovative and, more than that, propose concrete research programs for new kinds of theoretical work; hence, they are placed first as keynote presentations for the theoretical section of the volume. The essays in the second half of the volume—those of Deutsch, Smart, Mayeda, Staal, Chan, Ames, Cua and de Bary—take up comparative issues within specific cultural contexts and reveal some of the practical implications that a more sophisticated comparative philosophizing generates. To be sure, the essays in the second half refer primarily to specific regions (Deutsch, Smart, Mayeda, and Staal to South Asian traditions, and Chan, Ames, Cua and de Bary to East Asian traditions), but it should be noted that the regions are not in themselves the primary focus. The focus, rather, is on the manner in which research within a region can be appropriated and assimilated in terms of a broader, comparative enterprise that seeks critically to transcend older approaches to comparative work. To put the matter somewhat differently, the task of the new comparative philosophizing is to get away from talking *to* one another (along the lines of the tedious descriptivism of specialists) in favor of talking *with* one another (the type of critical and provocative interaction that occurs when specialists step away from their expertise and encounter one another as human beings). The essays in the second half of the volume represent, in our view, important steps in this new direction.

KARL H. POTTER

Metaphor as Key to Understanding the Thought of Other Speech Communities

ALL SORTS of people are continually attempting to interpret across boundaries. Whenever we go abroad we perforce get engaged in the enterprise. But likewise, we do so whenever we speculate on what an author we are reading meant. For that matter, we do so whenever we engage in conversation with one another, for the boundaries between what I intend and what you understand are just as much boundaries as the cultural and historical ones. And just as we know what it is to get clearer about what our neighbor is saying just now, we know what it is to get clearer about what people of other times and/or other cultures were and are saying.

I make these banal remarks in anticipation of an argument that might appear to show that no interpretation across boundaries is possible. We know that such interpretation is possible; and yet there is a line of thought pioneered mainly by Quine that may seem to preclude any such knowledge.[1] More precisely, it seems to refute the supposition that any methodology might be devised that would (beyond a certain point) enable us to interpret across boundaries in such a way as to achieve uniquely correct interpretations.

The argument I have in mind goes like this:

(1) Successful interpretation across boundaries requires that the meanings of sentences (utterances, speech acts) on one side of a boundary be uniquely equated with the meanings of sentences (utterances, speech acts) on the other side.

[1] See especially Willard Van Orman Quine, *Word and Object* (Cambridge, Mass.: M.I.T. Press, 1960), chap. 2.

(2) Unique equation of meanings across boundaries requires the use of analytical hypotheses.
(3) Use of analytical hypotheses involves indeterminacy of translation. So,
(4) Unique equation of the meanings of sentences (utterances, speech acts) across boundaries requires determinacy of translation. So,
(5) Successful interpretation across boundaries requires what it precludes, viz., determinacy of translation. So,
(6) Successful interpretation across boundaries is impossible.

One could give the message of this argument by saying that if interpretation across boundaries is possible it is so only in an indeterminate way, that is, that one should not hope for any precise method of interpretation. This statement in turn leads to the conclusion that such enterprises as history of philosophy, cultural anthropology, and comparative philosophy, along with the enterprise of translation, must be viewed as at best creative rather than descriptive in nature, that viewing them as "scientific" in method is a mistake, that there is no generalizable procedure for achieving precision in these fields.

Such a conclusion, if left there, leaves us with no way to explain of what successful interpretation across boundaries consists. If any interpretation is as successful as any other, or if anything that relates items across boundaries in some way or another is going to count as a successful interpretation, we are left without any canons of criticism to apply to such interpretations, and one can have no reason to appeal to any one of them for any systematic purposes other than, perhaps, amusement. In short, if this argument is allowed to stand the activities of practitioners of a good many disciplines are going to have to be viewed in a far different way than they expect us to view them. We should not consult historians for understanding what people in the past actually meant; we should not consult anthropologists for understanding what people in other cultures actually intend; we should not consult comparative philosophers for understanding what philosophers writing in other languages mean or meant to say; and we must take translations as fantasies.

Quine's thesis is about translation. A segment *P* of an investigator's home language *H* is said to be a *translation* of a segment *T* of some language *L* when it is true to say that the behavior occasioned by the utterance of *T* in *L* is similar to the behavior occasioned by the utterance of *P* in *H*. An *analytical hypothesis* in *H*, to the effect that *P* translates *T*, has the form "the behavior occasioned by the utterance of *T* in *L* is similar to the behavior occasioned by the utterance of *P* in *H*." Quine's thesis of the indeterminacy of translation is that it is not generally the case that only one analytical hypothesis is the correct one. But Quine does not say that translation is impossible. Certain utterances—of observation sentences, truth functions, stimulus-analytic sentences—can be translated or at least "recognized" for what they are. Quine's point is rather that, though the meanings of these sorts of utterances can be uniquely correlated with their translations across boundaries, such utterances make up only a small part of our linguistic output, and the constraints their translations place upon the possible analytical hypotheses about the remainder of the utterances to be translated are insufficient to determine any particular hypothesis among its rivals as being the correct one.

Nothing in the foregoing formulations requires that the boundaries in question lie between different languages, different cultures, or different times. What Quine has in mind as boundaries are those between "conceptual schemes," a notion with a notoriously vague principle of individuation. You and I, both being speakers of English, share a conceptual scheme at one level of analysis, but at another level you, being a physicalist, and I, being a mentalist, differ in our conceptual schemes. The latter difference may constitute a boundary; that is, it may dictate that you and I mean different things by our talk about minds, just as the linguist and the native may mean different things by their talk about *gavagais* (the linguist, say, meaning rabbits and the native meaning rabbit parts). To the extent that two speakers share the same conceptual scheme, categorize the world in the same manner—to that extent the meanings of their utterances may be similar and known to be so. Indeterminacy of translation is relative to the extent to which translator and translated share the same conceptual scheme.

If that is true one may well wonder why *linguistic* boundaries in particular are supposed to thwart understanding. If one can successfully interpret utterances within a shared conceptual scheme (allowing it to be a relative sort of success, relative to the level at which the conceptual schemes are deemed shared), why is it impossible that two speakers of different languages should share a conceptual scheme at some level or other? The evidence for successful interpretation is similarity of behavior, including nonlinguistic as well as linguistic behavior. We have been, without realizing it, assuming that difference in language does not merely constitute a possible kind of boundary, but in fact necessarily indicates difference in conceptual scheme. Such an assumption explains why Quine finds translating a problem. But difference in language is only one way to characterize the possible differences between the conceptual schemes of Jones, a twentieth-century American, and Devadatta, a fifth-century Indian. Who decided that it is a relevant difference?

The Quinian argument I offered is now seen to be an instance of a more general argument. The Quinian argument had to do with translation across linguistic boundaries. The broader argument would have to specify that successful interpretation across any boundaries requires the equation of something or other with something else of the same kind, so that some sort of conceptual scheme is shared. What kind that is depends in a particular inquiry on which boundaries we have in mind. The question becomes: what are the boundaries we should be interested in, and what are the related categories or kinds, instances of which are going to be compared and contrasted?

Just as there is, in the Quinian view, no absolute distinction between analytic and synthetic statements, so there should be, in his view, no absolute distinction between any categories. No boundaries should necessarily determine boundaries between different conceptual schemes. The determining considerations that dictate relative judgments concerning greater or less similarity of conceptual systems must stem from practical considerations. It depends how much these or those categories or boundaries matter to me, or to you, or to me and you jointly. Still, despite this relativistic stance on categories and boundaries, the Quinian view still takes scientific method very seriously. There is no incompatibility between a relativism of categories and boundaries and a science involving those categories and boundaries.

The Quinian view, as is well known, is a species of holism. Indeterminacy of translation is only a difficulty if the wrong units of analysis of conceptual schemes are chosen, the wrong units of analysis for the purposes intended. What enables us to interpret across boundaries is the overlapping of entire conceptual systems. But that overlapping cannot be easily analyzed into the relationship among parts of the schemes, because the understanding—the mutual interpretability—arises from the relations between the wholes and is frustrated by assumed boundaries among the parts. The problem of dealing with the Quinian way of thinking is to know how to study the whole without studying the parts. A "scientific" method for the disciplines under consideration—history of thought, cultural anthropology, comparative philosophy—needs to be pitched in terms of entire schemes that are specifically *not* to be thought of as determined by their parts.

Historians of thought tend to assimilate or to distinguish the thought of persons of the past from the thought of those of the present on the basis of the meanings of what they said and wrote, meanings determined by the presumed meanings of the component segments—words and sentences—of their discourse. Cultural anthropologists compare and contrast the specific pieces of behavior elicited in one culture by determinate stimuli with pieces of behavior elicited in another culture by the same determinate stimuli. Comparative philosophers compare and contrast the specific categories used by one philosopher with the specific categories used by another. In each case difference in conceptual system is *assumed* by the investigator, and differences between persons, cultures, or philosophers is thus made to fit differences in meanings of segments, pieces of behavior, and specific categories. In truth, the choice of boundaries across which to compare is the same choice as that among categories of investigation; as we saw, it is the practical concerns of the investigator which ultimately dictate these boundaries, they are not absolutely there to be discovered in the material investigated. If the categories chosen are too precise—calling attention to the parts rather than the wholes, and so creating a priori boundaries and the resulting indeterminacy—the requisite methodology would seem to be one that moves to categories not so dependent on the precise values of their components. Precision is a valued requirement in mathematical sciences, where the very point is to draw as many distinctions as possible. Not all sciences, however, are mathematical. Comparative philosophy, along with translation, history of thought, and cultural anthropology, are nonmathematical sciences in which too much precision obscures rather than furthers the inquiry.

FOR a number of years I have been associated with an effort to understand clearly what the notion of Karma means in Indian thought. Assisted by the Joint Committee of the ACLS-SSRC on South Asia, a number of us gathered in October 1976 to lay out a research agenda for this project. Included in the group were a number of native speakers of Indian languages, who kept insisting that what the word *karman* means is "action." The trouble was that the rest of us were not sure what "action" meant, and furthermore we were not sure that our Indian colleagues were using the term in the ways we supposed they might be. We were, that is, making analytical hypotheses, and the indeterminacy of translation was evident enough to us.

The project wound its way over time. Panels were held, papers read and printed, entire volumes published.[2] Lots of People had lots to say about Karma, much of it unconnected with what others had said and were saying. The project was sponsored by the joint committee as part of an entire research thrust oriented around the use of indigenous categories in the study of South Asian culture. Karma, we were sure, was such a category. But having decided that, nobody seemed able to or willing to figure out what category—what kind of category—it was.

The project has now worn down and dissipated. Just before it died, I had a sudden insight (I think it is an insight). Whereas the English word 'action' means various, though not all sorts of doings, it occurred to me that in context in Sanskrit philosophical works the use of words stemming from the root *kṛ* carries with it a series of expectations which are not the expectations we have when we hear the word 'act' or 'action' in English. They are much more like the expectations we have when we hear the word 'make'.

It came to seem to me that when a Sanskrit writer or speaker uses words stemming from *kṛ* he expects his hearer to associate a certain range of things with what is being referred to. To "make," that is, to *kṛ* something is to construct something. Furthermore, it is to take up those materials with a desire, an intention to produce something that will serve a certain function. I make a cake to eat, make a house to live in, make noises to be heard. So making carries with it the implication of a result that is intended by the maker to be useful to someone for some purpose. Frequently, though not always, the someone for whom one's making is useful is just oneself; sometimes one makes things for others' consumption. Arguably, whenever

[2] Two volumes emanating from the project have so far been published by the University of California Press. The first is *Karma and Rebirth in Classical Indian Traditions*, edited by Wendy Doniger O'Flaherty, which appeared in 1980. The second is *Karma: An Anthropological Inquiry*, edited by Charles F. Keyes and E. Valentine Daniel, which appeared in 1983. A third volume, edited by A. K. Ramanujan and Guy Welbon, is scheduled to appear in due course from the same publisher.

one makes things, whether for one's own or for others' use, one aims for a benefit for oneself: the making is part of a sequence of purposive activity designed eventually to satisfy a drive.

My suggestion, then, is that when Sanskrit users say or hear the words based on the root *kṛ* they naturally—in other words, as a reflection of their conceptual scheme—expect that it will be possible to identify a maker (*kartṛ*), some materials out of which the making takes place, a beneficiary for whom the making is intended, a purpose or purposes (*puruṣārtha*) being served by the making, an operation (*vyāpāra*) by which the making is carried out, and of course a resulting thing made (*karman*), which will serve the purpose or at least perform a function conducive to the eventual satisfaction ultimately sought. All this baggage, then, comes along with each use of a word in the *kṛ* family. So, for example, when in Indian thought we hear of something *kṛta*, we should understand that the reference is not only to some deed, something done, completed, but further that it refers to something made, produced from some materials by someone for somebody's purpose.

That *kṛ* means "to make" is not a new discovery. Dictionaries regularly offer "to do, to make" as the definition of the term. The insight I refer to involved a renewed realization of the standard definition, a recognition that took place in a certain context. A peculiarity about the conceptual system shared by users of classical Sanskrit is that just about all of the activities we would in English call "doing" are classed as makings. Most significantly, many sorts of thinkings are considered makings, that is to say, that are thought of in such a way that answers to the questions "who made it?" "out of what?" "for what purpose?" and so on are appropriate and answerable if asked. For example, in Vātsyāyana's *Nyāyabhāṣya*,[3] in explicating the concept of *pravṛtti* (usually translated as "positive ac-

[3] Vātsyāyana, *Nyāyabhāṣya*, on *Nyāyasūtra* 1.1.2. The translation follows that of Ganganatha Jha in Poona Oriental Series 59 (Poona: Deccasi College, 1939).

tivity"), Vātsyāyana provides the following table of illustrations:

- I. Wrong activities
  - A. Bodily (*kāyika*)
    - 1. *hiṁsā* ("killing")
    - 2. *steya* ("stealing")
    - 3. *pratiṣiddhamaithuna* ("illicit intercourse")
  - B. Vocal (*vācika*)
    - 4. *anṛta* ("lying")
    - 5. *puruṣasūcana* ("rude talking")
    - 6. *asambaddha* ("incoherent babbling")
  - C. Mental (*mānasika*)
    - 7. *paradroha* ("malice")
    - 8. *paradravyābhīpsā* ("desire for things belonging to others")
    - 9. *nāstikya* ("materialism")
- II. Right Activities
  - A. Bodily
    - 10. *dāna* ("charity")
    - 11. *paritrāpa* ("protecting")
    - 12. *paricaraṇa* ("service")
  - B. Vocal
    - 13. *satya* ("telling the truth")
    - 14. *hita priya* ("saying what is wholesome and agreeable")
    - 15. *svādhyāya* ("studying the Veda")
  - C. Mental
    - 16. *dayā* ("compassion")
    - 17. *aspṛha* ("entertaining no desire for the belongings of other people")
    - 18. *śraddhā* ("faith")

How many of these eighteen kinds of things would we happily term activities, doings? We have no trouble with the bodily kinds. They are the sorts of things conscious agents deliberately and believingly bring about, if given opportunity and ability. Of the vocal activities, the one that may give us pause is "incoherent babbling." One does not deliberately babble incoherently, and if one believes one is doing so his babbling is not incoherent but only intended to sound so. But perhaps too much should not be made of this single case of vocal action. It is not altogether clear what sort of example is actually envisaged, and generally we are happy enough to count linguistic activities as cases of activity or doing.

But a problem does seem to arise when we consider the list of mental activities. The category of mental acts is a great deal more restricted for us English speakers than is the category of *mānasika-pravṛtti* for Sanskrit users. I suggest that our general tendency is to view awareness as something that happens to us. Of course, there are plenty of clear-cut cases to the contrary. When I deliberately set out to solve an equation, say, I am engaging in mental activity, I direct my thoughts toward a solution to the problem. I can try to remember something long forgotten, and presumably I can succeed in doing so. Nevertheless, we would not normally suppose that desiring, for example, which appears on Vātsyāyana's list of *mānasa pravṛttis*, is a doing; it is rather a state of mind. So are malice, compassion, and faith, as well as absence of desire. Of course, we may think malicious thoughts, or think compassionate thoughts, or faithfully think on God. But it is rather peculiar to suppose that we do such things deliberately and believingly in a manner parallel to that in which we perform bodily or linguistic acts. To view a person as deliberately and believingly thinking a malicious thought is to suggest that he is manipulating himself in some arcane fashion. One who deliberately and knowingly thinks compassionate thoughts seems to be someone described as disciplining himself to be compassionate in his overall behavior, despite a character that makes compassion difficult. And deliberately to think on God faithfully is surely to be engaged in religious discipline. These are not cases of spontaneous awareness.

Although this particular list of Vātsyāyana's does not include perceiving among its examples of *mānasa pravṛtti*, a great many Sanskrit writers on philosophy speak of perceiving as a mental act. This seems most peculiar, since one cannot choose what one sees—if the tree is there before one, and one has operating sense-organs, sufficient light, and a functioning, attentive mind, one cannot help but see the tree. Even more passive in nature is hearing—if someone bangs a drum loudly inches from my ear, I do not need to act to hear the noise. Yet seeing and hearing are regularly counted as mental acts by Sanskrit users.

To sum up the thought process that led to my insight, it came to me that for Sanskrit philosophers acting is making, awareness (mental activity) is acting, and so awareness is making. And I realized that if that is correct the route to the theory of Karma and rebirth is straightforward. Every activity is a making of something for a purpose. In some cases it is obvious enough what is made and what is the immediate function; it is also fairly clear in such cases what the ultimate purpose is. Thus I make a cake for someone—myself or another—to eat, I make a pot for someone to use for holding water. The ultimate purposes in these actions are mundane—satisfaction of hunger and thirst drives, technological control of the sources of comfort. In other cases—notably in the case of mental acts—it is not so apparent what is made, who is being benefited, and what the overall purpose is. But the metaphor of doing as making leads to the expectation that there must be something made, someone benefited, and some purpose in the activity. So a theoretical construct—or series of them—is developed to satisfy the expectations. And so, the theory of Karma emerges.

In any activity, since by the metaphor it is a making, there must be something made. And since mental acts are notoriously free from any obvious—that is to say, publicly observable—products, the metaphor leads Sanskrit speakers to postulate an unobservable product, namely, a *karman* in the form of traces (*saṁskāra*). Furthermore, what is made must benefit someone in some manner. But it is often difficult to see in what way a mental act benefits anyone. The only beneficiary that seems affected in the relevant way by awareness is the agent himself, so it is presumably his purposes that are served in some way by the traces produced by a mental act. But that can only be so if those products—the traces—maintain themselves long enough that they can produce eventual results conducive to the agent's purposes. How long is long enough? As long as it takes to produce a situation in which the trace can help do, that is, make something that is relevant. This may take quite a long time. Indeed, a certain trace may not function fruitfully until after the death of the particular physico-mental apparatus that made it in the first place. And how does this trace function at the time of fruition? By providing the material for a new making by the agent in question, which making may be the making of a new physico-mental apparatus (a "body"), or the making by the agent of a new experience (*bhoga*), which normally in turn engenders further makings with their eventual results. In either case, the new making is not merely occasioned by the trace of the past making, but is also colored (*vāsita*) by it so that it properly reflects the moral quality of the original making. Thus if the original making was maleficent, the new making will be frustrating; while if the original making was beneficent, the new making will be satisfying. This accords with an obvious point about makings, which is that if they are done well the results are satisfying, while if done badly, the results are frustrating—the satisfaction or frustration corresponding to the extent to which the results made conduce effectively to the purposes of the beneficiary. So one who acts badly makes a trace that eventuates in a low embodiment, which, though it does conduce to human purposes (one cannot act at all without a body), does not conduce as effectively as a high(er) embodiment, and is therefore relatively frustrating by comparison with the higher embodiment. The same pattern applies with respect to experiences, which are comparatively frustrating (*duḥkha*) or satisfying (*sukha*) insofar as they feel conducive or otherwise to the experiencer's purposes.

What had I discovered when all this came to me? I think I discovered at work in the conceptual system natural to Sanskrit users one or several metaphors at work, in the sense of George

Lakoff and Mark Johnson's book *Metaphors We Live By*.[4] Their thesis is that a conceptual system is a coherent system of metaphorical concepts, where a "metaphor" is the "understanding and experiencing (of) one kind of thing in terms of another."[5] Lakoff and Johnson subject contemporary American speech to an analysis in which they show the pervasiveness of a number of fascinating metaphors, such as "Argument is war," "Time is money," "Happy is up," "Inflation is an entity," "Labor is a resource," "Theories are buildings," and the like. In each metaphor one sort of thing is understood in terms of another, so that certain aspects of the first thing are emphasized by the comparison and other aspects are hidden.

> For example, in the midst of a heated argument, we are intent on attacking our opponent's position and defending our own, we may lose sight of the cooperative aspects of arguing. Someone who is arguing with you can be viewed as giving you his time, a valuable commodity, in an effort at mutual understanding. But when we are preoccupied with the battle aspects, we often lose sight of the cooperative aspects."[6]

Thus "Argument is war" highlights the competitive aspects of argument and hides the cooperative ones.

Metaphors, Lakoff and Johnson argue, permeate our ways of talking and thinking about things. A map of the metaphors discernible in the commonly used expressions in our language community can therefore constitute a graphic explication of the conceptual system or systems shared by members of the community of speakers of American English. This seems to me to be a useful suggestion, and one that is applicable to the attempt to interpret across boundaries. If we examine the speech habits employed in a particular language community and discover the metaphors embedded there, we shall be able

[4] George Lakoff and Mark Johnson, *Metaphors We Live By* (Chicago: University of Chicago Press, 1980).

[5] Ibid., p. 5.

[6] Ibid., p. 10.

to provide an explication of the conceptual system at work in the thinking of that community's members.

In the light of the first section of my remarks one must emphasize that care needs to be taken with this approach. For example, I have just suggested a discrepancy between English and Sanskrit speech patterns and presumably between the conceptual systems underlying them, such that awareness is not regularly thought of as action by the English-speaking community, while it is in the Sanskrit language community. We might be tempted, then, to utilize the metaphor approach to say that in the conceptual system underlying Sanskrit usage "Activity is making," that "Awareness is activity," and that "Awareness is making." But that would presume that the English terms 'awareness', 'activity', and 'making' mean the same things as the respective Sanskrit terms *jñāna, pravṛtti,* and *kriyā.* To proceed this way would merely reintroduce the indeterminacy of translation and thus the suspicion of parochial interpretation having nothing to recommend it save the interests of the particular inquirer. But we do not have to proceed that way. We can say, rather, that in the Sanskrit conceptual system *Jñāna asti* [is] *pravṛtti, Pravṛtti asti* [is] *kriyā,* and *Jñāna asti* [is] *kriyā.* These equations are not translations but themselves express in Sanskrit metaphorical links characterizing the expectations of those who share a certain conceptual scheme. They are either part of a map that explicates the Sanskrit conceptual system, or else portions common to the several maps that explicate the several conceptual schemes shared by groups of Sanskrit users.

Metaphorical links of this sort seem to me to provide the sorts of categories I called for at the outset, categories that are not so distinct as to create a priori boundaries, because they are not to be understood in terms of breakdown into their components. What metaphors express are tendencies to behavior on the part of speakers and hearers that are not so firm as to be unbroachable. Any natural language is rich enough to provide the means for expressing relations that run counter to any particular metaphorical link that the language is capable of expressing. The currency of a metaphorical link in a conceptual system, then, does not preclude expression of its opposite; these conceptual relationships are neither a priori nor analytic, and what is being explored through them is not a logic, at least as logic is understood by modern logicians. The study of a conceptual scheme through its metaphorical links is, then, not an a priori or mathematical science but an empirical one capable of being carried out in as rigorous, "scientific" a way as any other.

I suggested that the boundaries across which we think we must interpret are the creatures of our own categories of investigation. We choose which boundaries we wish to interpret across; they are boundaries because we choose to believe that they are. I do not wish to be understood as suggesting that inquiry should not begin with the postulation of such boundaries: I suspect that is the only way we can begin. Answers, interpretations will not arise unless questions involving boundaries are asked. I am counseling that the relativism to human choice of the questions be acknowledged. I do not think that relativism leads to a stultification of rigorous interpretation, making it impossible to tell right answers from wrong ones. If Quine is right, there is a seeming boundary between the holistic nature of the objects of philosophical study—conceptual schemes—and the natural order of investigation, which is not holistic but piecemeal. Finding metaphorical links provides a way of seeing conceptual schemes in a manner that does not erect such a boundary, or at least does not erect it in so absolute a fashion as to invite skeptical arguments of the sort I reviewed at the outset of this paper.

ALL of this discussion suggests as a research program for comparative philosophy the identification of metaphorical links in the conceptual systems in which philosophical writings are and have been embodied. Let me conclude with a suggestion about what sort of results the method should eventually yield. Suppose we established that in a or the "normal" Sanskrit conceptual system *Jñāna asti pravṛtti*, *Pravṛtti asti kriyā*, and *Jñāna asti kriyā*, along with other metaphorical links further connecting the concepts of *jñāna, pravṛtti*, and *kriyā* with still further concepts. We would then be in a position to ask whether, for example, the Sāṁkhya and Advaita conceptual systems are a part of the one characterized by these links. It is well known that Śaṅkarācārya frequently uses the term *jñāna* to speak of *cit*, pure consciousness that is clearly not *pravṛtti* or *kriyā*. Now this manner of Śaṅkara's might be just that, a manner of speaking: he might, knowingly or unknowingly, have used one term in Sanskrit (*jñāna*) for something that is normally expressed by a different term (*cit*), without changing the metaphorical links that connect the things expressed by these terms in the "normal" Sanskrit conceptual system. Or he may instead have been (again, knowingly or unknowingly) recommending adoption of a different Sanskrit conceptual scheme in which the metaphorical links between what the "normal" Sanskrit speaker called "*jñāna*" and "*kriyā*" are other than they are in the "normal" system. We shall, in short, have to come to a point at which we develop principles of individuation for conceptual schemes, principles that are sadly lacking at present but which are unavoidable as investigative devices as long as investigation proceeds in the way human beings are prone to proceed. Note that I do not say *discover* those principles of individuation, for it is my view, once again, that boundaries and categories of investigation are justified pragmatically to reflect the purposes of the investigator.

The research program I propose is of a sort that could be jointly pursued not only by philosophers but by historians, language specialists, students of literature, cultural anthropologists, and indeed by most any kind of scientist who deals with linguistic and/or psychological materials. As philosophy is the queen of the sciences it seems appropriate that the program should start there. The method is one that is suggested in Lakoff and Johnson and no doubt in other work on metaphor, though a lot of what is said in the literature on metaphor has a rather more limited sense of the term in mind. The research must be carried on in the home language of each investigator—

what else?—at least to the point that it is mature enough to develop its own technical terminology. But, as I have tried to show, as long as metaphorical links held to exist in the scheme associated with a particular language can be expressed in that language, translation provides no more serious problem for this program than for any other. I urge the field of comparative philosophy to consider the proposed research program, perhaps by scheduling subsequent discussion panels, workshops, and so on, designed to make a start on it by exploring the methodology, or whatever seems appropriate.

HENRY ROSEMONT, JR.

Against Relativism

ARGUMENTS for relativism in one form or another are at least as old as Protagoras and Zhuang Zi, and the roots of contemporary conceptual relativism can be traced—retrospectively at least—to the writings of Hume and Kant.[1] In the twentieth century relativistic theses first rose to scholarly prominence with the Sapir–Whorf hypothesis of linguistic relativity, the claim that what and how we see the world is determined for us by the overt and covert structures of our native language.[2] This view leads naturally to a concept of ontological relativity, as seen clearly in the works of Quine,[3] and if we wish to follow such commentators as Richard Rorty, in other philosophers as otherwise different as the later Wittgenstein, Heidegger, and Dewey.[4] More recently arguments for conceptual relativism have swelled to a torrent, coming from the streams of history, psychology, anthropology, and literary criticism, in the works of Foucault, Lacan, Geertz, and Derrida, respectively, to name only some writers *au courant*.[5] Here the claims are that our historical periods and culture do the determining, to such an extent that they, when coupled with our language, construct the person—the subject—as well. And the full conclusion to these

[1] Richard Rorty has so argued in "The World Well Lost," *Journal of Philosophy* 69 (1972): 649–665.

[2] Benjamin L. Whorf, *Language, Thought, and Reality*, ed. John B. Carroll (Cambridge, Mass.: M.I.T. Press and Wiley, 1956).

[3] Beginning at least with the preface to *Word and Object* (Cambridge, Mass.: M.I.T. Press, 1960); and it has been an explicit theme since *Ontological Relativity, and Other Essays* (New York: Columbia University Press, 1969).

[4] Richard Rorty, *Philosophy and the Mirror of Nature* (Princeton: Princeton University Press, 1979).

[5] See especially (but not only): Michel Foucault, *The Order of Things* (New York: Pantheon, 1971); Clifford Geertz, *Local Knowledge* (New York: Basic Books, 1983); Jacques Lacan, *Écrits*, trans. Alan Sheridan (New York: Norton, 1977); Jacques Derrida, *Of Grammatology*, trans. Gayatri C. Spivak (Baltimore: Johns Hopkins University Press, 1976).

arguments appears to have come from the history and philosophy of western science, namely, in the works of Kuhn and Feyerabend.[6] Western science, as it turns out, has not been the building-block, linearly progressive affair we have always thought it to be; rather it has involved a series of fundamental cognitive reorientations on the part of its practitioners, which come to be accepted at least in part nonrationally, and which Kuhn calls "conversions" or "gestalt switches."[7]

This is a simplisitic outline of a complex congeries of arguments and positions,[8] but the skeptical implications of conceptual relativism in general should be clear: our basic cognitive framework—which ranges from our unreflective conception of what it is to be a human being to our assumptions, beliefs, and presuppositions about the general features of the physical universe—is overwhelmingly determined for us by a set of highly specific environmental circumstances ranging from social relations accompanying stages of history and of culture, to the syntactical peculiarities of our native tongue. To be is to be the value of a pronoun form—and an indexical at that.

[6] Thomas S. Kuhn, *The Structure of Scientific Revolutions*, 2d ed. (Chicago: University of Chicago Press, 1967); Paul K. Feyerabend, *Against Method* (Atlantic Highlands, N.J.: Humanities Press, 1975). See also their contributions to *Criticism and the Growth of Knowledge*, ed. Imre Lakatos and Alan Musgrave (Cambridge: Cambridge University Press, 1970), especially Kuhn's "Reflections on My Critics."

[7] Kuhn, *Structure of Scientific Revolutions*.

[8] At the very least it may appear that I have run together positions described as "antirealist" with relativistic positions. Statements of the former position generally have in common the claim that there is no be-all and end-all set of ultimately true statements about the world, which contrasts with the somewhat more modest relativistic claim that among and between different coherent sets of statements, there is no independent means of judging that one is superior to others. Each position, however, employs arguments also used by the other, and they all have very similar implications for comparative philosophers who work with nonwestern texts; so the fine distinctions between antirealism and relativism need not be drawn here. Further accounts of relativistic theses can be found in Bryan R. Wilson, ed., *Rationality* (Evanston, Ill.: Harper & Row, 1970); Martin Hollis and Steven Lukes, eds., *Rationality and Relativism* (Cambridge, Mass.: M.I.T. Press, 1982); and Michael Krausz and Jack W. Meiland, eds., *Relativism: Cognitive and Moral* (Notre Dame, Ind.: University of Notre Dame Press, 1982).

All of this bodes ill for philosophy and the human sciences in general, but the problem is particularly acute for comparative philosophers, who share a concern and commitment to bring western philosophical perspectives to bear on the study of nonwestern textual materials, and vice versa. If, however, the producers of those texts came from cultures very different from the contemporary West—and it is obvious that they did—and if the languages in which they wrote have phonetic, syntactic, and semantic properties very different from, say, contemporary English—and it is obvious that they do—then what reasons can be given for believing that we might ascertain, even in principle, what those texts said to the people who could read them at the time of composition? Can we really translate and interpret Sanskrit, classical Chinese, or other nonwestern texts without imposing our own linguistic, cultural, historical, ontological, and other categories thereon? Must these texts not ultimately be seen as a series of sophisticated Rorschach blots?

Of course translators, historians, anthropologists, literary scholars, and others who work professionally with nonwestern materials are not going to hold their research projects in abeyance until such questions are answered to the satisfaction of all concerned. They can rightfully say that their fields of study are established, that there is a generally agreed-upon body of translation and interpretation in each field, with accepted standards of scholarship therein; all of which is reflected in and reinforced by specialized professional societies and learned journals.

But comparative philosophers cannot ignore these questions, for whatever else they may do, comparative philosophers must do *philosophy*. Radically different definitions of the subject notwithstanding, all definitions must include the self-referential nature of philosophy: the discipline's foundations (or lack thereof) are an integral part of its subject matter. The skeptical questions raised by relativistic arguments, therefore, have to be addressed by everyone wishing to do comparative philosophy.

In what follows I will not attempt to prove that theses of

conceptual relativism are false for the same reason that I do not believe they could ever be proved to be true; logical proofs of the requisite kind are not to be found outside the language of *Principia Mathematica* and intertranslatable artificial languages purged of all connotative elements. Nor will I attempt to give anything like a full response to the manifold claims of relativism in a paper of this kind. Rather I will first take up some major themes in relativistic theses and offer some arguments and considerations, against a linguistic background, to show why it is more reasonable to assume that relativism is false rather than true. In the second part of this paper I will endeavor further to break the spell of relativistic theses by offering an alternative. I will also use this positive perspective in challenging the most deeply entrenched form of philosophical relativism, value relativism, and by so doing hope to suggest ways in which comparative philosophy can help to chart new directions for philosophy and the human sciences.

AT FIRST we must distinguish a few singulars and plurals. Language is a multiple blessing for Homo sapiens; indeed it is the single most distinguishing characteristic of the species and indicates a strong commonality among us. Language*s* are also a blessing because of the basic contribution they have made and make to the variety of ways of interpreting the world. But in one sense languages have not been altogether benign historically, because they have and do divide us (Babel has often been referred to as the "second fall"),[9] and it is the multiplicity and diversity of languages in the world that gives rise to conceptual relativism, a claim to which I will return later.

The other singular–plural distinction that needs to be drawn relates to the world just mentioned. I mean what I said, for there is only one. The relativist who speaks of our inhabiting different world*s* must be taken as speaking figuratively—and misleadingly—for there is not a plurality of worlds. Ways of viewing and responding to the world have, of course, varied

[9] James A. Boon, *Other Tribes, Other Scribes* (Cambridge: Cambridge University Press, 1983), p. 30.

greatly from time to time and from place to place, and we must be genuinely indebted to relativists for calling attention to the importance of this fact; but all of the variations must and do take place in the world; singular, following Rebecca West: "Art does not copy the world; one of the damned thing is enough."[10]

A basic way to combat relativism would be to hold, as my previous remarks may have implied, that there really is a world "out there," a "given" that we must struggle to apprehend directly and immediately, jettisoning our culturally imposed conceptual framework and linguistic categories to the best of our abilities. It is altogether consistent with the totality of our sense experience to believe that there is a material world external to us, Berkeleyan and more recent brains-in-vats arguments to the contrary notwithstanding.[11] Moreover, infants

[10] In *Languages of Art* (Indianapolis: Bobbs-Merrill, 1968), Nelson Goodman offers this quote (p. 3) as coming from Virginia Woolf, but says he could not find the citation. As I heard the quote, "thing" is in the singular.

[11] The relation between concepts and terms that express them has been a major source of philosophical controversy since Wittgenstein and cannot be fully considered in brief compass. The position taken herein is basically Chomsky's, against the background of which a few points should nevertheless be adumbrated. First, one sense of "having the concept *X*" is where *X* is the statement of a *rule* followed by the person said to have the concept. To the extent that "knowing a language" means "knowing the rules of a grammar," there does not seem to be anything wrong with saying that a person "follows the rules" of the language spoken—is rule guided—even though the person almost surely could not state the rules for that grammar as described by a linguist. Because it is concepts, and not rules or the possibility of a private language, that is the focus of this remark, it should not be read as either augmenting or detracting from the Wittgensteinian discussions of these latter issues offered by Saul Kripke in his *Wittgenstein on Rules and Private Language* (Cambridge, Mass.: Harvard University Press, 1982). For a response to Kripke, however, that is consonant with the present remark, see Noam Chomsky, *Knowledge of Language* (New York: Praeger, 1985). Second, a different, though related sense of "having the concept *X*" is where *X* is simply a predicative expression. Here anti-Wittgensteinians claim that one can have concepts without having terms to express them, and to claim otherwise is to be "unfair to babies." But we may attribute prelinguistic awareness to babies—it would be irrational not to—awareness of pain, heat, hunger, and so on, without talking of their having concepts; to be in pain is clearly distinguishable

must apprehend that part of the world constituting their immediate environment—evidenced by the responses they make to that environment—and such apprehension is surely unmediated by cultural or linguistic categorizations.

The ontological claim here may well be true, but the imperative to apprehend the "given" directly and immediately cannot be obeyed by anyone who, unlike infants, understands it;

---

from having the concept expressed by the open English sentence '. . . is in pain.' And on the basis of this distinction it can be maintained that people have both sensations and concepts and that we attribute specific sensations to people on the basis of either their behavior or their speech, but that we attribute concepts to them only on the basis of the latter. Third, following Jerry A. Fodor's *Representations* (Cambridge, Mass.: M.I.T. Press, 1981), p. 260, we may also distinguish "lexical concepts" from "phrasal concepts." The former "is one that is expressible, in English, by an open sentence with a morphologically simple—viz. a monomorphemic—predicate term. So, for example, GREEN is a lexical concept, since it is expressible by the open sentence '. . . is green.' " Phrasal concepts, by contrast, are expressible in English (and related languages) by complex predicate expressions in open sentences: '. . . drinks beer and belches.' Fodor then goes on to argue that perhaps *all* lexical concepts are learned holistically, which is to say that they have no internal structure that can be further analyzed; from which it would follow—contra the contemporary empiricist position in cognitive psychology—that the list of "primitive" concepts is almost as long as the *Oxford English Dictionary*, which, if true, requires reconsideration of a number of issues in formal semantics, epistemology, and the philosophy of mind. Whatever the outcome of this research, it has seemed appropriate in this text to take "concept" as Fodor's "lexical concept" and to use it as synonymous with "term"; with only a few exceptions not relevant here, all Chinese graphs of the classical period (to be discussed later in the text) are monomorphemic. Fourth, if it is warranted to see concepts and (predicative, including predicate nominal) terms as equivalent, the point is of importance to comparative philosophers. Working with texts the authors of which have long since passed to their reward, comparative philosophers cannot ask those authors for clarification, paraphrase, or elaboration; neither, of course, can we examine their behavior. All we have are the texts themselves, a finite corpus, and therefore the only way it can be maintained that a particular concept was held by an author is to find a term expressing that concept in his text. Thus we cannot say that so-and-so had a "theory of *X*," or that he "espoused *X* principles," if there is no *X* in the lexicon of the language in which the author wrote. (In the example following in the text, we replace *X* with "morals," and "the author" with "the early Confucians.") A more complete account of the several issues raised in this note will be given in my *Foundations of Comparative Philosophy*, in progress.

for such understanding is only possible within cultural and linguistic categories. Excepting perhaps the (interesting) case of the mystical trance state, mature human beings—competent language speakers—cannot apprehend the world unmediated by language. We must therefore reject the "myth of the given," for in a fundamental sense it is just that, a myth; and so is its occasionally invoked corollary, the claim that "language distorts reality."[12] The weakness of these claims becomes even clearer when we pluralize, for such claims must characterize languages as altogether passive elements fundamentally distinct from our sensory organs and cognitive structure, and hence in a very basic way independent of language speakers. But such a view of languages, and of human beings, is patently false.

By rejecting the myth of the given and the distorting nature of language claims, however, we seem to place ourselves right where the relativist wants us. If our languages must needs mediate, indeed inform, our perceptions and conceptions of the world, and if languages are indeed varied and diverse, then it follows that our perceptions and conceptions of the world must be equally varied and diverse. We all have our separate realities, and hence conceptual relativism.

I believe this argument is sound, but it does not prove very much. The most that it could establish is that up to the present, human beings have not concurred in the accounts they gave of the world they jointly inhabited, which is hardly news. The argument does not, and by itself could not show that it is impossible for all peoples to offer a fairly similar account at some time in the future; that is, that they could share the same view of the world in its natural and social aspects. They would in all probability have to become bilingual, maintaining their native language and all learning the same second language; a matter

[12] This claim is one of the more unfortunate ones that D. T. Suzuki regularly advanced in the many works he wrote introducing Zen Buddhism to western audiences. For discussion and references, see Henry Rosemont, Jr., "The Meaning Is the Use: *Kōan* and *Mondō* as Linguistic Tools of the Zen Masters," in *Philosophy East and West* 20 (1970): 109–119.

of enormous practical difficulty, perhaps, but not theoretically impossible.

There is more to say about this relativistic argument. If he or she agrees in rejecting the "myth of the given," if it is agreed that languages are dependent on language speakers, it follows that cultural, ontological, historical, and all other forms of relativity, excepting perhaps values, ultimately reduce to one, namely, linguistic relativity; from which it follows in turn that one's views of conceptual relativism will have to be grounded in one's views of human language(s) in general, and to matters of translation and interpretation in particular. To the extent that significant evidence for relativistic theses is significantly linguistic, the weight that the evidence can bear must be seen to depend on the strength of specific claims about what has been said (written) and can be said (written) in a language, and how well or poorly it has been or can be translated into any other language.

This is not to say, of course, that when you've heard one argument for relativism you've heard them all. Some relativistic theses are at least semi-independent of linguistic issues. Many moral relativists, for instance, believe that physicists do, or can, describe accurately a physical universe existing altogether separately from our perception of it. Conversely, a person might accept cognitive relativism in a strong form—standards of rationality can vary arbitrarily—and yet reject moral relativism (entering a caveat, Zhuang Zi can be argued to hold this position).[13]

But the central point remains: one's views on the nature of human languages, translation, and interpretation are crucial for evaluating relativistic theses. A person can fasten on the fact that various natural languages slice up natural environments in various ways phonetically, syntactically, and semantically and come to believe that there must consequently al-

[13] The caveat being that Zhuang Zi does not have the concept cluster of modern morals, to be taken up in the text below. A more contemporary statement of this position is Joel Kupperman, "Moral Realism and Metaphysical Anti-Realism," in manuscript.

ways be some basic indeterminacy of translation, with no way of ultimately reconciling differences. To such a person, relativistic arguments will seem persuasive.

The converse also holds: a person can believe that all natural human languages have the same expressive capacities; and therefore believe too that whatever can be expressed in any natural human language can be expressed in any other if the richness, variation, mechanisms for change, and other capacities of natural languages be fully exploited. To such a person, most relativistic arguments will seem unpersuasive.[14]

To see in another way how relativistic theses are inextricably linked to matters of language, translation, and interpretation, consider the following: we may safely assume, I think, that no two human beings, even identical twins raised together, have held exactly the same beliefs about everything, and therefore agreement and disagreement in beliefs is always a matter of, more or less, a scaling function. And the scale for any two individuals, or groups, is largely and most significantly ascertained by the extent to which they will affirm and deny sentences. In order to know that you do or do not share my belief on some matter, I must know that you interpret the sentences

[14] To speak of relativistic theses as "persuasive" or "unpersuasive" rather than true or false might suggest that what is going on here more nearly resembles rhetoric or debate than philosophy. It is philosophically important, however, to note that truth claims cannot be made, at least at the present stage of scholarly knowledge, for either relativistic theses or their denials. To be sure, a number of authors have endeavored to prove relativistic theses true, or false; but in the rigorous philosophical sense of "proof," all such endeavors have failed and must fail. Moreover, no consistent and thoroughgoing relativist would or could claim that relativistic theses—most of them at any rate—were true; the most that he or she could claim would be that the theses were true relative to some standard, which in turn would have to be relative to some culture at a particular time (which, if enough turns were taken, would probably reduce the notion of relative truth to incoherence). Most relativists—correctly—do not worry about this problem. At the same time, nonrelativists certainly could not prove—in the same sense of "proof" as before—to a skeptic that relativism was false, nor could they even show (yet) that there was sufficient empirical evidence to warrant fully the belief about the similar expressive capacities of all natural human languages.

we jointly affirm or deny in the same way that I do, from which it follows untrivially that I must know how to interpret your sentences (where "interpret" implies that I must not simply know what one of your sentences means, in isolation, but must also understand it against the background of other beliefs you hold).

There is a catch. I can only know how to interpret your sentences by assuming certain attitudes, assumptions, and beliefs on your part at the outset. At the minimum I must assume that when you assert a sentence, in general you are affirming it. I must also assume that what you mean when you assert a sentence very closely approximates what I would mean if I asserted (affirmed) the same sentence. At the same time, however, I cannot know of your attitudes, assumptions, intentions, or beliefs until you have spoken to me, and I have been able to interpret what you have said. And you must do exactly the same for me. Put another way, matters of translation and interpretation are wedded permanently to matters of beliefs, assumptions, attitudes, and intentions; no divorces are possible.

What follows from these considerations is that if someone had a view of the world altogether different from my own—if we shared, that is, no common perspectives—neither of us could ever come to know it. We must presuppose that we share some beliefs, assumptions, attitudes, and intentions—not an unreasonable presupposition, considering that we are both human—before either of us can begin to interpret any of the other's sentences and hence establish points of disagreement. Thus the possibility of a total failure of translation and interpretation—and consequently the possibility of radical conceptual relativism—is not one that should be entertained seriously by a rational person, for no rational arguments (in language) or empirical (linguistic) evidence could ever be adduced to show that the possibility had been realized.

Very well, a skeptical relativist may now reply, but what merit your arguments might have thus far is tied to the fact that you have been taking your examples from your own culture, or, at best, from cultures with languages assumed to be intertranslatable with English. But pass from English and related languages to one very different therefrom; pass, that is, to Quine's gavagai language, spoken by a people hitherto unknown to field linguists and anthropologists, and consider the following two points.[15] First, if the language, and therefore the culture of the people who speak it, are wholly unknown to us, by what right may we assume that some at least of their basic beliefs and attitudes mirror our own? Second, and more important philosophically, the present account has obfuscated the possibility, argued by Quine and others, that the speakers of this hitherto unknown language might assent and dissent to the same set of (translated) sentences that we do, yet have a very different ontological view of the world (rabbithood manifested again).

To these skeptical objections I want to make four replies. First, and most simply, consider specifically the gavagai example, a hitherto unknown collection of human beings into whose midst a field investigator walks behind a veil of linguistic ignorance. Intriguing as this hypothetical example is to contemplate, perhaps philosophers have contemplated it overlong, for in the real world there are no such peoples, no such languages. All cultures have intercourse with some other cultures, and consequently there is a linguistic web throughout the world. Certainly some cultures have very little intercourse with *us*, but that is an entirely different matter; even the recently "discovered" Tasaday of Mindanao had interpreters from day one.[16]

We should not think that while languages *A* and *B* are intertranslatable, and languages *B* and *C* are intertranslatable, and ditto languages *C* and *D*, nevertheless *A* and *D* may not be intertranslatable. And we should not think so because if *A* and *B* are intertranslatable, and if *ex hypothesi* some of the sentences to be translated into *A* and *B* are translations from *C*, it follows

[15] See Quine, *Word and Object*, especially chap. 2.

[16] A popular summary account of early encounters with the Tasaday is found in Kenneth MacLeish, "Stone Age Cavemen of Mindanao," *National Geographic* 142.2 (August 1972): 219–249.

that *C* may be translated into *A* if *B* can; and so on for *D*, and however many more languages we may want to add to the list. Again, there may be many practical difficulties here, but I do not see any theoretical ones.

The conclusion of this first reply: if there are no wholly different human languages—and therefore no wholly different human views of the world—wholly cut off from all other human languages, then there can be no wholly different human views of the world. (Later I will suggest why examples of Martians or other visitors from outer space should not be given the attention many philosophers have paid to them.)

Consider next the claim that two of us, speaking very different languages, might assent and dissent to exactly the same set of translated sentences (or to two translations of the same language) with radically different ontologies, both of which were perfectly compatible with "all the available evidence." To a significant extent the plausibility of this claim hinges on the notion of stimulus meanings with respect to linguistic utterances, a notion I do not think many linguists or psychologists would give credence to today.

But even ignoring this difficulty, just how genuinely plausible is the idea that two of us might affirm and deny *exactly* the same sentences, yet have fundamentally different views about the constitution of the world? If this way of putting the question seems overly rhetorical, it can be paraphrased: what follows from entertaining seriously the possibility of such a divergence of views?

What follows, as I see it, is that most scholarly efforts in the human and natural sciences would exhibit the same pessimism and near nihilism that is currently threatening much of philosophy. To see this point, take as example the attacks by Quine himself on Chomsky and other generative grammarians for their efforts to construct grammars of specific languages, and, more deeply, to describe as well the features of universal grammar.[17] Quine's argument is that there will always be an indef-

[17] W. V. Quine, "Methodological Reflections on Current Linguistic Theory," in Donald Davidson and Gilbert Harman, eds., *Semantics of Natural Lan-*

initely large number of grammars that are compatible with all the available evidence, and therefore Chomsky's effort to establish *the* abstract representation of a specific human cognitive capacity is no more than chasing a will-o'-the-wisp.

It is historically the case that at the time Quine and others argued against the generative grammarians in this way there were no grammars for any language that claimed to be correct—nor are there any now—and the question therefore arises, why should Chomsky or any other linguist cease to pursue research on the basis of their own theories because of the logical possibility that there might be other theories that would have the same descriptive and explanatory adequacy? Surely the heliocentric theory of the solar system is not the only one incompatible with the geocentric; any imaginative thinker could postulate others. Copernicus, Galileo, Kepler, and others, were certainly imaginative thinkers; should they have been deterred from advancing strongly the heliocentric theory? (That empirical evidence grossly underdetermines any and all theories of scientific interest is not at issue here, for this claim applies no less to physics and chemistry than it does to the human sciences.)[18]

In a related manner, the notion of "all the available evidence" is not above suspicion: for no scientific theory is all the evidence ever in, and in the case of language—Quine's focus—it never could be. Every day many things are said in all human languages that have never been said before. Moreover, our ability to seek new evidence, to construct novel experiments, to build fresh models, is no doubt limited, but limited more by our ingenuity than by anything else. And it is now almost a

---

guage (Dordrecht: Reidel, 1972), pp. 442–454. For additional citations of other philosophers who have followed Quine on this topic, and my replies to them, see Henry Rosemont, Jr., "Gathering Evidence for Linguistic Innateness," *Synthese* 38 (1978): 127–148.

[18] Donald Hockney, "The Bifurcation of Scientific Theories and Indeterminacy of Translation," in *Philosophy of Science* 42 (1975): 411–427. See also Noam Chomsky, *Rules and Representations* (New York: Columbia University Press, 1980), especially pp. 13–25.

commonplace, thanks to persuasive relativistic arguments, that what is to count as evidence is at least partially a function of the theory under examination (a point to be taken up again below).

My third and fourth replies constitute an answer to the relativist-skeptic's first question: by what right do we assume that speakers of languages very different from our own share any of our beliefs and attitudes? In passing it can be noted that we should begin saying "very different" in a somewhat softer tone of voice, for again there are not, in the actual world, any human languages (or cultures) altogether cut off from all others.

But more fundamentally, such an assumption underlying translation and interpretation is not a right but a requirement, for otherwise no translation or interpretation could ever go forward. Now, however much a relativist might wish to challenge this position, it is difficult to take the challenge to heart, because the writings of most of them show clearly that they hold exactly this position themselves.

Benjamin Lee Whorf advances the claim that Hopi metaphysics differs radically from all western metaphysical views, and he does so by describing Hopi syntax and semantics, and consequent Hopi metaphysics—in English.[19] Clifford Geertz makes the rather foreign concepts of Arabic *hagg*, Malaysian *patut*, and others, eminently intelligible to us—in English.[20] Thomas Kuhn argues that pre- and post-Einsteinian physicists held incommensurable (read "untranslatable") views of the nature of the physical universe by describing both of them—again, in English;[21] and Feyerabend not only does the same for pre- and post-Copernican astronomers, he then goes on to

[19] This claim runs throughout much of Whorf's accounts. Specifically, see "Science and Linguistics" and "An American Indian Model of the Universe," in *Language, Thought, and Reality*, ed. Carroll, pp. 207–219 and 57–64, respectively.

[20] Geertz, *Local Knowledge*, esp. pp. 181ff.

[21] One of the major narrative themes of Kuhn's *Structure of Scientific Revolutions*.

proffer quite intriguingly a very different world view he believes characteristic of Homeric Greece—once more, in English, though he surely could have done the same in equally or more elegant German.[22]

And so it goes, not only in straightforward English and German, but in the historical, literary, and psychological French of Foucault, Derrida, and Lacan as well, at least to the extent that their claims do not depend on the use of self-referential "arguments." In all these cases, which I am not the first to have noticed, the result is the same, upon reflection: to the extent that examples given on behalf of conceptual relativism are compelling, they compel us to reject the relativistic position. If relativism were in some strong sense true, the supporting evidence could not have been obtained, nor could it have been communicated to us—in clear English.

This point closes this critical line of argumentation against theses of conceptual relativism. Again, I do not claim to have proved those theses false, only to have sketched some lines of reasoning to show why it is more reasonable, plausible, to assume that they are false rather than true. I would like now to turn to a more affirmative line of thought, by advancing some hypotheses incompatible with theses of relativism; and I hope thereby to further weaken the notion that we are, to quote Geertz, "all natives now,"[23] and at the same time to challenge the most deeply entrenched relativism of all, value relativism, namely, traditional aesthetics and morals.

A GREAT deal of work that has been carried on in the social and behavioral sciences over the past fifty years or so may be seen to fit roughly into one of two categories. The first has focused

[22] Feyerabend, *Against Method.*

[23] Although in *Local Knowledge* Geertz makes clear his entering "more complexly into" relativism (p. 157), the methodological thrust of much of that work applies, I believe, no less to comparative philosophers than to anthropologists. I would endorse, in other words, *what* Geertz says we should do as comparativists, but dispute with him about *why* we should be doing it. See also n. 41 below.

research and attention on the manifold differences between and among human beings, especially at the cultural level. The second has focused research and attention on the similarities between human beings as a species, and all other forms of sentient life. There are interesting exceptions, but in general we have been urged to see ourselves as almost wholly other than Huichol shamans, Renaissance Venetians, Ptolemaic astronomers, Zande witches, sixteenth-century French physicians, and the authors of the Upaniṣads, on the one hand, and on the other, to acknowledge our very close kinship with the other anthropoids (we are the naked ones), and other organisms as well, from pigeons to planaria.[24]

Many interesting insights into human behavior have issued from this work, which we would be ill-advised to ignore; but at the same time the most interesting research, to my mind, has come from one of the exceptions: linguistics, especially as conducted by generative grammarians. Working with a very different model of what it is to be a human being, these linguists seek similarities—in the ability to acquire and use languages—between the peoples of the world past and present,[25] which simultaneously requires an appreciation of the stark differences that seem to obtain between Homo sapiens and all other life forms.

[24] The former theme has been the dominant one in anthropology for several decades, and, under Bloomfield's influence, in linguistics as well until the mid-sixties. And see as well all of the works by Foucault and others cited at the outset of this work. The second theme is of course the theoretical foundation for virtually all work in experimental psychology (else why would work with animals occupy such a prominent place in that discipline?), and it has achieved no little popular support from such works as Konrad Lorenz's *On Aggression*, trans. Marjorie Kerr Wilson (New York: Harcourt, Brace & World, 1966)—contributing to his winning the Nobel Prize—those of Desmond Morris and Robet Ardrey, and, more recently, Edward O. Wilson's sociobiology, one example of which is *On Human Nature* (Cambridge, Mass.: Harvard University Press, 1978), which won a Pulitzer Prize.

[25] These ideas were articulated first and foremost in the writings of Noam Chomsky, beginning with his *Syntactic Structures* (The Hague: Mouton, 1957). He has been extending these ideas beyond language at least since *Reflections on Language* (New York: Pantheon, 1975).

These linguists search for common (meta-)principles, abstract and complex, that, they believe, underlie the diverse particular grammars of the many natural human languages, as mentioned earlier. The set of these principles is known in the literature as "universal grammar," and it is clear to those who use the term what it means, but to my mind it is an unfortunate expression, because "universal" commonly suggests "throughout the universe," whereas the intended sense is "for all human beings, physiologically and mentally constituted as they are." I want to focus on this concept, because it is the foundation of my alternative to relativism. And to keep it in mind, I want to alter and borrow simultaneously from Greek and Latin—with apologies to classicists—and coin the ugly word 'homoversal' to signify "for all human beings, physiologically and mentally constituted as they are."

In arguments that spring from the work of Chomsky and other generative grammarians, it has been held that there are other cognitive and sensory "grammars" (homoversal principles) that operate in other domains, such as facial recognition, numerical intuition, personality discrimination, and the like.[26] It has been suggested, for example, that because of our biological endowment, the task of learning how to recognize and distinguish human faces is fundamentally different—in kind, not in degree—from that of learning how to recognize and distinguish other commonly perceived physical objects such as trees or automobiles.[27] And it differs in kind in the same way that learning to speak and understand our native language differs from learning FORTRAN or COBOL.

These ideas may be more easily appreciated if, following ethological research, we distinguish triggering from shaping enrivonmental stimuli.[28] When we want to housebreak a kitten, we organize its environment in a certain way, perhaps employ some rewards and punishments; we must, that is, "teach"

[26] Chomsky, *Reflections on Language*, pp. 20ff.

[27] See my "Gathering Evidence for Linguistic Innateness," for a discussion of this subject.

[28] Sources are cited in Lorenz, *On Aggression*.

the kitten to use the litter box by shaping its environment, which shapes the cat's behavior in turn. No such teaching or shaping is necessary, however, when we want to play with the kit; we simply wriggle a finger, or jiggle a piece of string in front of it, and it will pounce. The game is underway the first time it is played. In this case we would say the wriggling finger or string are triggering stimuli, eliciting a response from the kit determined by its biological structure and organization; and the pouncing behavior will be uniform across all cats, physiologically and mentally constituted as they are.

Against this background I may put my constructive reply to relativism in the form of a question that I answer affirmatively, albeit tentatively: may the concept of homoversal principles be extended to be applicable beyond the cognitively specific domains of languages, faces, and so forth, to other domains, specifically the domains traditionally circumscribed—vaguely—by the terms 'aesthetics' and 'morals'?

Prima facie this question may appear absurd but I hope as we go on it will seem less so. Again, by using the term "homoversal" I want to keep attention drawn to the physiological properties and the organization of the mind—ultimately brain—of Homo sapiens. And I want thereby to get away from "universal" or "absolute." Thus, to take some simple examples, it is difficult to imagine that the value human beings generally attach to love would attach in the same way to other intelligent organisms if they were self-reproducing. Similarly, the duties and satisfactions that center on parenting and nurturing the young would be radically different, probably nonexistent, if our offspring were self-sufficient twenty-four hours after birth. And if seeing human faces triggers one kind of specifiable response in us, then perhaps seeing a human face contorted in agony triggers another specifiable response, no less genetically based and only minimally influenced by cultural factors under normal conditions of care and nurture. Further, even the most hardened aesthetic relativist would have to agree that the different kinds of things we call beautiful would be very different indeed if we had insect visual systems, rather than the system we do in fact have.

Parenthetically, it can now be seen why I do not attend to "*gedanke* experiments" involving efforts at communications with Martians or other creatures from outer space; all of these examples suggest that we are looking for principles holding "throughout the universe," while I want to stay closer to human beings, with their specific cognitive and sensory systems; about which, it is becoming increasingly clear, we still have a great deal to learn.[29]

We turn now to value relativism. In the discussion thus far the terms "objective" or "objectivity" have not been used, because it is difficult to use them without simultaneously conjuring up their opposites, "subjective" and "subjectivity," dichotomies that contribute significantly to the theses of relativism, even for objective relativists; indeed, I would argue that this dichotomy is the ultimate source of relativism in the history of modern western philosophy. Imagine, for instance, trying to make a case for moral relativism making no references to an inner, personal, private, subjective world.[30]

Like the speakers of most of the world's languages past and present, therefore, I will continue to try to get along without using these terms except simplistically at the outset to state two major claims of value relativism: the shibboleth that "beauty is in the eye of the beholder," and "morals are subjective." The first statement I think false, and the second involves two concepts—morals, in addition to subjectivity—that should be sent the way of phlogiston. Herein these topics can-

[29] For research on the (species-specific) human visual system, which I believe to be supportive of the claim about homoversals, see David C. Marr, *Vision* (New York: W. H. Freeman, 1982).

[30] Not a few philosophers, from Hume to Hare, have taken a subjectivist position on morals while either implicitly or explicitly denying moral relativism. But, first of all, it is by no means clear that these denials are effective; and, second, they clearly imply that the morality of modern western culture is, must be, the standard for consideration. A more complete account of this point is in my *Confucianism and Contemporary Ethics*, forthcoming.

not be taken up in detail; only a sketch of alternatives can be offered, again against a linguistic background.

To people raised in the musical tradition of Bach and Mozart, classical Chinese music sounds rather cacophonous at first. But from this and numerous similar examples it does not necessarily follow that our preferences in music are strictly determined by environmental conditioning, that is, that our responses to music are simply shaped. One might on the contrary hold that the set of possible sound concatenations—their pitch, intensity, harmonic relations—is, for human beings, a highly restricted set; that many possible forms of music simply cannot be appreciated by human beings due to their biological endowment. In one sense this view is obvious: no tune will be produced, pleasing or otherwise, that consists solely of sounds (notes) inaudible to the human ear, however much dogs may dance to it. And even John Cage never attempted to write a concerto for four fingernails and blackboard.

An even stronger view might be advanced as a hypothesis for investigation, namely, that even within the aural spectrum certain patterns of sounds will be intrinsically more pleasing to human beings than other patterns. There surely will be a wide range of patterns, but it might be a restricted range nevertheless; perhaps when anything goes, nothing can go far.

It also seems to me that classical Chinese music fairly quickly loses its cacophonous qualities (my sample is admittedly small) and becomes quite pleasing to hear, just as Bach and Mozart come fairly quickly to be appreciated by Chinese. One might hold, therefore, that a comparative study of western and Chinese classical music might go some way toward establishing abstract constraints for the apprehension of beautiful music. The *initial* lack of appreciation for the music of another culture should no more surprise us than our initial inability to understand the language of the culture when it is first spoken to us. The phonetic, phonological, syntactic, and semantic properties of Chinese certainly differ from those of English; it is nevertheless the case, on the basis of the generative model of language I wish to defend, that both Chinese and

English will exhibit identical abstract principles and constraints.

The analogy between music and human languages should not be pressed too far.[31] It is not being maintained that music must have a grammar, or be a language, but rather that the hypothesis that all pleasing music shares substantive abstract principles, within which notes and chords trigger responses in human beings, is not absurd. Such a hypothesis may well be false, and as put forward here it is surely vague and oversimplified; but it does not seem to be an unreasonable speculative direction to take in research. And if I may be permitted some additional speculation, the hypothesis can be more sharply focused, though I do so with much diffidence, being rather ignorant in the field of music.

One of the reasons that classical Chinese and western music each sound strange initially to persons brought up in the other tradition lies in their having different tonic scales. Still another scale—twelve-tone—has been developed and worked with by Arnold Schönberg and his followers. This music has now been with us for well over half a century, and I have several acquaintances who are very fond of it. These people have something else in common: they are all accomplished musicians. Among them, and commonly now, it is being lamented that twelve-tone music is becoming increasingly difficult to include in musical programs, much as the musicians themselves wish to do so. Thus my question for comparative musicologists: might there be properties shared by Chinese five-tone and western eight-tone music that are absent in twelve-tone music? Might it be that the many people who come to appreciate twelve-tone music do so in a fundamentally different *way* from the way they come to appreciate the others, again, akin perhaps to the fundamentally different ways we come to know our native language and FORTRAN?

Following through on these speculations in other areas, we

[31] But see Ray S. Jackendoff and Fred Lerdahl, *A Formal Theory of Tonal Music* (Cambridge, Mass.: M.I.T. Press, 1981).

might suggest that similar principles might be found in the visual arts: perhaps the possible set of shapes, textures, and color combinations pleasing to the human eye is also restricted by principles as yet wholly unknown. To be sure, much variation will be seen within the constraints, just as the set of grammars for natural languages is varied; more than three thousand languages are still spoken today—all with the same abstract constraining principles, if the generative model of language is correct.

There may be, to put the case differently, certain combinations of shapes, textures, and colors that other organisms, differently endowed biologically, could perceive as beautiful, but not be so appreciated by human beings; and at the same time there may be certain combinations of colors, textures, and shapes that we can perceive, but which simply jar our sensibilities. Continued exposure to such forms might inure us to their ugliness, and it is possible that the repeated association of these forms with something else experienced as pleasant—in other words, shaping stimuli—might make some people have a favorable attitude toward those forms; but that will not warrant saying they are beautiful.

Thus Socrates might not have been mistaken in the thrust of his claim that if two people said of the same object that it was beautiful, and that it was ugly, then one of them was mistaken. Surely there will be degrees of beauty, just as there are degrees of rhetorical elegance and grammatical acceptability within human languages. But according to this hypothesis certain objects may be wholly lacking in beauty, just as some strings of morphemes are wholly ungrammatical, and not every possible combination of audible noises is a possible human language.

What I am suggesting, in short, is that much of what has traditionally been studied under the label of aesthetics might become a field of formal study not unlike linguistics—which, too, must be ultimately grounded in biology—requiring that specific abstract principles be postulated, evidence gathered for their confirmation or modification, and so forth; much of aesthetics, in other words, might be brought more directly into the purview of the human sciences, with comparative philosophical research making signal contributions thereto.

I WOULD also argue that the concept of abstract homoversal principles might be fruitfully applied to the realm known—in the West, at least for the past three hundred years—as "morals." That is to say, there may be abstract principles and constraints governing our responses to, and evaluations of, human conduct in all of its varied manifestations. Perhaps, for example, seeing a fellow human being contorted in agony does indeed trigger empathetic and sympathetic responses in every normal human being, and those cases in which the responses are not manifested will be accounted for by overriding shaping stimuli generated by adverse environmental circumstances (if, every time I wriggle my finger and the kit pounces, I immediately strike it with a rolled-up newspaper, the kit will eventually stop pouncing).[32]

[32] To many people, perhaps the most compelling argument from anthropology for moral relativism will seem to be obscured by my focus herein on the *concept* (term) "morals"; namely, the description of the Ik people given by Colin M. Turnbull in *The Mountain People* (New York: Simon and Schuster, 1972). Therein he describes, for example, the cackling of adults when children stumble into a campfire and burn themselves. But what Turnbull describes no less compellingly is the utter starkness of the environment in which the Ik were forced to live, away from their traditional lands, with no traditional knowledge of how to survive in it. Thus the negative shaping stimuli to which the Ik were constantly exposed after their "resettlement" must be taken significantly into account in evaluating the actions of these people. Not unrelatedly, it should be clear to students of Chinese thought that my suggestion of empathetic responses to perceived human suffering is almost precisely similar to the argument made by Mencius (2A6), in his language, of the child who was about to fall into a well. It should also be noted that my claim about homoversals is absolutely general. That is to say, it is not necessarily the case that the triggering stimuli in the example generate an empathetic, sympathetic response. It is possible that the response could be what we would call "sadistic"; it is simply my own view that there is more evidence suggesting the former as a hypothesis than the latter. For some behavioral-science research suggestive of my hypotheses of homoversal principles, see, for example, Paul Ekman, ed., *Emotion in the Human Face*, 2d ed. (New York: Cambridge University Press, 1983); Carolyn B. Mervis and Eleanor Rosch, "Categorization of Nat-

If there are such homoversal principles—if human perceptions of conspecifics are fundamentally different in physiological and psychological structure, function, and effect(s) from human perceptions of everything else in the world—then the existence of such principles will have implications for ethics: ethical theories derived from empirically specifiable theories of human nature will be very different from ethical theories based on one or another of the variant concepts of practical reason.[33] Clearly it is the task of practitioners of the human and biological sciences to postulate and test concrete hypotheses of homoversal principles, but there will be much for philosophers to do as well, especially comparative philosophers.

One contribution comparative philosophers can make to this enterprise is to ascertain and describe the theories of human nature—explicit or implicit—contained in nonwestern philosophical and religious texts, theories that serve as the (or a) ground for the ethical systems promulgated in those texts. In order for this research to be fruitful, however, it will be necessary for comparative philosophers not to be bound by the vocabulary of contemporary western moral philosophy. In the first instance "ethics" must be clearly distinguished from "morals," which will simultaneously serve to challenge the overall conceptual framework within which philosophical arguments both for and against "moral" relativism have taken place, and serve an additional challenge to relativistic theses. One such challenge follows.

One of the strongest arguments advanced on behalf of moral relativism is based on anthropological evidence from other cultures. We do not need to question initially the reliability of the wealth of ethnographic data that appear to dem-

ural Objects," *Annual Review of Psychology* 32 (1981): 89–115; Mark Seligman and John Hager, *Biological Boundaries of Learning* (New York, 1982); plus the works of Marr, Fodor, and Chomsky cited previously.

[33] For discussion, see Bernard Williams, *Ethics and the Limits of Philosophy* (Cambridge, Mass.: Harvard University Press, 1985), and David Copp and David Zimmerman, eds., *Morality Reason and Truth* (Totowa, N.J.: Rowman, 1985), especially the essays by K. Baier, K. Nielsen, and J. Narveson.

onstrate the regularity with which a particular human action has been loathed by one people and at least tolerated, if not applauded, by another. But this evidence by itself will not do what a moral relativist might think it does; there is a logical point involved.

The farther we get from modern English and related western languages, the farther do we get from lexical items that correspond closely to the term "moral." All languages of course have terms for the approval and disapproval of human actions, and also terms for concepts employed in the evaluation of those actions; but a great many of the world's languages have no words that connote and denote uniquely a set of actions ostensibly circumscribed by the pair "moral–immoral," as against the nonmoral.[34]

The simplicity of this linguistic fact should not obscure its philosophical significance: speakers (writers) of languages that have no term corresponding to 'moral' cannot logically have any *moral* principles (or moral theories), from which it follows that they cannot have any moral principles incompatible with other moral principles, our own or anyone else's.

Put another way, we might disapprove of an action that members of another culture approve. But if our disapproval rests on criteria that involve concepts (terms) absent from their culture (language), and if their approval rests on criteria that

[34] Imagine attempting to describe uniquely the set of human actions that should be evaluated as moral or immoral, distinguishing them from those actions for which the evaluations would be inappropriate—to someone not raised in any of the modern western cultures. What would be central, and possessed by all members of the set? But this question cannot be answered unless we assume the correctness of some particular philosopher's view: motives more or less for Kantians, consequences for utilitarians, intrinsic worth, perhaps, or piety for many Christians. The most that we could say was that under particular circumstances, virtually any human action *could* have moral consequences. This is probably true, but notice that it is not particularly helpful to someone from another culture who did not already have the concept of morals in advance. What might be said of ethical thinkers from other cultures (slightly misleadingly) is that every human action *does* have what we—not they—would call "moral" consequences.

involve concepts (terms) absent from our culture (language), then it would simply be a question-begging, logical mistake to say that the members of the two cultures were in basic *moral* disagreement; the term is ours, not theirs. The ethnographic argument for moral relativism gains force only if it can be shown that two different people(s) evaluated a human action in the same way—invoking similar criteria grounded and exhibited in the same or very similar concepts—and that one approved the action, and the other disapproved.

It may seem that a big fuss is being made over a little word: why not simply find the closest approximation to the English 'moral' in the language (culture) under investigation, and proceed with the analysis from there? This is exactly what most anthropologists, and not a few philosophers and linguists, have done. But now consider as a specific example the classical Chinese language in which the early Confucians wrote. Not merely does that language contain no lexical item for 'moral', it also does not have terms corresponding to 'freedom', 'liberty', 'autonomy', 'individual', 'utility', 'rationality', 'objective', 'subjective', 'choice', 'dilemma', 'duty', 'rights', and probably most eerie of all for a moralist, classical Chinese has no lexical item corresponding to 'ought'—prudential or obligatory. (And we should suspect that the vast majority of other human languages that do not have a lexical equivalent for 'moral' will not have equivalents for most of these other modern English terms either; which could hardly be coincidental.)[35]

No, it is not only a term corresponding to 'moral' that must be sought in other languages if we are to speak cross-culturally about morals, for the sphere of contemporary western moral

[35] The notion of "concept cluster" that follows is important for translation matters here, because arguments that endeavor to show that *dao* (道), or *li* (禮), or *yi* (義), or some other single Chinese graph might appropriately be translated as 'morals' cannot succeed unless one is also willing to offer Chinese lexical candidates for 'subjective', 'rights', 'choice', and so forth—an altogether question-begging philological effort. See Rosemont, *Confucianism and Contemporary Ethics*, for further discussion, and n. 11 above.

philosophy is designated only roughly by the single term itself; a clear delimitation requires the full concept-cluster of terms just adumbrated, plus a few others. Now if contemporary western moral philosophers cannot (or do not) talk about moral issues without using these terms, and if none of the terms occurs in classical Chinese, it follows that the early Confucians could not be moral philosophers, and we will consequently be guaranteed to miss what they might have to tell us about ethics if we insist on imposing upon their writings the conceptual framework constitutive of our contemporary moral discourse. (And the same may be said, mutatis mutandis, of members of all other cultures who spoke or wrote about basic human conduct descriptively and evaluatively.)

To some, these arguments may still appear to be making too much of narrowly logical and linguistic claims about the word 'moral', or 'morals'. It can quickly be objected that one meaning of 'morals' is such that it is simply synonymous with 'ethics'. Consequently if it is legitimate to speak of "Confucian ethics," it must be equally legitimate to speak of the early Confucians as "moral philosophers," fine analytic distinctions aside.

But this objection ignores a simple fact: within the field of contemporary western moral philosophy, the term 'morals' is almost uniformly taken as circumscribing the culturally specific concept-cluster listed above, now referred to as "rights-based" theories and principles.[36] In the several and varied

[36] David B. Wong, *Moral Relativity* (Berkeley: University of California Press, 1984). To be sure, some contemporary western moral philosophers are questioning the "rights-based" concept cluster of modern morals, turning away from highly abstract rules, logical principles, and calculations, turning instead to qualities of personal character, in many ways attempting to reinvigorate the concept cluster surrounding the Aristotelian virtues. The significance of this shift notwithstanding, it is almost certainly the case that non-western ethical systems will not be better described by an updated Aristotelian terminology than by the terminology of "rights-based" moral theories; more will be needed. For the trend away from the latter in contemporary philosophical work, see Philippa Foot, *Virtues and Vices* (Berkeley: University of California Press, 1978); James D. Wallace, *Virtues and Vices* (Ithaca, N.Y.: Cornell University Press, 1978); Williams, *Ethics and the Limits*; Christina H. Som-

accounts put forward by writers in this field, moral issues involve the weighing of rational arguments on behalf of putative universal principles, which are possible options for guiding the specific actions of freely choosing, autonomous individuals. In this field the early Confucians, along with most other non-western thinkers, will not be found; nor, for that matter, will Aristotle: Alasdair MacIntyre has described cogently how the "rights-based" concept cluster of morals developed in modern western culture, and how very far removed it is from the ethical reflections found in the *Nicomachean Ethics*.[37] It is by no means just the early Chinese we will fundamentally misunder-

---

mers, ed., *Vice and Virtue in Everyday Life* (Orlando, Fla.: Harcourt Brace Jovanovich, 1985). See also the reference to MacIntyre in the following note.

[37] Alasdair MacIntyre, *After Virtue* (Notre Dame, Ind.: University of Notre Dame Press, 1981). By relying on clear and simple English prose, MacIntyre is well able to bring out the differences between Aristotle's virtue-based theory and contemporary rights-based theories, which employ a fairly technical vocabulary; and by so doing, he dissolves the apparent paradox of the exposition and/or advocacy of incommensurable belief systems. The paradox can be stated as follows: if two ethical conceptual frameworks (concept clusters) are taken to be total, and as sufficiently dissimilar as to be irreconcilable, then we could only make a case for the superiority of one framework to the other by assuming or presupposing the correctness of some at least of the ethical concepts embedded in the framework claimed to be superior. But on the first horn, if these assumptions or presuppositions are accepted by one's audience, it would seem that arguments would not be needed to command conviction. On the other horn, if the relevant assumptions or presuppositions are not accepted by one's audience, it would seem that no arguments could command conviction. Either the assumptions or presuppositions will be accepted by one's audience, or they will not; in either case, it would seem that arguments are not simply irrelevant, but altogether worthless for commanding conviction. It is something akin to these considerations that led Donald Davidson to say, "Most of our beliefs must be true." And if what is meant by "alternative conceptual frameworks" is totally and incompatibly different, then the claim is correct and does imply the conclusion of the paradox. However, Davidson's use of "our" is ambiguous. If it simply refers to mature English (and related modern western language) speakers, it is unexceptionable. But if "our" refers to contemporary western moral philosophers, his claim is suspect; and it is only the latter, and not the former, that MacIntyre (and comparative philosophers) challenge, so the seeming paradox is resolved. Donald Davidson, "On the Very Idea of a Conceptual Scheme," in *Proceedings and Addresses of the American Philosophical Association* 47 (1974): 5–20.

stand if we impose the concept cluster of contemporary western moral philosophy on ancient texts.

Thus the objection that one of the meanings of 'morals' is "ethics" can be turned against the objector: if one grants that in contemporary western moral philosophy 'morals' is intimately linked with the concept cluster elaborated above, and if none of that concept cluster can be found in the Confucian lexicon, then the Confucians not only cannot be moral philosophers, they cannot be ethical philosophers either. But this contention is absurd; by any account of the Confucians, they were clearly concerned about human conduct, what consequences would flow from that conduct, and what constituted the good life. If these are not ethical considerations, what are?[38]

If the concept cluster that dominates contemporary western moral philosophy is correctly seen as only one (or several) among many possible ethical positions, we must reflect on a number of consequences that follow from making this distinction. In the first place, while the distinction does not completely vitiate arguments presented on behalf of ethical (or cultural) relativism, it does call into question a number of their premisses; clearly the "moral" counterarguments given here are not confined to the ancient Chinese language, as already noted. Retranslations and reinterpretations must be carefully made before the extant ethnographic data can be called forth

[38] One could, of course, go even farther in making this objection, claiming that the Confucians were not philosophers at all, from which it would follow trivially that they could not be moral or ethical philosophers. But until there is greater agreement than exists at present about what is philosophy and what is not, it is difficult to take such a claim seriously; again, it is merely culturally question-begging. In a not altogether different context, Rorty has said, in *Philosophy and the Mirror of Nature* (p. 370), "This 'not really a philosopher' ploy is also used, of course, by normal philosophers against revolutionary philosophers. It was used by pragmatists against logical positivists, by positivists against 'ordinary language philosophers,' and will be used whenever cozy professionalism is in danger. But in that usage it is just a rhetorical gambit which tells one nothing more than that an incommensurable discourse is being proposed."

again in support of relativistic theses. Ethical relativism may turn out to be true, but it is not entailed by moral relativism.[39]

Second, making this distinction shows that nonwestern materials, despite the ever-increasing sophistication of comparative scholarship, continue to be approached from a strongly Western perspective. To be sure, no comparative scholar can come to another culture as a tabula rasa. One need not be a committed relativist to admit that pure (culture-free) intellec-

[39] Unfortunately, we do not have to trek to exotic lands to find examples of *moral* relativism; they are in abundance in contemporary American society. Abortion is a prime example. Within the modern conceptual framework (concept cluster) of morals, with its concomitant concepts of duty, autonomy, rights, choice, self, and freedom, it may not be possible to resolve the issue of abortion. One might want to argue that abortion is fundamentally a legal and not a moral issue, but for good or ill the vocabulary utilized in discussing the issue is the concept cluster of modern morals. It is difficult to see how the matter could be otherwise, for when one side says that basic human rights are at stake, and with rights being at the center of our concept cluster of morals, then we cannot but have a paradigmatic moral issue. Nor can it be objected that abortion is an instance of moral conflict, not moral relativism, for this objection misses the point: an abortion is a human action tolerated by a fairly large group of people, and loathed by another large group; precisely the same situation described in all ostensible instances of moral relativism based on anthropological evidence. The examples can be multiplied: animal rights, euthanasia, the rights of the not yet born to a healthy environment, genetic engineering, to name the most current. More generally, where the moral and political spheres are seen to overlap—justice and fairness—there is a good deal of prima facie evidence for relativism in recent philosophical writings; individual rights and social justice may not be altogether compatible concepts. And discussion of the grounds for the proper conduct of foreign policy are neither nonmoral nor noncontroversial. Perhaps all of these ethical and related issues can be well settled within the conceptual framework of modern morals. That framework has been deeply ingrained in western thinking for a long time; it was an integral element of the ideology undergirding the American and French revolutions. But perhaps that framework has served all the constructive purposes it can serve and is now becoming a hindrance rather than a help to the continuing human search for how better to live, and to live with one another in this complex world. In either case, it might prove salutary to consider alternative concept clusters, for just as no Renaissance astronomer could give up the Ptolemaic conceptions of the heavens until the Copernican had been articulated, just so we cannot clarify, modify, or abandon our modern conceptions of ethics as morals until there are alternatives to contemplate.

tual endeavor is a myth: physicists and physicians, scholars and scolds, plain men and philosopher queens are one and all ineradicably influenced by their cultural and historical circumstances. But it must equally be admitted that there are degrees of culture-boundedness, degrees that are in principle capable of being measured by all. Anthropologists of the late nineteenth century, for instance, made intelligence the determining characteristic of culture, and it was certainly a step toward reducing the Victorian English chauvinism underlying that concept when the focus shifted to learning as the determining characteristic.[40]

Still another consequence of distinguishing different concept-clusters is that among comparative philosophers, the most common (and often useful) method of working with nonwestern materials has been to address, as the most basic methodological question: to what extent do these texts suggest answers to philosophical questions that vex us? The moral of the "moral" illustration, however, is that the methodological question needs to be reformulated, both to reduce the investigator's temptation to read into the texts those issues by which he or she is already seized, and also, thereby, perhaps to generate some answers to the methodological question that are not altogether dependent for their plausibility on the investigator's cultural determinants. Reformulated, then: to what extent do these texts suggest that we should be asking very different philosophical questions?

By asking this latter question comparative philosophers can hope to revitalize philosophy in general by articulating alternative conceptual frameworks, showing how, why, and that they make sense; and by so doing begin to develop a new conceptual framework that embodies the insights from a multiplicity of cultures, which can assist the ongoing work of hu-

[40] George W. Stocking, Jr., *Race, Culture, and Evolution* (New York: Free Press, 1968).

man and biological scientists to solve the puzzles of what it is to be a human being.

OF COURSE my hypotheses about homoversal principles are just that, hypotheses, and highly speculative ones at that; and because none of them has been tested, I certainly cannot say that any of them are true. But a superiority of this position over the relativist's can be argued on the ground that it opens questions—philosophical and scientific—instead of begging them. To be sure, relativistic theses have done much to reduce the chauvinism implicit (when not explicit) in the work of a great many western scholars in the humanities, and in the social and behavioral sciences; the "white man's burden" is slowly but surely becoming as heavy to bear conceptually as it is economically and politically.

But theories are needed to guide fresh observations and research, and relativistic theses are sterile in this regard. If we assume conceptual relativism in one of its contemporary guises to be correct, it would always be correct; the questions asked herein, the hypotheses advanced, could not even arise, which would ensure that no one would look for evidence either to support or to invalidate them. And it would ensure likewise that evidence in support of them probably would not be recognized as such even if it stared us in the face, which is unlikely. If there are abstract homoversal principles of the kind suggested, they will be abstract indeed and will interact in highly complex ways with our other cognitive and sensory systems. Consequently, evidence for the specific properties of these principles will surely not merely be lying around waiting to be noticed by a casual observer, as the case of language illustrates clearly. For a technical example, consider the following two sentences:[41]

[41] The examples are modified from Chomsky's discussion of the syntactic elements involved in *Knowledge of Language*, pp. 101–110. That interesting theories do not seem to be generated by relativistic theses is suggested by Clif-

(1) This book is too difficult to understand without reading it.

(2) John is too narrow-minded to believe it [some idea, doctrine, etc.].

We interpret (1) as "this book is too difficult [for us/(any *x*)] to understand without [our/(any *x*)] reading it." Similarly, we interpret (2) as "John is too narrow-minded [for John] to believe it (the idea)." In both (1) and (2), then, we supply missing subject noun phrases in order to understand them.

Now if we omit the final pronoun in (2), the meaning changes significantly: "John is too narrow-minded to believe" means "John is too narrow-minded [for us/(any *x*)] to believe." This is a curious circumstance: omitting one constituent of the sentence alters our interpretation of other constituents omitted in both sentences. That is to say, in this case the appearance or nonappearance of a final pronoun form determines how we interpret subject NPs not audibly or visually given in the sentences. But this is not always so, for dropping the final pro-form in sentence (1) does not change the interpreation at all: "This book is too difficult to understand without reading" means just what (1) means.

The formal linguistic analysis of this phenomenon is rather technical, but the point of the illustration is not: what is crucial for analyzing these sentences is not physically present in them, and therefore linguistic reasearchers could not possibly focus thereon unless hypotheses of a highly specific, abstract, and restricted kind showed them where to look and what to be looking for.

In sum, if there are homoversal principles to govern our responses to and evaluations of human conduct, a great deal of sophisticated research must be undertaken to ascertain what specific form(s) they take. Much of this work, as in aesthetics

ford Geertz, sympathetic to them, in his "Anti Anti-Relativism," *American Anthropologist* 86 (1984): 263–278. See also n. 23 above.

as well, will have to involve a variety of disciplines, the members of which work together cooperatively and speak a multiplicity of languages. Again, in all such research comparative philosophers will have a key role to play, because they work with nonwestern texts that discuss at length other views of the world, of beauty, of human nature, and of the analyses and evaluation of human conduct. These discussions are carried out in languages very different from our own, which I personally consider not only a blessing but as containing the most exciting prospect of all for comparative philosophy.

My earlier arguments against conceptual relativism were obviously grounded in the belief that whatever can be said in any one natural human language can be said in any other if the full richness, variation, and capacity for change in human languages be exploited; and it is to nonwestern texts that I think we should now turn for much of the enrichment and change. While I do believe there are homoversal principles of the kinds suggested, I do not believe they can be well described or accounted for in the language I am now using. Some western philosophical concepts will—and should—remain with us; some others will have to be stretched, bent, or extended significantly in order to represent accurately nonwestern concept-clusters; and still other western philosophical concepts will, I think, have to be abandoned altogether in favor of others not yet extant, but which will issue from future research as new (or old) concept clusters are advanced. If we are seeking new perspectives in and on philosophy, if the discipline is to become as truly all-encompassing in the future as it has mistakenly been assumed to have been in the past, we must begin to develop a more common philosophical language to take its place alongside the other languages of the world.

An idealistic vision perhaps, but it is one that not only philosophers can share, they can share it with practitioners of the human and biological sciences as well. Even if successful, of course, such efforts would not put universal or absolute relativism universally and absolutely to rest. The most we would ever be able to say is that our way of viewing the world, our place in it, and our responses to and evaluations of others were true relative to Homo sapiens.[42] But with that kind of relativism perhaps we can all come to live—together.[43]

[42] The concession to absolute relativism is that any and all scientific views of the world, including views of what it is to be a human being, are all of them human views.

[43] For travel subventions that allowed me to present this paper at the international conference I am indebted to the Society for Asian and Comparative Philosophy and to the Faculty Development Grants Committee of St. Mary's College of Maryland. For their close reading of the paper—which is reflected in this revised draft—I am grateful to Roger Ames, Eliot Deutsch, John Hawthorn, Danielle Macbeth, Joan McGregor, and Graham Parkes, all of the Philosophy Department of the University of Hawaii, and to David Finkelman of the Department of Psychology at St. Mary's College of Maryland.

DAYA KRISHNA

Comparative Philosophy: What It Is and What It Ought to Be

ALL COMPARATIVE studies imply simultaneously an identity and a difference, a situation that is replete with intellectual difficulties, which give rise to interminable disputes regarding whether we are talking about the same thing or different things. One may cut the Gordian knot by deciding either way, but the situation would reappear again as it is bound up with the comparative perspective itself and not with any particular example of it. One wonders how long we shall go on "naming," for the process is unending and ultimately "everything is what it is, and not another thing." Or, if we do not like "names" as they hardly give us any knowledge and if we opt for "descriptions," which give us "facts," then they too are as unending as the "names," for, as the Jains taught us long ago, they are a function of the *dṛṣṭi* that we have or the point of view that we adopt.

"How similar is the similar?" is a question that can always be asked and hence is the bane of all comparisons, infecting them with an uncertainty that is irremediable in principle. Yet bare identity is not interesting to anybody. "$A = A$" hardly makes one move forward and "$A = B$," as everybody knows since the work of Frege, raises problems that seem insoluble at least to pure theoretical reason. As for the practical reason, particularly not of the kind that Kant called "pure," it has never had problems with the difficulties that the pure or even impure theoretical reason has raised—a situation that has earned philosophers the dubious privilege of being considered the most impracticable people in the world.

But comparative studies are not just comparisons. They are comparisons between societies, cultures, and civilizations.

Across the boundaries defined by the "we" and the "they," the world of comparative studies is inevitably an attempt to look at what, by definition, is "another reality" from the viewpoint of that which is not itself. The contradiction lying at the very foundation of comparative studies is sought to be glossed over by the appeal to the universalism of all knowledge and the identification of the knowledge with the privileged "us" from whose viewpoint all "other" societies and cultures are judged and evaluated. The roots of this privileged position have generally lain in the political and economic power of the society of which the viewer happened to be a member. The anthropological studies from which most comparative studies have arisen were, by and large, an appendage of the extension of some western European countries' political and economic power over the globe during the past three hundred years or so. As this expansion was accompanied not only by phenomenal growth in some of the traditional fields of knowledge but also by demarcation and consolidation of new areas designating new fields of knowledge, the feeling that the claim that all "knowledge" discovered by the West held universal validity was justified. It was seen, therefore, as a universal standard by which to judge all other societies and cultures anywhere in the world, not only in those domains of knowledge but in all fields, whether they had anything to do with them or not.

Comparative studies, thus, meant in effect the comparison of all other societies and cultures in terms of the standards provided by the western societies and cultures, both in cognitive and in noncognitive domains. The scholars who belonged to these other societies and cultures, instead of looking at western society and culture from their own perspectives, accepted the norms provided by western scholars and tried to show that the achievements in various fields within their cultures paralleled those in the West, so they could not be regarded as inferior in any way. This acceptance of bias hindered the emergence of what may be called "comparative 'comparative studies,'" which might have led to a more balanced perspective in these fields.

Further, the so-called comparative studies were primarily a search for facts or a reporting of data in terms of a conceptual structure already formulated in the West. The questions to which answers were being sought were already predetermined in the light of the relationships that were regarded as significant or the theories that were to be tested. Where cultures were seen as autonomous it was more in terms of values embodied in the institutions of the culture than in terms of conceptual structures defining the cognitive terrain itself. Philosophy is, however, nothing but the conceptual structure itself, and hence any attempt at comparative philosophizing is bound to lead to an awareness of an alternative conceptual structure, a different way of looking at the world, a different way of mapping the cognitive terrain than that to which one is accustomed. Yet, however natural such an expectation might be, it is not what happened. How could one allow for the possibility of an alternative conceptual scheme when what was "possible" was itself determined by the conceptual scheme one was born into?

Comparative philosophy, thus, has been bogged down from the very beginning with the question of whether there is anything that can be called "philosophy" outside the western tradition. It took a fairly long time for scholars to realize that the so-called histories of philosophy they were writing about were mainly histories of western philosophy and not of philosophy outside the western hemisphere. Bertrand Russell was the first person to acknowledge explicitly, in the very title of his work relating to the history of philosophy, that it was a history of western philosophy and not of philosophy in general. But even today the problem remains the same. Shall we acknowledge what exists outside the western tradition as "philosophy" or not? The question has repeatedly been raised with respect to Indian and Chinese philosophies, the two major traditions outside the West. Recently, the same debate has erupted around the question of whether there was such a thing as "philosophy" in Africa. Surprisingly, the question has never been raised with respect to Islamic philosophy, presumably because it derived its inspiration directly from the Greeks and self-consciously built upon their work. In fact, most histories of western philosophy have a chapter on Arabic philosophy, but mostly they treat it as important in the context of the West's access to Plato and Aristotle before they came to be directly available in their Greek sources, or else as an interlude with little interest for the development of mainstream philosophy in the West.

The debate regarding the status of philosophy in China or Africa or even in the Arabic world is not the subject of discussion here for the simple reason that I know little about the philosophical tradition in these cultures. A discussion of the Indian case, which I know a little better, may, however, be expected to throw some light on the problems of comparative philosophy as it has developed to the present day.

The first and foremost question that has engaged all those who have been seriously concerned with the so-called philosophical tradition in India relates to the issue of how it can be regarded as "philosophy" proper when it is supposed to be primarily concerned with *mokṣa*, that is, liberation from the very possibility of suffering, which is a quintessentially practical end and has hardly anything theoretical about it. To this question is added the consideration of how any cognitive tradition can be regarded as genuinely philosophical that accepts the authority of revelation or of some superhuman authority which is supposed to have an overriding authority over both reason and experience. In fact, *The Encyclopedia of Indian Philosophies* officially underwrites the necessary relationship of Indian philosophy with *mokṣa* and maintains that the former cannot be understood without the latter. It is, then, no wonder that Indian philosophy is not taught in the philosophy departments of most western universities, for neither the students nor the teachers in these departments are presumably seeking *mokṣa*. The relegation of Indian philosophy to departments of Indology and its effective segregation from all active philosophical concerns of the day speaks for itself. The other side of the coin is attested by the so-called revival of interest in Indian philosophy on western campuses in the wake of interest in such subjects as Transcendental Meditation, Yoga, and the like.

Yet, one has to square this widespread impression about Indian philosophy with the fact that in any work of Indian philosophy *pūrva-pakṣa* (the opponent's position) has necessarily to be presented and refuted before one can establish one's own position. The counterposition, it should be remembered, is not merely stated but is presented with not only all the arguments that have already been proposed in its favor but also those which one can imagine to support it in any way whatsoever. If one simply asserted something and could not provide any reason or *hetu* for it, one opted out of the philosophical arena and ceased to be counted therein. Even the *sūtras* of the various philosophical schools, which are supposed to be the foundational works for them, not only give reasons for the positions they hold but also refute counterpositions. Further, all reasons are not regarded as equally valid; a great deal of thought went into determining what was valid reasoning and how to distinguish it from what was fallacious.

Moreover, the history of the debate on any philosophical issue documents, thinker by thinker, the development of the argument and the flaws pointed out by each in the position of the others. There was, however, in this matter no static repetition of positions but a modification of one's position in the light of opponents' trenchant criticism or even a more sophisticated reformulation of one's position in the light of those criticisms. The great debate between the Buddhists and the Naiyāyikas, which started from Dignāga in the fifth century after Christ and ended sometime around the eleventh century, is evidence of this process. This period of about six hundred years saw on the Buddhist side such well-known figures as Dignāga, Dharmakīrti, Dharmottara, Śāntarakṣita, and Kamalaśīla. Ranged against them were Uddyotakara, Kumārila, and Prabhākara of the Mīmāṁsā school, Vācaspatimiśra, Jayanta, Udayana, and Śrīdhara. After the disappearance of the Buddhists from the Indian scene, there was the great debate between the Advaitin and the non-Advaitin, whose last great representatives were

Vyāsatīrtha on the side of the latter and Madhusūdana Saraswati, on the side of the former. Along with this were the radical and revolutionary developments in Nyāya after Gaṅgeśa from the twelfth century, which lasted to the seventeenth century. During this period of almost five centuries there were at least thirty-six thinkers whose names are known and who by their works contributed to the development and refinement of logical thought in India—a development that set new norms for intellectual precision such that no study remained unaffected by it.[1]

From the fifth century to the seventeenth century is a long period indeed, and to find evidence of a fairly high degree of hard-core philosophizing with continuous interchange of argument and counterargument between the participants resulting in a cumulative sophistication of the positions held is an intellectual achievement of the highest order of which any culture might be reasonably proud. Yet, the general picture of Indian philosophy is that it can hardly be regarded as philosophy proper in the western sense of the word, because it is primarily concerned with *mokṣa* and cannot rid itself of its ties to revelation, which it regards as authoritative over and above both reason and experience. Moreover, this privileged sense of the word, to which the West lays a monopolistic claim and which is supposed to provide the standard in terms of which every other "philosophical" enterprise would have to be judged, is supposed to characterize it *uniformly* from the time of Thales down to the present. But as everybody knows this is a false claim, and for long stretches of time what passes for philosophy in the West could not be characterized as such if the definition were to be as strictly enforced there as it usually is in the case of nonwestern cultures. To treat Plato and Aristotle as exclusive parts of the western patrimony and to reread retrospectively the whole of the western tradition in terms of what has

[1] See M. Chakravarti, "History of Navya-Nyaya in Bengal and Mithila," in Debiprasad Chattopadhyaya, ed., *Studies in the History of Indian Philosophy*, 3 vols. (Calcutta: K. P. Bagohi, 1979), 2:146–82.

happened there since the seventeenth century are the usual means through which this claim is upheld. However, surprisingly enough, it is not only western scholars who perpetrate this deception; many nonwestern scholars also accept it unquestioningly.

The Indian scholars who have concerned themselves with philosophy, for example, not only have swallowed the bait hook, line, and sinker but have tried to gain respectability for Indian philosophy either by discovering parallels to most of the western philosophical positions in the Indian tradition or by taking pride in the fact that philosophy in India was no mere arid intellectual exercise engaged in logic-chopping for its own sake, but concerned with the deepest existential issues of the bondage and liberation of man's innermost being. Indian philosophy, thus, either had everything that western philosophy had to show in terms of the utmost sophistication of epistemological and ontological reflection or had the special, unique characteristic of being spiritual and concerned with *mokṣa.* It was conveniently forgotten that if philosophy is an enterprise of the human reason, it is bound to show similarities across cultures to some extent and, similarly, as a human enterprise it is bound to be concerned with what man, in a particular culture, regards as the summum bonum for mankind.

The inevitable position of the privileged terms in any comparison can only be overcome if the terms functioning as a standard for comparison are deliberately changed to provide a different standard. Normally, this diversity would naturally have been provided by the fact that each culture would have seen the others from its own point of reference and thus been the subject and object of comparison, in turn. But due to political and economic factors, such a situation has not come to pass, as the intellectuals of the observed cultures have themselves internalized the western categories and standards of intelligibility so that they observe, understand, and compare their own cultures in terms given to them by the West. To adopt a well-known expression from Sartre, all nonwestern cultures have been reduced to the status of "objects" by being observed and studied by western scholars in terms of western concepts and categories, which are treated not as culture-bound but as universal in character. In a deep and radical sense, therefore, it is only the West that has arrogated to itself the status of subjecthood in the cognitive enterprise, reducing all others to the status of objects.

The problem is further complicated by the fact that most of the discussions about Indian philosophy are carried on in the European languages. Perforce, therefore, the Sanskritic terms have to be translated into their western equivalents, giving the latter a magisterial status in deciding what the former mean or ought to mean. The converse situation normally does not take place; but recently when at Poona the experiment was tried of translating some issues in Russell and Wittgenstein into Sanskrit so that responses might be elicited from persons trained in philosophy in the traditional manner, the difficulty became apparent. How were the pandits—philosophers trained on the Sanskrit classics in the traditional manner—to make sense of what Russell and Wittgenstein were saying? As most of them did not know English, the matter had to be translated into Sanskrit, but then those Sanskrit terms carried the usual connotations associated with them and resisted the imposition of new meanings upon them. Earlier, a similar experiment had been tried in the pages of *The Pandit*, a journal published in Banaras in the nineteenth century, with results that have, as far as I know, not been clearly analyzed before.

In any case, the problem remains of how to translate one conceptual structure in terms of another, particularly when it is not only in another language but also has a history of sophisticated development of its own over millennia. The point is important, for there was a time in which difficult philosophical texts were translated from Sanskrit into Tibetan, Chinese, and later from Chinese into Korean or Japanese. But in most of these cases, because there was no equally developed native philosophical tradition one could coin new terms without coming into conflict with already well-settled ways of thinking about things. Even in such a situation, as Nakamura has shown, the translation had to come to terms, if not with the intellectual then at least with the new country's cultural ethos.[2]

However it may be, the only way in which even the first steps can be taken toward any solution of the problem is to look at it from both sides, to see how each looks when seen from the point of the view of the other. No culture or tradition can be assigned a privileged place in this game of observing the other or understanding, judging, and evaluating it in terms of itself.

But there are not just two cultures in the world. It may be difficult to say with any certainty how many there are or even to give some agreed criterion in terms of which one may determine the distinction or demarcation between cultures. Also, it is not necessary that each culture have a distinctive identity in all the domains or even that it might have been creative in all of them. But there can be little doubt that whatever dimension of a culture we may choose to consider, it has been creatively pursued by more than one culture, each of which has made major contributions to it. But if this be so, each would have to be seen from a plurality of standpoints. Such an expectation at the present would almost be utopian. Most countries today are only aware of the West, in terms of which they see, measure, and judge themselves. They are not even aware of its neighbors, even though they might have made the most impressive contributions in the fields in which they may be interested. Of course, there are historical reasons for the situation as it obtains today, and while these reasons continue to operate it is difficult to see how they can be overcome except by the joint effort of scholars in a discipline who belong to diverse cultures and yet are aware of the need for transcending their culture-centric predicament.

The problem of the self-identity of an intellectual tradition within a cultural area, moreover, runs against the claim to universality that all truth professes. But the claim to universality,

[2] Hajime Nakamura, *Ways of Thinking of Eastern Peoples*, rev. ed. Philip P. Wiener (Honolulu: East–West Center Press, 1964).

it should be remembered, is only a claim, and it has hardly been fulfilled by any of the existing claimants to the title. It is only by tacit agreement that the western models are universal, not culturebound as all others are. There is, of course, the other problem of how to compare alternative conceptual structures or decide between them. The Kuhnian approach argues the incommensurability of alternative conceptual structures even within a tradition with a common language, culture, and history. But when these latter differ radically, how can one even think of comparing, contrasting, or judging them? Yet, the judgment of incommensurability involves not only the fact that the two have been compared, but that each has been intelligibly grasped and understood. The consciousness that does so has thus the capacity for intellectual empathy that through conceptual imagination can enter a different world of intelligibility and feel, if not at home, at least not alien in it.

The decision between alternative conceptual structures is made, it has been urged, not on grounds of logic or evidence but in terms of their fecundity for suggesting significant research programs, particularly these days, when the number of persons engaged professionally in research is so large and is increasing day by day. Of course, what is ultimately supposed to decide between alternative theories or conceptual schemes is the Darwinian struggle between them, which results in the survival of the fittest. It is conveniently forgotten that survival is a function of many factors, including those which happen to be primarily political and economic, and that unlike biological forms, cultural forms never die unless their embodiments are destroyed without leaving any traces or copies and beyond the possibility of all retrieval. Further, there is a difference between domination and survival, which those who bring evolutionary considerations into the comparisons of cultures tend to forget. They also tend to assume gratuitously that what is dominant today will remain so forever.

But the idea that a choice has necessarily to be made between alternative conceptual structures, whether they be rooted in different cultures or not, itself need not be accepted. Conceptual structures may be seen as tools for the organization of experience and for giving it meaning and significance. Each available conceptual structure thus shows the limitations of the others and suggests an alternative possibility unexplored by them. Also, they may be seen as drawing our attention to those facts of our experience which have been neglected in other perspectives and to ways of organizing and patterning experience that were not seen by them.

This view, it may be urged, brings the whole cognitive enterprise perilously close to the artistic one and, if taken to its logical conclusion, would make us give up the truth claim altogether. The parallel with the arts may, however, not be seen as a danger signal warning us that we are not on the right track, but rather a sign, at least for those who value the world of art very highly, that things are not far wrong, even if they are not completely right. Concepts can never be simply images or symbols and can hardly ever be simply a matter of feelings and emotions. The questions of truth and falsity can never be allowed to remain absent for long, even though they may be intractable in nature. Yet, what we should remember is that the cognitive enterprise is as unending as any other enterprise, and that though the truth claim must inevitably be made, it is equally certain that it shall remain unresolved in time. The future will always be there to show us not only the limitations of our knowledge and the falsity of our claims but also to bring to our notice new horizons, undreamed of before.

It is true that the diversity of conceptual structures is rooted in the historical isolation of cultures with little communication, if any, between them. The isolation has been fostered by geographical, political, and linguistic factors, which have simultaneously facilitated interaction within certain peoples and hindered it among others. Trade and religion have generally tried to cross the boundaries for material or spiritual profit, but they have seldom achieved notable success unless backed by political power. Behind the individual stamp conferred on a culture by this development in relative isolation, however, lies the accident of what struck the great minds as problems requiring solutions or as questions requiring answers at the very beginning of civilization.

Absolute beginnings, it is true, can never be determined with certainty, but there can be little doubt that at the beginnings of all the recorded civilizations there stand outstanding individuals who posed the problems, raised the questions, and laid down at least the direction in which possible solutions or answers might be sought. It is this distinctiveness in what is perceived as a problem or the direction that is chosen for its solution that marks out one tradition from another, and which is what is (or should be) significant for other cultures or traditions.

There is, of course, an objective universality of human reason on the one hand and of the conditions of human living, on the other, which ensures that there would be a fair repetition amongst the problems perceived and the solutions proposed. But this universality can only be of momentary interest except for those who have identified themselves so much with a particular section of humanity that the only paramount concern for them is to prove that all worthwhile things originated with them and were borrowed by others. Basically, their conviction is that what was not originated by them or their ancestors could not possibly be worthwhile, or even if it were, it must surely be inferior to what they themselves have produced or discovered. But just as one travels to find a renewed sense of wonder and novelty, so does one make conceptual journeys to other cultures to look at the world through new conceptual frames.

The interesting approach in comparative philosophy would, then, be to search not for similarities but for differences. But even the differences are philosophically interesting only when they are articulated not in terms of the doctrines held, but in terms of the problems perceived and the solutions attempted. Ultimately, it is the arguments given for a certain position that are of interest to a philosophical mind, and in this respect the Indian philosophical tradition is especially rich because its very format of presentation consists of giving the arguments of the opponent first and then the establishment of one's position by their rebuttal.

To search for the distinctive philosophical problems seen as problems or for distinctiveness in the solutions offered to similar problems is not only to see the alien tradition in a new way but to enrich oneself with the awareness of an alternative possibility in thought, a possibility that has already been actualized. The awareness of this alternative actualized possibility may, one hopes, free one's conceptual imagination from the unconscious constraints of one's own conceptual tradition. Thus comparative philosophy has the chance to function as a mutual liberator of each philosophical tradition from the limitations imposed upon it by its own past, instead of being what it is at present, the imposition of the standards of one dominant culture upon all the others and the evaluation of their philosophical achievements in terms of those alien standards.

BEN-AMI SCHARFSTEIN

The Contextual Fallacy

THE FALLACY that I propose to analyze consists of a misplaced emphasis on context, on the attempt to understand something in the light of a presumably unique, original perspective or context, in the absence of which everything is taken to be misunderstood. Yet the very attempt to understand something in particular requires us to detach it at least somewhat from whatever background we find it in, to turn it over in our minds, and to relate it to our present interests. We may at moments enjoy the fantasy of living in the thoughts of someone long dead; but if we did live there, we would not have the chance or ability to live in our own thoughts and their relation to those of the long-dead person, who may, for our present purposes, be considered a philosopher. In any case, the fantasy is only that, and the exact restoration of the past philosopher in ourselves no more desirable than it is possible. The truth seems to be that the problem of context is more easily dealt with in practice than in theory, and in practice our habits often lead us to disregard it as an explicit problem. It is forcibly raised, however, by some historians, especially the revisionists among them; by social anthropologists, who may be shamed by their fieldwork or impelled by their rebelliousness into relativism; and, with a different kind of intellectual and emotional pressure, by textual scholars. Nationalism, too, makes an issue of it, for no tribe or nation can accept its history as viewed by outsiders, whether religiously motivated missionaries, colonial administrators, or others. To the nationalists, often, there is some pure source and a true way of imbibing from it, representing it, and living out its effects.[1]

[1] Much of this essay is based on a book in process, on comparative aesthetics. The essay is so general that it seems best to me not to provide a bibliog-

Let me confine the problem for a moment to textual scholarship. Those who deal with the history of thought, especially that of distant periods or cultures, commit themselves to the discovery of the exact meaning of the texts that interest them. Experience has taught them how unlikely it is that the words of the texts convey just what we might take them to mean here and now. To verify the accuracy of the text, one begins with the history of its transmission and a comparison of the oldest versions. Whatever else is attributed to the same author and those close to him must be kept in mind as part of the relevant environment. Committed to such a subtle, nuance-filled, and endless task, a scholar is likely to be antagonistic to the generalizations of those who do not know and possibly do not care about the nuances of his text. Furthermore, the scholar acquires a sense of proprietorship over the text, like that of a priest dedicated to the keeping and interpretation of traditional formulas. Comparisons with texts distant in the time and place are often made by persons who do not command the at least double scholarship required, and the comparisons are discouraged as tending by their very nature to disregard context and destroy nuance. If we find such difficulty in understanding what is relatively close to us, the scholar implies, why confuse ourselves by comparing this half-known thought that we hardly know at all?

This antagonism, nourished by examples of pretentious ignorance, tends to make students of comparative thought cautious; and caution slips easily into hypercaution, which deserves the name because it is sterile. For those interested in comparative thought it is therefore important to recognize that an extreme emphasis on context can be unreasonable and intellectually expensive enough to be considered a fallacy.

A little reflection should persuade us that understanding is often injured if we try to confine it to appreciation of the nu-

raphy. However, for those who are interested, I cite Benoit B. Mandelbrot, *The Fractal Geometry of Nature* (New York: W. H. Freeman, 1982); and R. J. Maeda, "The 'Water' Theme in Chinese Paintings," reprint from *Artibus Asiae* 33.4 (1971):247–290.

ances that make texts or anything else unique. Taking things out of context is essential, not only to abstract learning, but to life itself. To take things intellectually out of their immediate context is only to continue what happens at every moment of our lives, when ordinary perception convinces us and memory confirms that some one thing or event resembles some other, previously experienced. The very perception that discloses uniqueness discloses similarity. If it were not for the perceptual ability to disregard differences, our experiences would never become cumulative, we would never learn from them, because there are inevitable differences in any of the experiences we undergo. The question is not whether the differences exist, because they do, but what we should make of them; and the answer often lies in the conscious or unconscious decision to pay no attention to the context, or, more accurately, to make use only of the criteria that fit our need at the time, that is, to intuit or hypothesize or discover the context that is most pertinent to our need.

Let me continue to justify decontextualization (or recontextualization) by a brief word on identity and difference. It would take us too far afield to discuss them in terms of the ancient and still current philosophical debate on nominalism and realism. I shall therefore remain on a more commonsense level, though the philosophical issue, on which I take an intermediate position, is obviously relevant.

In terms of depth of abstraction, mathematics comes first. If we, human beings, have learned or conceived of objects of thought that remain always identical with themselves and subject to absolute rules of comparison, the objects are those of mathematics. Physics, too, is deeply abstract. It currently assumes that particles of a certain kind are identical with all others of the same kind, or, if the particles decay or otherwise alter, with all others in the same state of decay or alteration. The theoretical context of mathematics and physics is sufficiently strong and uniform to make everything in their domains subject to the same assumptions and rules and, in this sense, exactly comparable—to exaggerate, though not intolerably, the assumptions and rules are context enough.

The exaggeration that is tolerable for pure mathematics and theoretical physics becomes harder to maintain for applied mathematics and experimental physics; and when we turn to biology and, beyond it, to culture, everything shows itself to be different from everything else. Examined with enough care, even identical twins are observed to be different, at times grossly so. For that matter, it is reasonable to hold that a person in different situations or at different times is distinctly different from what he was—the view can be held without any Buddhist, Humean, or other self-estranging assumptions: a human being plays different roles, develops, responds in ways that surprise even himself, and shows the effects of an imperfect integration. The individuality of any one of us cannot be put in an exact, sufficiently rich generalization or given a brief, coherent, sufficiently varied description, so that the logical tautology that says that a person is identical with himself is misleading if taken to mean that a person can be summed up or his responses predicted on the basis of the tautology and what is known or supposed of him. An individual in fact is far denser than the individuality posited by theories of personality. Not only is he incommensurable as a whole, but he cannot be explained as simply the emergent result of a unique configuration of structures identical with those that make up other individuals. As immunologists have discovered, every cell in the body distinguishes between the cells that do and do not belong to that individual and rejects alien cells or materials, much as ants reject ants from other nests and clean out alien materials. It appears that learning is possible for individual cells, which may, that is, have a sort of memory. The biochemist Daniel Koshland contends that bacteria acquire and continue to show characteristics of their own, that they too, in other words, are individuals. Therefore everything biological, from human being to bacterium, is profoundly different from the atomic and subatomic particles that make it up.

However, the individuality of at least everything biological is no reason to forget how profoundly and pervasively similar everything is. As sheer concepts, individuality or uniqueness, on the one hand, and generality or sameness on the other, are of course mutually dependent, and they remain so when applied in order to clarify our thought or guide our reactions. The profound and pervasive similarity between biological individuals is demonstrated by mathematics, physics, biochemistry, ethology, and social sciences. If everything were not profoundly similar, if there were not pervasive lines of identity and similarity running through existence, existence, if it could exist otherwise, would be unthinkable chaos. Profoundly different though a human being is from subatomic particles, he is profoundly like them, even identical with them, in the sense that they make him up; and the discovery of the likeness and connection is the prolonged work of science, whether conceived from the bottom up, as a philosophy of reduction suggests, or from the top down, as is suggested by a philosophy of emergence; for we and quarks are identical. Although all of our cells may be biochemically identified with ourselves as individuals, their rejection of alien cells is explained, it appears, by the electrochemical properties of the cell surfaces, in other words, by the selfsame electrochemical principles. Cellular "memories" may vary, but how and perhaps why they vary is explainable, we hope, by identical principles, including that of cellular "learning." The involvement goes beyond physics. Like every other living thing, the human being is in a sense profoundly involved in, even identical with, mathematical relationships, which are immanent in his structures, his actions, and his understanding. In this sense, we are mathematics come alive.

An old paradox, which I remember under the name of Plato's Paradox, goes to the length of saying that things that are as different as possible from one another resemble one another in being as different from one another as possible. A variant of this paradox of identity would require anyone arguing that contextual differences made a comparison impossible to explain just what the decisive contextual differences might be;

and this explanation would of course be a form of the very comparison the impossibility of which it was taken to show.

Considerations such as these lead me to insist that any objects of thought can be compared legitimately. There is no general, abstract question of the legitimacy, but only whether a particular comparison has led to anything intellectually useful, pleasurable, or enlightening. The comparison may turn out not to have met these natural demands; but its failure ought not be assumed a priori. A far-reaching comparison is best viewed as an experiment that can be judged to have succeeded or failed only after it has been made. The cultural distance it spans makes the challenge the greater and the success, if it comes, the more interesting. But whether the comparison is judged to have succeeded or failed, it is always made in *some* context, if only that which expresses the purpose of the decontextualizer. Laboratory experiments owe much of their difficulty to the difficulty of forcing things out of context. Often even the laboratory apparatus refuses to function as the experiment demands. Often the subjects do not yield to the attempt to force them out of their natural patterns of life. Laboratory experimenters used to complain that ethologists were anthropomorphic and imprecise, while the ethologists complained that the experimenters were subjecting animals too much to human preconceptions and not allowing them to express their own nature, to which they quickly reverted, sometimes in the laboratory itself. Birds were thought mechanical and stupid because they lacked a cerebral cortex, which in the human being was associated with intelligence, and because on certain tests they responded with a damaging automaticity; but then it was discovered that the birds' ability to learn was primarily located in another anatomical area, the hyperstriatum, and that some birds, such as crows, were extraordinarily adaptable and, by that widely accepted criterion, intelligent; and that birds might outrank mammals, even primates, in their ability to generalize concerning shapes (to identify related shapes among others). By now experimenters and ethologists have reached a fruitful modus vivendi and are sometimes joined in the same person. Decontextualization takes place, because it must, but with more awareness of the particular animal's nature. Typically, ethologists, who make prolonged observations of the same small group of animals, give each animal an individual name and learn to react to it as an individual; but, like all other scientists, they are in constant pursuit of generalizations.

If you are careful, to particularize is to be safe, while to generalize is to endanger yourself intellectually, to lay yourself open to the charge that the generalization has missed something—the very point of a generalization is a useful disregard of details. The fear of generalization is implanted in all of us, for good reasons and bad. In part the fear is based, I think, on the acceptance of implicit and explicit models of thought that are either too cautious or too simple. The too cautious are those which imply, like some local histories or biographies, that everything they deal with is unique and can be grasped only as such, even though the language in which they convey this old, far from unique thought is based on the shared meaning of the same words. There is a very common confusion between the living inside a person's skin, being that person, and grasping what kind of person we are describing. While the relation of any person to himself (a term I use despite Wittgensteinian objections) is unique and privileged, the person in question may be confused, inconsistent, and, in important ways, less known to himself than to others. To use a medical analogy, a person may suffer from an autoimmune disease, in which he is identified biochemically as alien to himself, for which reason some fraction of himself attacks another portion of himself. If to understand someone required us to be experientially identical with him, we would run into the difficulties I have mentioned, reaching to the extreme of a chaos of incomparable events that would not share even the same sense of "event." To such hyperindividualizing, my answer is also, therefore, that if all the objects of thought and all persons were wholly unique, the attempt to describe them as such would necessarily fail because it was addressed to persons who would appreciate the uniqueness only on the basis of their own, quite different, quite unique experience. Aristotelianism faced this kind of difficulty in establishing in what sense, if any, God could be said to know unique, individual objects of thought. Those who, like the Indians (of India), tend to believe in the reality of "supernormal" perception, have other answers, the intellectual basis for which is likely to be a belief in the essential identity of everything, which knows itself in everything as soon as it sees through the veil that obscures understanding; but this belief exacts a high intellectual price.

The overly simple models are perhaps more insidious in their influence. They are related to our inclination to equate with exactly scientific reasoning. That is, we are likely to have been educated to feel that a relation between a cultural generalization and its presumed instances should be like that between a regular geometrical figure and an approximation to it; or between a law of physics and something formally derivable from it; or between a simple statistical curve and something that finds its place more or less on the curve.

It appears to me that if we feel the need to think in terms analogous to those of exact science, we should find ourselves models that are more intellectually useful, not only because they create a chance for a closer approximation, but because they serve the imagination better. The models must be more complex, that is, scientifically more difficult to deal with, or, in the case of a different emphasis, more vague in an intellectually useful sense of vagueness. As possible examples, let me give the models of turbulence, of a "cascade," and of a cloud.

A turbulence—an unsmooth flow, one containing eddies—is unstable and hard to deal with mathematically. It seems that, like the wind, it is made up of a succession of bursts themselves made up of smaller bursts. A turbulence model would surely fit in with the views of the world as constituted by the entanglement and disentanglement of forces of various kinds. We see visual illustrations of such turbulence in Chinese paintings of water, as we see them in the currents, waves, and storms drawn by Leonardo or the waves drawn by Hokusai. The useful sense of turbulence is that of a flowing, shifting, forceful balance, the regularity of which is easier to perceive than to analyze intellectually.

The "cascade," which is unturbulent, can serve as a model for whatever breaks up into fragments like itself, the fragments breaking up into others like themselves, for example, the Chinese hierarchy of human, political, and political-cosmic relationships and the structures within structures of Indian mythology, and all the microcosmic-macrocosmic pairs that show a universe with a texture, so to speak, the same at every level.

Maybe clouds, with the geometrical irregularities, varying densities, holes, and vague boundaries, would make interesting, useful models. The indefinite boundaries of clouds seems to me particularly useful because they may weaken our often excessive tendency to subject indefinite phenomena to the logic of "yes" and "no" and to search for intellectual devices that will classify everything human on one or another side of a sharp intellectual boundary. A cloud may have a clear shape on the background of the sky or of other clouds, and yet, in a clear sense, it may not begin or end at any very definite line, or begin or end at all. In this definite indefiniteness, this separation by merging, a cloud resembles all kinds of cultural traits and entire subcultures and cultures. Like these, it may unite symmetry with asymmetry and so stimulate a cloud-clear analysis of complex and indefinite relationships. As an exercise, I suggest analysis of the ways in which a particular philosophy or philosophical school resembles a cloud.

It may encourage those with a technical cast of mind that a mathematics (of "fractals") is being created, and that "fuzzy logics" are being designed to help make our thought less vague or more exactly vague. Because my own cast of mind is not especially technical, I want to do no more than suggest that the imagination should be drawn on more to improve our intellectual grasp of human culture.

Decontextualization, like laboratory experiment and like analysis generally, requires us to simplify the objects of our thought, and we may easily forget the objects' great density in fact. It would therefore be helpful if we could keep in mind models that would encourage a representation of the density itself. The point may be made by considering the process of reproductive printing. A picture printed without any screen or textural gradation—a woodcut, for example—gains in salience but loses the ability to represent differences in density or color. A reproduction made with the help of a screen but in one color only allows for differences in density but restricts the information given by hue. For a maximum of color information, three or, more usually, four screens must be used, each screen being based on a photograph taken with the appropriate color filter. The granulations (usually differentially sized dots) of the different colors, which establish the varying color densities, are printed above or alongside one another to create intermediate colors and more subtle gradations of density. A picture in a single, ungraded color is like a dichotomous classification—a black shape, say, against a white ground. The single screened color produces a more subtly varied image, but is one-dimensional in hue. It resembles a description of a group of people in terms of a single trait or dimension, for example, religion. Each additional color adds a dimension of hue and an alteration, perhaps, of shape or area, such as we get, analogously, when we add to the description of the group's religion descriptions of its economic life, its family and other social structures, its aesthetics, and so on. Each added hue adds to the density and accuracy of the picture, every hue being modified by the presence of every other. A clear analysis is like a photograph made through a certain filter. If we want to end with a rational reconstruction of the object of our analysis, we should analyze it in its different dimensions, as if photographing it through different filters. To fit together, to allow their superimposition, the analyses must be uniform in some respects. This uniformity is approximated when the same person or group makes them all; but when the analyses are made by different persons or groups, with no artificial coordination established among them, the superimposition—that is to say, the summation—is internally discordant and suffers from its own autoimmune disease, the image-destroying war among its elements.

To understand the density of human beings is to preserve one's modesty in characterizing them. No one has a full grasp of the workings of even a single cell in a human body, let alone a human's philosophical views; and it does not usually help us to understand his philosophical views if we insist on confining our study to the single cells of his body. It is necessary for us to be clear about context and to try sometimes to come as close as we can to being sufficient. At the same time, we should not allow our interest in context to stand in the way of distant and radical comparison. Contextualism is too easy a refuge from analysis. It prevents a more than instinctive understanding of even individuality and context. The parochialism it encourages is itself a form of misunderstanding, intellectually little but myopia raised to the status of virtue.

Apart from its myopia, contextualism is subject to practical and theoretical limitations. If we assume that nothing can be understood outside of its particular context, the same must be true of the doctrine of contextualism, and the context of the doctrine must, in turn, be set into context, and so on. So, too our personal act of setting something into context must be set into context. To avoid this ordinarily unhelpful regress, we use the doctrine as if it itself had no context. In other words, we usually decontextualize it and use it directly to get closer to what we take to be the truth. Yet even the unselfconscious application of the idea of context may in fact create distance rather than closeness. I mean that to describe the context of a philosophy is, among other things, to resist the claims of that philosophy and perhaps to defend oneself against the direct reactions that it arouses. In this sense, to establish a technical context may be the very act by which we decontextualize emotionally, refuse to participate emotionally. The fullest attempt to understand distant thought may be, in effect, both to insert it into and extract it from context. Local detail and nuance make an object rich in texture but may obscure its shape against its background and make it difficult to compare. If we disregard its nuances and extract it, so to speak, from its context, we get a clear but sparsely textured shape. It we are able to think of it both in and out of its local context, the intellectual image is, in different ways, both rich and sparse, vaguely shaped, and clearly shaped, and therefore intellectually dense.

Having argued that decontextualization is legitimate and necessary, I would like to end with suggestions for wide-ranging comparisons of the sort that a resolute decontextualization makes possible. I begin with two wide, vague suggestions that stem from my interest in both anthropology and philosophy. The first is the attempt to grasp the philosophy that is latent in mythology, as compared with the latent or open tendency of philosophers to mythologize, in other words, to depend on metaphors, parables, and sometimes fancy cosmologies. I am referring to Plato, the Neoplatonists, and the Neopythagoreans; but mythologizing is characteristic of many other, later philosophers, and sometimes, I think, the dependence on metaphor and parable-like example is crucial. My suggestion recalls the interest in mythology of Schelling and, in our century, Jung, Cassirer and Eliade; but comparative philosophers have done almost nothing with the theme, certainly not in a contemporary frame of mind.

The second wide, vague suggestion is the comparison of so-called "primitive" or "tribal" thought with the thought of philosophers. The work of many anthropologists is relevant, among them the Dane, Rasmussen—with his reports on Eskimos, some of whom sound not unlike Sartre or some other existentialist—and the American, Radin, with his book *Primitive Man as Philosopher*. The riddles and dilemma tales of the Africans, which they accompany with discussion, stand comparison with the earlier Socratic dialogues and with Buddhist, especially Zen, parables and philosophical concepts, as well as with those of the Jains. The elaborate cosmology of the Dogon, of the Sudan, stand comparison with the cosmology of the Pythagoreans and the Stoics. And, if we are interested in the roots of a rational, scientific attitude toward the world, we may take notice that the Kung of South Africa have been described as sharing and using it, at least in relation to the animals they hunt.

A related, somewhat narrower subject is that of the theories of origin and structure, some microcosmic-macrocosmic, some more or less numerical, some composed of polar opposites. Another subject to which anthropology, comparative culture, and philosophy are all relevant is that of theories of Ideas, resembling Plato's theory. Primitive analogies may include the Iroquois notion of "elder brother" or prototype in the sky; the Navaho notion of the "inner form" of plants, animals, and certain inanimate things; and the developed Dogon notion of the power of the word and the shape. Then there are such magically charged words or essences as we find in the Sumerian *me*, the cosmic rule or power; the various reifications of the principle of order or justice, such as the Egyptian *maʿat*, the Indian *ṛta*, the Iranian *aša*, and the Greek *nomos* or *dike*; and, naturally, apart from *Idea* itself, *Brahman*, *Tao*, and *Logos*, and other conceptions of what we may call *Substance*.

To go on, there is still no developed philosophical comparison of different views of atomism or discreteness, on the one hand, and of continuity on the other; or of what Europeans call "matter" and "form"; or of the philosophical uses of the notion of infinity in its quantitative sense or in its sense of perfection. Each philosophical culture has had its partisans of paradox and paradoxicality, its skeptics, and its partisans of political trickery or ruthlessness. The relationship of skepticism and mysticism is still unexplored in comparative research. So is the nature of basic assumptions and fundamental rules, and even of techniques of argument; or of the symmetrical development of schools engaged in long-continued rivalry; or of systematic versus antisystematic philosophy. My own psychological orientation attracts me to such unexplored subjects as ambivalence, which is the desire to negate and affirm simultaneously, or to keep incompatibles together, or as the functions of emotions, whether anger or humor or any other, in philosophy.

I assume that in all such subjects comparative research could be particularly fruitful because it supplies us with analogous facts in different contexts and therefore draws us on to more general and fundamental explanations.

The suggestions I have offered, to which everyone in the field of comparative philosophy could easily add, are only meant to emphasize what enormous wealth is there almost for the asking. Those who begin such research will no doubt make the errors and gain the satisfactions of pioneers.

The truth is that every philosophical school, religion, culture, or style and form of art has undergone a repeated process of contextualization, decontextualization, and recontextualization. It is by this process that human culture grows and renews itself. I suggest that if, as comparative philosophers, we are bold, imaginative, and precise enough, we shall discover worlds of which we have only imprecise hints at present. I think we should be led at least as much by our sense of adventure as by our fear of making mistakes. Mistakes are, in any case, inevitable, so why not make them, in the course of our own adventuring among thoughts, and allow others the pleasure of correcting them?

I want only to add that although our adventuring may exhilarate us and, we hope, increase our own and others' tolerance, it will never inspire much agreement among us. In the exact sciences there are relatively effective long-term constraints that limit individuality and subjectivity. These constraints are weak among philosophers. Neither the exercise of scholarship, nor the elaboration of methodology, nor the dependence on intuition can inspire much agreement among us as philosophical scholars or scholarly philosophers. We can no more produce identical philosophies than poets can write identical poems. Because this is apparently a fact, the contrary dream is an impossible one. It would be easiest on us if we accepted our inevitable disagreements as simply a heightening of our intellectual adventure. Like travelers, each of us sees the terrain through eyes that are his alone. Yet, like travelers listening to one another, we are, after all, quite similar enough to appreciate and profit from our differences.

CHARLES HARTSHORNE

Śaṅkara, Nāgārjuna, and Fa Tsang, with Some Western Analogues

IN THE past two decades American thought has made some progress toward a global perspective. By American thought I do not refer to the way the vast majority of Americans think. Ours is still a narrowly western-oriented population. The big, powerful countries are not, alas, as enlightened as the best of the smaller countries. Bigness favors smugness and collective conceit. But thanks to the Society for Asian and Comparative Philosophy, also to the Center for Process Studies, we are making some progress away from our western provincialism.

How does one interpret across cultural boundaries? Being multilingual certainly helps. In many small countries one must be at least bilingual to prosper. One sees this in Belgium, Switzerland, Holland, Sweden, Denmark, Norway, Finland, Austria. Important as language is, however, in philosophy a good deal can be done through translation. My wife, Dorothy C. Hartshorne, has become an expert on the history of Japanese art in Japan with only minor use of the Japanese language and a very little use of my German, and I feel that I have acquired some grasp of Japanese, Chinese, and Indian thought, also of ancient Greek philosophy, almost entirely through English. How far is this possible?

In philosophy concrete examples are important. Plato's cave is the same whether in Greek or in English. The Indian rope mistaken for a snake is not different in English than in Sanskrit, ditto dreaming as opposed to waking experience. Seeing with eyes or hearing with ears, or the distinction between a living and a dead body, are the same in any language. The basic phenomena that set philosophic problems are universal and interlinguistically recognizable. In all languages we are born of mothers and our bodies eventually stop functioning. In many higher languages there is some formulation of a superanimal form of consciousness, immune to death and birth, an all-surpassing, encompassing reality, relation to which is the key to life's meaning. In all too there is recognition of the relations of temporal succession, togetherness (remoteness or nearness) in space, and of cause and effect. In all too there are ways of distinguishing between desirable or acceptable social relations and undesirable, unacceptable ones, between selfishness and generosity, fairness, or love; also, among aesthetic values: beauty, ugliness, the comic or humorous, and others.

In ancient India and China many of the essential philosophic issues were definitely encountered. Positions were taken that anticipate to a significant degree doctrines that have emerged in recent centuries in Europe and America. I shall choose three illustrations. One is the most monistic form of Hinduism, the Advaita Vedānta of Śaṅkara. A second is the Mahāyāna Buddhism of Nāgārjuna. The third is the development of the second by Fa Tsang in the Hua Yuen tradition in China.

Śaṅkara's doctrine of *māyā* is the "ignorant" view that reality is a multiplicity of beings in space and time, in contrast to the enlightened view that qualityless Brahman, a blissful, unchanging nonmultiplicity, is all there is. In modern Europe, F. H. Bradley comes the nearest to Śaṅkara's thought. Kant's denial that the reality appearing in our experience is, in itself, spatial or temporal prepared the way for Bradley. Hegel's criticisms of the pluralism of Leibniz helped also. Let us consider the reasons given for the Advaita doctrine.

According to T.R.V. Murti, a basic monistic argument is "the dream argument." In modern European thought, beginning with Descartes, we find the reasoning that on awakening from a dream we dismiss the things we dream of as unreal, mere false beliefs. How then do we know that waking experience is not similar to dreaming in the unreality of its contents, even though there is more order in waking appearances, and we and others experience it in mutually supportive ways? (If I see a tree you can see it when and where I can, while what we dream of will show no such concordance.) I hold with Bergson, who stands out for his penetration in this matter, that the dream argument rests on a false description of dreaming.

It is simply false that the real physical world we all share is entirely absent from our dreams. In my dreams, for example, I am there, and in your dreams you are there, and we are realities not only for ourselves but for each other. What are these individuals, I, you, that dream of themselves in various apparent situations? Do we dream of ourselves as mere disembodied consciousnesses, or as embodied ones? In my dreams I have a body, however vague its outlines may be. If so, then one part of the actual physical, spatial reality is given in the dream. You, watching me dream—psychologists say this means that my eyelids move—can check on the state of my body. We will both be experiencing one and the same portion of the physical world. Nor is this all. Suppose I hear a noise in the dream and seem to see something I take to be an electric fan making the noise. I awaken and hear the same sound, but now I realize it comes from a plane overhead. You confirm my conclusion that while I had the dream the noise of the plane was sounding. We agree that in my dream the extrabodily environment was given, partly as it really was. That I interpreted it as the noise of a visually appearing fan does not refute our contention. For since my eyes were closed or there was almost no light, my visual imagery was not being controlled as it normally is by external stimuli, so I was reduced to guessing what the visual aspect of the situation was. Hundreds more examples could be given. We dream of being cold or wet and we are; of being erotically physically excited and we are; of suffering from an itch and the mark of an insect bite is there where we were scratching. It is hard to believe how little, before Bergson, the facts of this matter were correctly reported by philosophers. I myself had to read Bergson to begin to notice such things. My conclusion is definite: the wholly nonrealistic view of dreaming is baseless. There is no such phenomenon. The supposition that there is, as an argument against realism, begs the question. Bergson shows how the inclined position, the soft support of the mattress, the sound of one's breathing, the relative lack of kinesthetic sensations—as when one wants to run from something but does not move—all have their mode of givenness in dreaming.

Other arguments for antipluralism used in India, in my opinion, also beg the question. That one can confuse a rope and a snake proves nothing against belief in a real physical world. The rope in the case supposed is real, it definitely resembles a snake in shape, and this explains the confusion. True, one must grant that human visual and other intuitions are not absolutely distinct and infallible, but in my view this only means that we are not as God is believed to be. It is entirely compatible with the reality of the physical world.

A third argument is likewise inconclusive, to put it mildly. I have read a dissertation on Advaitism that runs as follows: the real is the permanent or indestructible; nothing that we see, touch, hear, smell, or empirically experience is indestructible; therefore nothing is real. Let us see. Some insects have life-spans of a few days at most, some particles have statistical or half-life spans of a few quintillionths of a second. To define reality as the absolutely permanent implies that there is no real difference between brief endurance and long endurance, or between brief endurance and zero endurance. But we all show by our behavior that we see these as real differences. We want life-spans longer than most insects and even than most nonhuman animals. To define 'real' so as to nullify these distinctions is merely to misuse words, or if you prefer, to beg the question at issue.

More precisely the fallacy is to identify two clearly distinct concepts, existence and actuality. Real persons or things exist, whereas states, experiences, or events occur or happen. I call such occurrences actualities, not existents. The distinction between real and unreal applies to both. Charles Dickens really existed, his Mr. Micawber did not, except as an idea in the minds of Dickens and his readers, or as symbolized by the words in his books. An event described in a history book may or may not have really, actually occurred as described. Moreover, the alleged axiom, namely that only the permanent or indestructible is real, is acceptable in application to occurrences, but to existing things or persons only as sequences of actualities that I call careers. Thus the career of Dickens is indestructible, nothing can ever cause it not to have happened or make it longer or shorter than it was. To say that things or persons are unreal unless they endure forever is to compliment ordinary beings by attributing to them as a right what is a unique excellence of deity. Only God, I believe, could assimilate into a unitary consciousness an unlimited sequence of experiences. The finitely enduring is not to be made unreal by an arbitrary definition of the word real.

One thing is clear: my judgment that Śaṅkara's case is unconvincing is not explained by my lack of intimacy with the language and culture of India. For many Indians, for example Rāmānuja, Mādhva, Śrī Jīva Goswāmi (with millions of followers in Bengal) have judged similarly. I have known two followers of Śrī Jīva and felt at home with their way of thinking. The point is that philosophical differences are within, almost as much as between, cultures.

A philosophical problem that arose in India concerned relations between reason and intuition. Pluralists and antipluralists—the usual word was antidualist, even two realities being too many for monists—both parties agreed more or less that mere argument cannot settle such issues. All arguments have premises, and one cannot accomplish an infinite sequence of arguments for the premises of arguments. Disputants who agree on nothing can settle no dispute by arguments. Some orthodox Indian monists say that only a guru who is already enlightened can enable us to achieve enlightenment. We shall then have by intuition or direct experience the essential insight, which we may extend by argument into a philosophy that furnishes answers to whatever further questions may arise.

If argument cannot settle everything, how do we know where the boundary is between what argument can and what it cannot adjudicate? Do we know this by argument or by intuition, or in both ways? Many answers have been given to this question. It is still moot in western philosophy. Buddhism has been especially subtle at this point. Nāgārjuna, as I incompletely know him, tried to show that there were no concepts neutral to the issues between him and his opponents in terms of which relations between empirical entities, for instance between causes and effects, or earlier and later events, could be formulated without logical absurdities. This was an argument to settle limits or argumentation.

Nāgārjuna proposed, and I salute him for it, that we exhaust the logically possible answers to philosophical questions. How, for example, are causes and effects related? Are causes and effects similar or dissimilar to each other, or both similar and dissimilar, or neither? These seem to be all the possibilities, and Nāgārjuna thinks he shows that none of the four options makes sense. Conclusion: reason, ordinary secular thinking, cannot tell us what causation is. Similarly, suppose we ask the causal question in terms of the concept of dependence and its negation. Causes and effects may depend on each other, be independent of each other, or have both or neither of these relations. Nāgārjuna finds difficulties in each of the four options. Same conclusion: rational metaphysics is impossible. For the truth one must turn to direct experience as enlightened by disciplined living and meditation. Has Nāgārjuna proved his case against rationalism? I hold with Robinson that he has not, but that he has given us a good start by his effort to exhaust logical possibilities—a good start, but no more.

Eighteen centuries later and far off in space, F. H. Bradley also considered temporal and causal relations and found them to defy rational analysis. His options were in terms of the concepts 'internal' and 'external' relations. A relation is internal to a term if it is constitutive as necessary for the term; external if it is not necessary. Internal relations are constitutive of terms, external are not. Bradley did not consider the options, both internal and external, neither internal or external. It is clear, however, that if a relation is constitutive of a term the term depends on it and on the other as relatum for the relation. Hence Bradley's problem is Nāgārjuna's. He also dealt with the concepts of similarity and its negative. And Bradley also reached the antirationalist conclusion, by purportedly rational argumentation. Was the argument rationally cogent?

I find a common fallacy in these widely separated thinkers. A relation between two terms is really two relations, the one of *A* to *B*, and the one of *B* to *A*. Neither Bradley nor Nāgārjuna takes this duality into account. I have examined both with this fallacy in mind, and I say, and experts on Nāgārjuna in India could not, as far as I could see, refute me, that Nāgārjuna assumed that whatever the relation of cause to effect, the relation of effect to cause would be the same. Partly he was misled by the nominal truth that if *A* differs from *B*, then *B* differs from *A*. But suppose that when *A* exists, *B* does not yet exist. Then *A* will have no relation to *B*, for there will be no such thing as *B*. Later, when *B* comes into existence, it will differ from *A* unless *A* has entirely ceased to be. And this problem is one of the metaphysical issues about time. Is a past event simply unreal? In that case history is about nothing.

The doctrine of process philosophy, clearest in Peirce and Whitehead, and in me as a close student of both, is that events have for themselves constitutive relations to their predecessors, but not vice versa. Past events are realities, not unrealities. This doctrine is missing both from Bradley's and from Nāgārjuna's accounts. Hence they clearly begged the question. They both assumed the falsity of the creative-preservative doctrine of becoming. They overlooked time's arrow, the asymmetry of temporal relations, and committed the fallacy of misplaced symmetry. Another way to put the matter is that both thinkers refuted only a static view of multiplicity. They spatialized time, as Bergson puts it. Relations of dependence in space are indeed symmetrical, but not those in time.

Do effects depend on causes? Of course. Do we depend on our ancestors? Of course. Do causes depend on effects? Of course not. Do we depend on our descendants? Whatever our descendants turn out to be, we are what we are. But it is absurd to say that whatever our ancestors were, we are what we are. Without them we would not have been, period. But our existing now is absolute fact, which no occurrence or nonoccurrence in the future can nullify. There is nothing in Bradley's argumentation or in Nāgārjuna's to refute what I have just said. It is the indispensable foundation of any tenable rationality. All our living implies a real past, immune to alteration, and a merely potential future, the exact characters of which are in the process of being created, step by step, beginning now. How could the career of Caesar have depended on us? How could we not have depended somewhat on the acts of Caesar? We all know we cannot influence the past; we all know it influences us. The one-way relatedness is the keystone rejected by many builders.

There is one assumption that partly explains Nāgārjuna's mistake. He assumed that the complex can be analyzed into the equally or absolutely simple, which is also an assumption of symmetry. If *B* depends on *A* but not vice versa, then whatever the complexity or simplicity of *A*, *B* is one degree more complex, for in it is relation to *A*, whereas *A* lacks relation to it. Logicians tend to overlook or dismiss such distinctions. They want to view things "from the standpoint of [pure] eternity." They had better remember not only that they are not God but that even God (according to many recent theologians and some not so recent) does not view things from a purely eternal standpoint.

Logicians may say all they wish that for every relation we can formulate a converse relation. Thus I think about Caesar and Caesar is thought about by me. But whereas the relation attributed to me cannot be omitted from the description of me without obvious loss there is no scintilla of evidence that the supposed relation of being thought about by me was in Caesar. The converse relation in this case is mere verbiage; it tells us nothing about the world beyond the fact stated in the first formulation. If I had been a contemporary of Caesar's and among his acquaintances, then his being thought about by me could have been a constituent of his actuality. To know me fully is to know all that has influenced me; the converse principle is invalid. For absolute knowledge we would appear as more complex phenomena than our ancestors. The complex cannot be reduced to a bundle of simples.

In Fa Tsang we see a somewhat different version of the Mahāyāna odyssey. Instead of an equal rejection of every rationalization of relatedness, we find a tilting toward the monistic side. The terms of relations are indeed mutually dependent, "interdependent." Rafters of a building, he says, depend on each other. The symmetry of space justifies *this* statement. But then Fa Tsang goes off the deep end and commits a howler. He says, rightly, that there cannot be a second without a first, or a third without a second. But he also says that there cannot be a first without a second, or a second without a third. Were this true, a couple with two children must go on and have a third child, and so on. What is true is that to count one is to imply the idea, the possibility of counting two, and to count two the possibility of a third. But if a couple has an actual second child then it has or has had an actual first child. Counting has the temporal asymmetry built into it. C. S. Peirce was right when he used Firstness and Secondness as symbolizing and actually illustrating independence and dependence, respectively. In my experience some contemporary Japanese Neobuddhist philosophers are still imprisoned in Fa Tsang's mistake. Again I am not preferring the West to the East, for Brand Blanchard and some other westerners would agree with Fa Tsang. So would the Stoics and Spinoza have done.

Stcherbatsky interprets Theravāda Buddhism as an extreme pluralism and Mahāyāna as an extreme monism. If he is right, then Buddhism has never found a truly middle way. In this failure it resembles western thought as it has mostly been, at least until recently. The mistake, in East and West, has been the assumption that the available options are alike symmetrical.

David Hume proclaimed as a truism, "What is distinguishable is separable." He took this to mean mutually separable: either term can be without the other. He forgot that distinguishability of two terms assumes both terms. When *A* only is real there is no sameness and no difference between *A* and *B* for there is no *B*. Then *A* does exist on its own. Its successor *B* does not exist merely on its own but only thanks to its predecessor *A*. The successor relation is internal and constitutive, but the predecessor relation is not. It is only a backward way of affirming the one real relation, *B*'s having *A* as its own past condition.

Since Fa Tsang knew as well as anyone that many couples have only one or two children, it is imaginable that all he meant by his cryptic saying is that each moment of becoming is bound to have a successor, not necessarily the successor that in fact ensues. No event can be the last event. If this was his meaning, I wonder if any scholar has documented this interpretation. The ones I have known or read did not. And I infer that this includes Stcherbatsky, for otherwise, in the case of Fa Tsang at least, the Mahāyāna was not an extreme monism.

If the Russian scholar was right about the extreme pluralism of the Theravāda, its pluralism was like that of Hume, mere succession not only without interlinkage but without one-way linkage. Bertrand Russell, Hume's disciple, along with many disciples of both Hume and Russell have taken this view as their ontology. Naturally, then, they had no metaphysical account to give of causal dependence, and we find Russell simply postulating certain metaphysically arbitrary rules from which the possibility of inductive inference follows.

In his early period Russell was a determinist, as was Hume. Logically, metaphysically, anything might happen at any time and place; but for some totally inexplicable reason we have up to now been able partially to predict the future, so well indeed that, Hume thinks, we should accept strict causal determinism as the truth. Indeed, in his critique of the idea of God, Hume assumes this determinism, and his conclusion depends on it. Metaphysically the world could have been utterly chaotic, but in fact it is absolutely ordered. Whitehead said of this combination of doctrines that it seemed to him "wonderfully irrational." Although we have, it is said, no understanding whatsoever of causal linkage in itself, yet we are to admit such linkage in the most extreme, symmetrical, all-determining power. Therefore, if God is the ground of cosmic order, God must be the all-determining power, all evils are divinely produced, and God's goodness, in any sense intelligible to us, must be given up. To worship God, then, is to worship sheer power, not goodness. Admit the partial indeterminacy of becoming and the argument against the goodness of God fails. Creaturely freedom may be the explanation of evil, not the lack of goodness in God.

The partially intercultural nature of philosophy can be illustrated in many ways. The denial of self-being to temporal realities, the *śūnyatā* doctrine of Nāgārjuna, seems based on the idea that we depend not only on our ancestors but on our descendants as well, that the linkage is symmetrical. For if we only depend on our ancestors, how does this contradict our truly being what we are? Nothing can ever make our ancestors not have been, and what we needed from them we have and always will have had. No danger threatens in that direction. It would be very different if we depended in the same strict sense on our descendants. As we, inhabitants of the second half of the twentieth century, know, there might even not be any descendants or posterity of humankind. This consideration brings out the truth that we do in a sense depend on having descendants, not on the ones who happen to occur but on having some individual descendants, or some posterity or other that can make some use of our having existed and acted as we have. Our belief that there will be such individuals certainly does influence what we now are. But it is our present belief that it does so, not any subsequent events. In contrast, our ancestors influence us whatever we believe, and they influence animals too primitive to have beliefs on this level. There is still a profound asymmetry in the relationships.

A western parallel to Fa Tsang, as I have interpreted him, is Josiah Royce's acceptance of universally internal relations, symmetrical interdependence. Royce gives a formally fallacious argument for this view. He attacks a realistic theory of knowledge according to which the objects of experience are real independently of us as experiencing them. Objects are independent of subjects. It follows, says Royce, that subjects must be independent of objects. This is a non sequitur. Caesar, my object, does not depend on my thinking of him, but I do in my actual state depend on Caesar. Royce covers up the logical gap by declaring, "It would be contrary to the whole spirit of realism to admit that subjects depend on objects." If the realism in question is that of Hume and his many disciples, then Royce is correct. If "the distinguishable is (symmetrically) separable" then subjects can as little depend on their objects as the objects can depend on them. And it would follow that no experience can establish the reality of what is experienced. But realism as such should take dependence to be unilateral.

Royce concludes that all relations are internal so that past, present, and future, the near and the far, are interlocked in an all-inclusive system that Royce interprets as the Absolute Experience, timeless but inclusive of all time. Unlike Bradley and Mahāyāna Buddhism, Royce holds that the word of determinate interlinked multiplicity in space and time is entirely real, and so is the equally determinate absolute consciousness. There is no real indeterminacy or indefiniteness, and the timeless divine definiteness is all-inclusive. Our volitions, however unfortunate or unhappy their results, are eternally willed as necessary to the perfection of the absolute whole. The problem of evil in its worst form is thus involved. Of course Royce could not convince his cultural community by this paradoxical extreme. Buddhism did well not to justify evils as divinely willed. But is the alternative to accept the idea of absolute indeterminateness, the "undifferentiated," as the source of all definiteness and as somehow one with salvation or Nirvana? Bradley's absolute seems to me scarcely distinguishable from the *śūnyatā* doctrine. For if there are no terms in relation, whether internal or external, in what sense can there be definiteness, real differentiation? I find Bradley more nearly consistent than Royce, and nearer to Buddhism. What all these people seem to have missed is the essential role of one-way dependencies, internal for one term, external for the other. A theist must reject both symmetrical extremes, whether of dependence or of independence.

Still another western partial parallel to the far eastern views under consideration here is Bergson's argument for the necessity of relying on intuition in metaphysics. He too was an antirationalist, not as extreme as some critics have supposed but extreme enough to get into trouble. Duration, he believed, cannot be expressed in conceptual terms, such as unity or multiplicity, taken as subject to logical rules. He held that logical thought reduces temporal succession to a spatial array of mutually external items, "juxtaposed" to one another, while the truth is that successive states of becoming "interpenetrate" one another. Note the assumption of symmetry. In fact, successive experiences in memory embrace their predecessors but not their successors. So here is one more philosopher who is apparently unable to get it into his head that asymmetry is as real as symmetry and even more fundamental. Analysis shows that symmetry is in principle a special, zero case, the case in which some difference reduces to zero. Neighbors in space interact, but the action of *A* on *B* is one relation and that of *B* on *A* is another. Both actions involve a temporal difference between cause and effect and this, as we have seen, is one-way. If *A* and *B* know each other, *A*'s knowledge of *B* is not simply *B*'s knowledge of *A* read backward. In formal logic, biconditioning, the symmetrical case—called equivalence—is defined through conditioning as the general principle, which is normally one-way. With mere equivalence we could only go from the same to the same. The power is in the asymmetrical principle. What Bergson missed is precisely what logic might have taught him. Even in aesthetics symmetry is not the principle or the ideal. Absolute symmetry is dead aesthetically, as artists know. I never saw a church uglier than one I recall with two towers indistinguishably alike. The Greeks said that the circle is the most beautiful of curves. In truth, it is only the simplest, most symmetrical one. Great aesthetic value is not found in extreme simplicity or symmetry. It takes no genius to achieve that.

One more East–West parallel. Some Buddhist writers have noted that what in the West has been called the "negative way" in theology has its analogue in Hinduism and Buddhism. As Aquinas said, we know what God is not rather than what God is, so Buddhists tell us that we know what Nirvana is not, and Advaitists tell us what Brahman is not. Qualityless Brahman is said to be more real that qualitied Brahman. I believe that both East and West made a bad mistake in their undue reliance on negation. Independence, is *not* more than, superior to, more real than dependence; absoluteness or nonrelativity is not more than relativity; the simple is not more than the complex. Quite the contrary is true. The dependent and complex is more than and includes the independent and simple, the relative is more than and includes the absolute, what in some aspects becomes is more than and includes what in no aspect becomes. The positive is more than and includes the negative. Is this a paradox? Rather, its denial is paradoxical. How is one to get more by abstracting from experience positive properties found in it?

There are many ways of grounding the position taken in the previous paragraph. In knowing an insect I am conditioned by the insect, for as Aristotle and all his followers agreed, apart at least from God, knowing depends on what is known for its possibility. Aristotle, wanting to make deity independent, with intellectual honesty sadly lacking later, refused to allow that God knows contingent details of the world, for this knowledge would make God somewhat dependent on those details. If the world had been otherwise, God would have had to have a partially different knowledge. Medieval theology, entirely without refuting Aristotle's reasoning, for religious reasons attributed knowledge of all things to God, yet verbally asserted the absolute independence of deity. This stance I can only view, with Spinoza, as cheating: he too wanted to make God wholly noncontingent and independent, and also omniscient. So he denied the contingency of the world. All action is divine action, and it is all necessary. There is no contingency. Aristotle had a God ignorant of much that we know, but he did preserve the integrity of his concept of knowledge. Aquinas had a God knowing all truth, but he had no intelligible concept of knowledge to use theologically. Spinoza had a God knowing all truth, except, alas, that there was no truth genuinely applicable to concrete actuality, for that is pervasively contingent. Moreover, it is far more reasonable to define necessity as what any possible actuality would include than to define possibility as that the nontruth of which is not necessary, that is, by a double negation. Every moment of life we assume more or less consciously that the future is a matter of options, possibilities, limited by certain impossibilities and necessities. The sheer denial of contingency is contradicted pragmatically, whatever words we use. If we do not know what possibility (irreducible to necessity) is, we know nothing much metaphysically.

The negative way I take to be a clear failure. In twenty-five centuries it has given us little that is usable in life or science. The physicists nowadays commonly admit the reality of contingency, of chance, or randomness. The list of speculative philosophers who have dealt creatively and pertinently with metaphysical problems since Hegel, overwhelmingly consists of those opposed to the essentially negative view of God as wholly independent, noncomplex, immutable, and so on; it is opposed to determinism, the wholly symmetrical view of causation. The evolutionary scheme is radically asymmetrical; biology is wonderfully knowledgeable about the past of life but makes no pretense of predicting much about its future, nor is it trying to show that chance variations are really not that but necessary results of deterministic causality.

The reader may have noted that the word asymmetrical is negative. Yes, but the open secret of the matter is that the idea is positive and it is symmetry that is negative, for it is the absence of difference between items compared. Thus, equality is symmetrical and it is a double negative, *A* neither larger nor smaller than *B*. Moreover, it is largeness that is most positive, for the large can contain the small, not vice versa. Asymmetrical order is directional order; symmetrical order is nondirectional. Thus the equality of *A* and *B* is the same as the equality of *B* and *A*, but *A*'s being larger than *B* or containing *B* is not at all the same as *B*'s being larger than or containing *A*.

The negative way pretended to be modest about human capacity. We cannot know what God is, but we know very definitely and precisely what God is not. How modest is that? We tell God, you must not change in any way whatever, no matter how excellent the way. For we are so unassuming that we know precisely how impossible it is that there could be any form of change or growth so excellent that it must qualify deity. Do we really know this? I challenge anybody to justify this claim. It will not do to argue, as Plato (who, I think, really knew better) once did, that God is perfect and hence could only change for the worse, hence cannot change at all. So we know exactly what absolute perfection would be and that it is a logically possible idea. The class of all classes sounds like a possible notion but has been proved self-inconsistent. Has anyone shown that the combination of all possible excellences makes any better sense? I am confident no one has or will. If God is absolutely perfect and we know what that means, then we know positively what God is after all. Take it how you will, the negative way cannot maintain itself against criticism. The experiment of more than two thousand years has reached a result, and the result is negative. The negative way is to be negated.

If the reader is surprised at the passion with which I put these things, I will tell him why I do so. I regard the failure of medievalism as a tragic, humanly very costly failure. Its God was supposed to be a God of love. But as there was no genuinely coherent idea of knowledge applicable to the God medieval theology defined, so there was, even more obviously if possible, no genuine idea of love thus applicable. There was a lot of cruelty in the medieval scheme, and the Protestants, alas, did not find the remedy for centuries. They too believed in a hell and in a God whose omnipotence determined all, monopolized decision making—though how free decision could take place in sheer eternity they could not (and no one can) explain.

I wish to make a final return to the East and Buddhism. To

seek a middle way between eternalism and temporalism was sound, but a movement that splits into a radical pluralism and a radical monism has scarcely solved all the problems. We need a moderate pluralism and a moderate monism.

Buddhism exalted love but just short of the highest exaltation. There was something still more ultimate and good, the undifferentiated. Note, a negation. It was also called the undivided. Or nonbeing. In love there is unity and multiplicity, both equally real, as I see it. Some loves are more inclusive than others. Everyone has a kind of inborn love for the members of one's own body, what someone has called one's "animal republic." But this republic is a small part of the cosmic whole. For what is outside that body our sympathetic response to its weal or woe, its need or advantage, is less constant, and at best covers only limited portions of reality.

Plato hit upon the tremendous metaphor of the World Soul, the consciousness related to the cosmos as yours or mine is to your or my body. Obviously this is an analogy in which the difference spanned is vast. But it is the only other great analogy that we have besides the usual one taken from interpersonal relations, a parent related to a child of that parent, a ruler related to a citizen, or a teacher related to a pupil (Kierkegaard's favorite). In our tradition (apart from Plato) this analogy is almost the only one used. Its limitations are obvious. Plato's analogy may have its limitations, but they are widely different from those of the other analogy and may, therefore, help us to correct the faults of the other, and vice versa.

My last word is about the negative way. Taken as the whole story it is a dismal failure, but taken as enabling us to abstract an important aspect of the idea of deity it can be largely adopted. Whitehead's primordial, or purely eternal, aspect of deity is indeed immutable, independent of all contingent alternatives, in certain senses simple, absolute, infinite, and undifferentiated. But it is, by itself, a mere abstraction, as Whitehead says. The concrete fullness of the divine life has all the positive attributes the negative way rejects. It is dependent on all for it knows and loves all, therefore it rejoices with our joys and grieves with our sorrows. It contains all but does not determine all, indeed does not absolutely determine any creature, for all have some freedom. Hence conflict and suffering are not deliberately chosen by divine will. God does not punish or reward, but makes it possible for creatures to benefit or harm one another. Only so could there be a world, according to this philosophy. Leibniz's phrase "spiritual automaton" for a monad is nonsense. In quantum physics there are no sheerly mechanical actions. Theology ought to have anticipated this. It had no business to conceive God as supreme freedom (unsurpassable by others) unless it was willing to conceive creatureliness as also freedom, but in unsupreme, surpassable forms.

If I have ended with a negative to distinguish God, please note, I qualify this negative with a positive; God is unsurpassable by others but is self-surpassing, as each new creature adds something to the divine fullness of life. God is all-surpassing, self-surpassing, a doubly positive idea. Process theology is indeed a positivism, in a new meaning of the word.

RAIMUNDO PANIKKAR

What Is Comparative Philosophy Comparing?

COMPARATIVE studies are still fashionable today because they belong to the thrust toward universalization characteristic of western culture. The West not being able any longer to dominate other peoples politically, it tries to maintain—most of the time unconsciously—a certain control by striving toward a global picture of the world by means of comparative studies. Yet, this very thrust toward homogenization and "global thinking" may boomerang into decentralization and pluralism once the wisdom of other cultures becomes better known. Paradoxically enough, comparative philosophy, which has an inbuilt trend to overcome the plurality of cosmo-visions, may end by legitimizing mutually irreconcilable systems and becoming the stronghold of pluralism.

I shall offer a definition of comparative philosophy and argue that it is different from all other comparative studies by virtue of the subject matter under comparison. And this uniqueness finds its paradoxical expression in my thesis that, strictly speaking, comparative philosophy is an impossible independent discipline, which nevertheless thrives in the very recognition of its impossibility.[1]

NĀGĀRJUNA saw a number of systems (*dṛṣṭis*) before him. He undertook to criticize them all, but he did not do comparative philosophy! Similarly, Aristotle frequently began his work by describing the opinions of his predecessors, but his philosophy was not comparative philosophy. Descartes was bewildered by the multiplicity of philosophical systems in his time and ex-

[1] This is the thesis of my paper "Aporias in the Comparative Philosophy of Religion," *Man and World* 3–4 (1980): 357–383.

cogitated a method to get rid of all those doubts; but he would not have dreamt of writing comparative philosophy. Śaṅkara and Thomas Aquinas were aware of the wide disparity of opinions and made of this fact an argument for the convenience of *śraddhā* and *fides*, respectively, but they did not do comparative philosophy. If comparative philosophy is to have a status of its own, it should be neither a mere history of philosophy nor simply philosophy based on the critique of previous philosophies. Otherwise, we give only a new name to an old discipline. In that case, every critical philosophy is comparative philosophy because it compares itself with other systems of thought and builds on those analyses.

Comparative philosophy has an illustrious forerunner to which it owes much of its existence and which is, at least partially, responsible for its success: comparative philology. The birth of comparative philology in the middle of the past century was the means for western scholarship to shed the shell of provincialism and to broaden the understanding of something so fundamentally human as language. Comparative philology is possible, though it does not pretend to be a metalanguage. Max Müller's inaugural lecture at Oxford University was delivered in 1868. But twelve years earlier he had already written about "comparative mythology."[2] And it was Pope Clement V in 1311 who erected in four European universities (Paris, Oxford, Bologna, and Salamanca) as well as in Rome, chairs of Hebrew, Chaldean, and Arabic.[3] From that moment on the ferment did not die. but comparative philology has a subject matter quite different from that of comparative philosophy.

The independent status of comparative philosophy should be distinguished from the conventional notions of comparison used by all systematic thinkers. We need to express our thoughts against the background of some other opinions explicitly or implicitly stated. Every philosopher, willy nilly,

[2] Max Müller, *Chips from a German Workshop*, 2 vols. (New York: Scribner's, 1902), 2:1–141.

[3] Cf. Concilii Viennensi (1311–1312), decretum 24, *Conciliorum oecumenicorum decreta*, 3d ed. (Bologna: Istituto per le scienze religiose, 1973), p. 379.

stands in dialogue with the surrounding philosophical world (or some other ancient one). When Kant writes his Critique he does it as a "Copernican revolution," reacting against the previous forms of philosophizing; when Śaṅkara exposes his system he equally enters in open polemics against the *karmakāṇḍins*, the Buddhists, and others. In this sense every philosophy is comparative philosophy because it compares itself—and seemingly successfully—with other philosophical views. But this is not the specific understanding of comparative philosophy as an independent discipline from the philosophy of one thinker or one school. We sit on the shoulders of our predecessors; but the contemporary concept of comparative philosophy pretends to be an autonomous discipline. It claims thematically to compare two, or more, or all philosophical views and give them a fair treatment without—at least ideally—necessarily subscribing to any of them. In this paper I examine the claim of comparative philosophy to be an independent discipline with its proper method and subject matter, which liberates us from the limited horizon of one single philosophical view and encompasses all—or most—of them, making us really "citizens of the world," "inhabitants of this planet." This is the illusion I would like to dispel: "World Government," "Global Village," "One Technology," "World Market," "Civilization," *lingua universalis*, one single world view, a universal philosophy called comparative philosophy; in short, the monomorphism of a monolithic reality.

We may ask now: what is the status of the question about comparative philosophy? From the name itself we may assume that comparative philosophy is a kind of philosophy. We may also assume that comparative philosophy is that philosophy which results from or deals with comparing philosophers. We ask then: what kind of philosophy is comparative philosophy? And immediately we have to ask further: what is the status of the question about philosophy? Is it a philosophical question? Or does the question not belong to philosophy? The questions about the ultimate foundations of poetry, geography, walking, or loving do not belong to poetry, geography, walking, or loving. They belong traditionally to philosophy. Now, the question about philosophy either belongs to philosophy itself or to a sort of metadiscipline that disclaims to be philosophy, for a member of a set cannot encompass or evaluate the whole set. What is it, then? One may answer that it is linguistics or history. But then we may still inquire about the status of linguistics or history and begin all over again. We would need a particular linguistic or historical theory as the basis of comparative philosophy. But what would be the criterion for choosing one particular linguistic or historical theory over any other one? It would require a special comparative linguistics or history based on something else, and so on ad infinitum.

We may well accept, then, that there is a human activity that asks about the very nature of asking and reflects about those final questions. Traditionally, philosophy deals with this problematic. We may then answer the query not just by saying that to enquire about philosophy is a philosophical question, but by saying that this type of enquiry is the specific and constitutive feature of philosophy itself. Aristotle had already suggested as much when speaking about that science which looks into its own foundations.[4] "How to know the knower?" and not just things, asked similarly the *Bṛhadāraṇyaka Upaniṣad.* It is interesting to remark, incidentally, that Greece asks impersonally about the nature of knowledge. Greece wants to know knowledge. India asks with a personal and existential urge about the nature of the knower. India wants to know the knower.[5]

Here begins the classical problematic inherent in the very nature of philosophy. On the one hand, it wants to tackle ultimate questions about the nature of reality. On the other, it asks the further question about the nature of its own enterprise. It asks about its own asking. "Philosophy starts in reflective consciousness," the post–Kantian K. C. Bhattacharya

[4] Cf. Aristotle, *Metaphysics* 1.2 (982b8).

[5] Cf. *Bṛhadāraṇyaka Upaniṣad* 4.5.15; 2.4.14; 3.4.2.

used to say,[6] echoing the Vedas ("What I am, I don't know") and Vedanta ("What am I?") as well as Augustine ("Quaestio mihi factus sum") and many others.

Comparative philosophy is a peculiar kind of philosophy comparing philosophies. The difficulty is, what kind of philosophy is it? A philosophy that passes judgment on all the others, or a metaphilosophy that amounts to another philosophy? The dilemma seems insurmountable.

Having reflected on the word 'philosophy' we should now ponder on the meaning of 'comparative'. Grammar cannot easily be whisked away. Why do we say 'comparative philosophy' and not 'compared philosophy' as the Romance languages say (*filosofia comparada* and not *comparativa*), or 'comparing philosophy' (*vergleichende Philosophie*, not *vergleichene*) as the Germanic languages suggest?

"*Comparing* philosophy" would be a philosophy that thematically proceeds by means of comparisons with other philosophies from the standpoint of the one philosophy that undertakes the comparisons. "*Compared* philosophy" would be the result of the process of a philosophy comparing itself with other philosophies. Is this all that there is in "*comparative* philosophy?"

Perhaps the entire phrase is an elliptic expression standing for "Comparative Science of Philosophy," as we have *vergleichende Literaturwissenschaft* or *science comparée des religions*. These two latter sciences may exist, but do we have a "science" that compares philosophies? Is this "science" not already "philosophy?" This question is the essential one.

THE first answer is simple. Comparative philosophy is philosophy, and qua philosophy is not better off than any philosophy. It is simply another philosophy with the limitations of all the rest. If there is no universal language, there is also not a

[6] K. C. Bhattacharya, "The Concept of the Absolute," in G. B. Burch, ed., *Search for the Absolute in Neo-Vedanta* (Honolulu; University Press of Hawaii, 1976), p. 175.

universal comparative philosophy. But we have to qualify this statement in a critical way.

The question about comparative philosophy may be a philosophical question. But it is a specific one. It does not inquire about the nature of reality, or about the essence of questioning in general. It asks about one very particular and still problematic kind of philosophy, namely the so-called comparative philosophy. The specific question should be clear. Comparative philosophy is that alleged philosophy which compares existing philosophies. The question about comparative philosophy asks not only about its epistemic status and its philosophical characters, but also about its locus in the philosophical enterprise. The problem at hand is the second one. What do we ask about when we ask about the nature of comparative philosophy?

We ask about how one philosophy relates to another, or how several philosophical schools relate to one another or how they envision one or many particular problems, how these problems interrelate and how we can compare them, so that a certain typology may emerge which may lead us to a deeper understanding of what is the case. We ask how people have interpreted the task of philosophizing and what presuppositions they brought to this task. But in so doing we become aware that we are also doing the same, namely, bringing our own assumptions to bear on our research. Therefore a critical comparative philosophy will have to ask about the kind of philosophy or philosophical attitude it assumes when doing comparative philosophy.

In the contemporary scene we find several interpretations of comparative philosophy. They all depend on the implicit philosophy that underlies the inquiry. I shall examine five types: transcendental philosophy; formal or structural philosophy; linguistic philosophy; phenomenological philosophy; and dialogical or imparative philosophy, endeavoring to understand, compare, and eventually evaluate the vision of different philosophical schools regarding philosophical problems.

A working definition of comparative philosophy may run as

follows: the philosophical study of one or some problems in the light of more than one tradition. But, obviously, what one understands by philosophical study depends already on the kind of philosophy one is espousing. Furthermore, even for choosing the traditions under study we use already certain philosophical categories of understanding—thus the need to clarify the issue of the implicit philosophy in any comparative philosophy.

I shall argue that all of these options give us a different type and understanding of comparative philosophy, but ultimately none is a satisfactory basis for a truly independent comparative philosophy. Yet, all of them together will give us a panorama of the strength and weaknesses of this (new?) discipline, which is still searching for its own identity and justification. And, as I have said, its nature consists in striving for an ideal recognized as impossible.

Whatever philosophy may be, *comparative* philosophy has to be comparative to be true to its name. It has to put on a universal scale the different self-understandings of the diverse philosophies. To compare is an activity of the human mind that takes a stance neutral to the things to be compared. Any comparison has somehow to transcend its subject matter. For any comparison three things are required: at least two *comparanda*, and the *comparans*, which is a third element that has to be equally distant from and outside the *comparanda*, the things to be compared. And here already looms unambiguously the idea of *transcendence*, which some philosophies would like to avoid. If philosophy is an ultimately human affair, comparative philosophy could only be handled from a superhuman standpoint. It would need an Archimedean fulcrum outside the contending parties. Now, without explicitly recurring to a transcendent deity, comparative philosophy appears thus to be a sort of transcendental philosophy. It appears as a philosophy that studies the possible conditions of its own philosophizing, which questions the very status of all philosophical assertions in the light of the unity of consciousness in the very act of knowing. It claims to be that philosophy which underlies the ultimate activity of the human mind reflecting on its own functioning. It would be a priori philosophy, and in that sense a metaphilosophy.

This is a valid critical philosophy. But can it be called *comparative* when it assumes already a conception of philosophy that may perhaps be the most comprehensive one, but is certainly not universal? The point of vision of comparative philosophy has to be surely transcendent, but it needs to be also neutral, unbiased.

We may have here a valid evaluation of philosophies and I may be able to draw *for myself* a convincing comparative philosophy. But the name 'comparative philosophy' seems improper, for it should be fair to the philosophies compared, and some of them will not accept my judgment about them because it is based on a scale of values they do not recognize. In other words, I have to compare philosophies when trying to sort out my own philosophy, but is this *comparative* philosophy, or only homework for my own philosophy?

One may retort that transcendental philosophy, which claims to be a sort of a priori of philosophies, could well perform the job of comparing philosophies, for it provides a proper platform, even if not accepted by all the philosophies concerned. This may be a convincing comparative philosophy for me, but it does not fulfill one of the constitutive rules of comparative philosophy if the latter has to have any specific identity. The subject matter of comparative philosophy is not the traditional object of philosophy—namely reality, what is the case, truth, or the like—but only a very specific aspect; that is to say, it should not reduce the knowers or understanders to objects known or understood (by us). Comparative philosophy cannot accept a method that reduces all those visions to the view of one single philosophy.

Historically speaking, comparative philosophy developed as an offshoot of comparative religion, and the latter was based on the belief in the transcendence of reason vis-à-vis all religious phenomena. As a result, reason was considered qualified to evaluate religions, so it could proceed to their comparison based on a transcendental, rational scale. Similarly, assuming that philosophies are also the product of reason, a kind of pure reason would be qualified to act as the *comparans* in the realm of philosophies. The two major objections to such an interpretation are, on the one hand, the very many aspects and forms of rationality, and, on the other, the fact that many philosophies do not understand themselves to be just *opus rationis*, without for that matter being irrational.

A transcendental philosophy may be too ambitious to perform the role of comparative philosophy. Perhaps a simply structural or formal philosophy may better do the job. Comparative philosophy may then be a kind of formalized analysis of the common patterns present in the diverse philosophical systems. And, in fact, many of the efforts at construing a genuine comparative philosophy take this form nowadays.

I shall not criticize this attempt here on its own merits. But it has a heavy set of presuppositions. It assumes that anatomy is sufficient for physiology, as it were. It assumes, further, that relations between philosophies or philosophical opinions can be formalized in a kind of algebra as if the inner dynamism of philosophies were all dependent on mathematical laws. In other words, it assumes the translatability of philosophical insights into formalized formulas, it equates mathematical coherence with full-fledged human understanding, and so forth. What transcendental philosophy claims to do in the realm of consciousness, this more formal philosophy wants to perform in the field of patterns. We may thus arrive at common structures and even be able to formulate some laws and detect some patterns of behavior or thought. We could describe useful structural paradigms of the ways different philosophies have proceeded in their attempts to decipher the nature of reality. We could arrive at a kind of comparison of the structural patterns that underlie several philosophies and from this point of view at a typography (rather than typology) of philosophical systems, but this could not be called philosophy. It is rather structural analysis.

But structural analysis offers only a reductionistic basis for comparative philosophy. Why should reality comply blindly with structural laws? Why should the laws of the mind be identical with the laws of reality—if it makes sense to speak of the latter.

Further, structural analysis does not address itself to most of the issues that traditional philosophies ask. Transcendental philosophy is too much of a philosophy, as it were, to perform the task of comparative philosophy. Structural analysis is too little of a philosophy for the same task. Yet both are useful, the former to give us a more sophisticated philosophical understanding of the variety of philosophies, the latter to unveil patterns and structures of the human spirit functioning in diverse contexts.

A third option is that of linguistic philosophy, which is not synonymous with linguistic analysis. Each philosophy can be equated with a language. After all, every philosophy uses language, and we are able to understand several languages and even compare them under different perspectives. Yet, the difficulty lies again in the fact that the chosen perspective, whatever it may be, is not philosophically neutral to perform the role of a truly comparative philosophy.

The great merit of this option, however, is that it shows the relative autonomy (rather *ontonomy*) of each philosophy and its relative completeness. Each language is somewhat autonomous and internally complete. This option makes us aware that in order to understand we do not need properly to compare, for we do not bring the *comparanda* on a neutral scale, but bring one *comparandum* into the field of intelligibility of the other; in other words, we translate. Translation means finding the corresponding equivalences (homeomorphic equivalents) between languages. But in order to discover the equivalences, we need a third element that bridges the several universes of discourse. We require a triple understanding: the grasping of the meaning of a word in one language, its English equivalents (if English is the other language), and a creative intuition that will allow the translator to float for a while above the languages before landing on the right or approximate expressions. Each translation transforms both the host language by the new shades of meaning and associations of the newly translated word, and the language from which the translation is made.

But even when translation obstacles are surmounted, the real problem for a linguistic comparative philosophy lies elsewhere. It lies in the problem of really understanding contradictory statements. We may be able to speak the language, say, of the *ātmavādin*s and with some skill we may succeed also in speaking the language of the *anātmavādin*s. But when it comes to comparison after exposing the arguments of either side we will have to stop at two basically incompatible visions of reality. We may even conjecture that psychology, geography, upbringing, or other factors have predisposed peoples or cultures to take one of the visions, but this hypothesis will not bridge the gap. We should then compare the stances from a third independent platform, which is ours but not theirs. At best we will have an exposition of the different systems, a kind of history of philosophy linguistically based. But it is not yet comparative philosophy. A list of contradictory statements does not make philosophy. Yet we may have gained very valuable philosophical insights.

Very often what occur under the name of comparative philosophy are single comparisons of the way a particular philosophical problem is envisaged by more than one philosophical school. We may study, for instance, the different uses of and conceptions about *pramāṇas* in the classical Indic *darśana*s, or the theory of causality among philosophies, eastern and western, that have used this theory. We may compare, criticize, and illuminate different aspects of the problem of causality by drawing from the various insights of the systems concerned.

A certain phenomenological method underlies this option. Phenomenology here is the implicit philosophy. We compare phenomena, concepts, as states of consciousness against a common background offered by a phenomenological analysis, and may reach important cross-cultural insights. This method is a fruitful contribution to comparative philosophy inasmuch as it offers us transversal visions of similar problems in different philosophical systems, but it cannot give us a substitute for a truly independent comparative philosophy for two main reasons. The first one is that each particular problem plucked out of its proper *humus* or context does not represent the real problem of the philosophical world-view concerned, but only our interpretation of it (modern scientific causality applied to astrology, for instance). Second, not even the sum total of all the philosophical problems would give us the unity of vision that most philosophies have. What we have at most could be called a certain philosophy inasmuch as phenomenology is philosophy. But a phenomenology of philosophies is not the same as comparative philosophy.

A fifth option is what can be called dialogical philosophy or imparative philosophy. The main difficulty with comparative philosophy is precisely its point of departure, its stand. And any effort at comparing philosophies starts consciously or unconsciously from a concrete philosophical position. What we have in fact is a philosophical stance that opens itself up to other philosophies and tries to understand them from the initial perspective—though it changes in the process. This enterprise is only possible in dialogue with other philosophical views. It should further cultivate an attitude of learning from all of them. In medieval Latin this process was called *imparare*: thus the name of 'imparative philosophy', in order to stress an open philosophical attitude ready to learn from whatever philosophical corner of the world, but without claiming to compare philosophies from an objective, neutral, and transcendent vantage point.

Imparative philosophy suggests that:

(1) We should first be aware that most philosophies regard themselves as unique and often as ultimate. Thus we cannot justifiably compare, that is, bring together (*com*) on an equal (*par*) footing, that which purports to be unique and uncomparable.

(2) We may instead *imparare*, in other words, learn by being

ready to undergo the different philosophical experiences of other people.[7]

(3) This learning is reflective and critical, because it takes into account the cumulative human experience up to the present time and subjects everything to a critical scrutiny with all the available tools of analysis, thus maintaining an openness and provisionality for the time being. Imparative philosophy would be that philosophical attitude which is convinced that we cannot escape taking a stand somewhere when we philosophize, and that such limitation makes our philosophizing relative to similar enterprises undertaken from different angles. Imparative philosophy does not pretend to possess a fulcrum outside time and space and above any other philosophy from which to scrutinize the different human philosophical constructs.

(4) Imparative philosophy is critically aware of the contingency of its own assumptions and the unavoidable necessity of resting on both limited and still unexamined presuppositions.[8] We are not the only source of (self-) understanding.

(5) It is constitutively ready to question its most basic foundations if this is requested by any other philosophical school. Nothing is nonnegotiable.

[7] *Imparare* is a nonclassical Latin verb *in* + *parare*. *Parare*, to prepare, furnish, provide. *Comparare* has the same sense of making things ready, thus to arrange. *Paratus sum*, I am ready, disposed. We may note that there is the *par* (*paris*), equal, from which comes the *comparare* of comparative religion; and the *paro*, I set, I put, from which the *imparare* of *imparative* religion is derived. The *imparare* of imparative religion suggests the opposite to the *dis-antepare* of medieval Latin, from which comes the Spanish *desamparo*, dereliction, despair. Imparative religion does not formally compare, but brings together, piercing the appearances and overcoming the dispersion and despair of the prima facie antagonistic tendencies and tenets.

[8] We are conscious of our assumptions, not of our pre-sub-positions. We may discover what we have in front of us (*pre*) but not what lies at the very basis (*sub*) of what we 'suppose'.

(6) It makes the search for the primordial ground of philosophizing its first thematic concern.
(7) It is open to a dialogical dialogue with other philosophical views, not only to dialectical confrontation and rational dialogue.
(8) It tries, furthermore, to form its philosophical view of reality by systematically taking into account the universal range of human experience inasmuch as it is possible to do so in any concrete situation.

I have already indicated that such an imparative philosophy may be the best way of performing one of the aims of so-called comparative philosophy, namely to overcome provincially chauvinist views, to cultivate tolerance and understanding of the richness of human experience, but I still wonder if that can be strictly called comparative philosophy.

There may be other implicit philosophies in other existing comparative philosophies, but these examples may suffice to show that there is not an independent comparative philosophy as a discipline of its own.

We may ask, further, whether we would not have a proper comparative philosophy by a combination of all the implicit philosophical attitudes. The answer is a clear no, for what this question raises is whether we could have a comparative philosophy of comparative philosophies. It would simply shift the problem to a third-degree comparative philosophy of second-degree comparative philosophies, and so on ad infinitum, for there is no reason whatever why the comparative philosophy of comparative philosophies should be only one.

What we actually have is a plurality of philosophies and of comparative philosophies. If truth is one, how can there be a plurality of philosophies, each of them claiming ultimate truths? Comparative philosophy is consciously or unconsciously prompted by such questions.

We could formulate it this way. Can we pass from a de facto *plurality* of philosophies (or comparative philosophies) to a de jure philosophical *pluralism*? This problem is an important one in our times and a central philosophical question with very practical and vital consequences in all the branches of human activity. It is obvious that philosophical pluralism cannot be just a superphilosophy, a kind of metaphilosophy, for practically every philosophy claims to possess an ultimate character in its own sphere. Further, by its very nature, pluralism does not allow of any supersystem or metaphilosophy. Pluralism is not concerned with multiplicity or diversity as such, but with the incommensurability of human constructs on homologous issues. The problem of pluralism touches the limits of the intelligible (not just for us but in itself). It poses the greatest challenge to the human spirit. It touches the shores of the ineffable and thus of silence.

THE comparison of philosophies implies an understanding of them; or, in other words, the process demands a proper hermeneutical activity. I submit that the proper method here is a special kind of hermeneutics different from the morphological and the diachronic types. I call it "diatopical" hermeneutics.

Diatopical hermeneutics is the required method of interpretation when the distance to overcome, needed for any understanding, is not just a distance within one single culture (morphological hermeneutics), or a temporal one (diachronic hermeneutics), but rather the distance between two (or more) cultures, which have independently developed in different spaces (*topoi*) their own methods of philosophizing and ways of reaching intelligibility along with their proper categories.

The great problem in such a hermeneutical approach is the peculiar type of preunderstanding necessary to cross the boundaries of one's own philosophical world. This problem already exists within a single culture. But in our case we have something specifically different. Here we are under a different *mythos* or horizon of intelligibility. We understand because we are within a hermeneutic circle. But how can we understand something that does not belong to our circle? If I smile to a monkey in sign of friendship the ape is likely to attack me. He sees my teeth and interprets my behavior as a sign of wanting to bite him. If I move the head vertically up and down some people will understand that I agree, and others that I disagree. Something limited was considered a suitable symbol of perfection for the Greeks, because it was intelligible. In India it would be the opposite. In other words, how do we communicate prior to handing down (this is tradition) the key to deciphering our message? And how are we to understand the meaning of the clue given to us? By what other symbol? Can we ask for an ultimate key?

If we take other philosophies seriously as sources of self-understanding and independent views of the universe, we cannot minimize this problem and assume that everybody speaks Indo-European or lives in a Euclidean geometrical world, or in an animistic universe. The West may have rejected on the mental plane the idea that humankind has come from Adam and Eve as a single couple, but many of its spontaneous reactions still come from the acceptance of that myth. So we speak of a universal reason and of the unity of human nature, though we mean, obviously, our own conception of universality, reason, and human nature. Diatopical hermeneutics has to proceed without necessarily assuming these myths as a priori conditions of intelligibility.

In a word, how do we cross the boundaries for the first time toward another totally independent culture? It may be retorted that the question is rhetorical, for this "first time" is already gone. We have already entered into contact with one another. Granted that this is mostly the case, yet in a nonabsolute sense there exist cultures and philosophies that have created their own understanding of the universe without major historical influences. The problem is theoretical and serves to clarify the very principles of diatopical hermeneutics, for we have constantly to deal with people who have misunderstood what another philosophy is trying to say. They have interpreted it according to their own categories and missed the point of the original philosophy. In point of fact to dispel misunderstandings is one of the major tasks of comparative philosophy. What cheap opinions are still in circulation in the world today, outside selected minorities, regarding African religions, for instance, or even concerning the great historical religions!

Taking a hint from Vedic wisdom, as developed mainly in Mīmāṁsā, I would like to propose the *apauruṣeya* insight as a main principle of diatopical hermeneutics. The *apauruṣeya* insight says that the Vedas have no author not because there is no scribe or poet who uttered those words for the "first time," but because they are primordial language containing primordial words and, thus, with no need for some author behind them to explain what they mean. If this were not the case the author should again explain the meaning through another language, and so on ad infinitum. The Vedas stand for the primordial symbols by means of which we know what is existentially important and by means of which we come to know also other things. The sense of a symbol is in the symbol itself. If we were to need another symbol to explain its sense, this second "thing" would be the real symbol. *Apauruṣeya* stands for primordial language, a language that does not need another form of language in order to communicate what it means.

The human being is an *animal loquens*, but we do not speak language. We speak *a* language, and other people speak other languages which we do not know. The primordial language is hidden in our respective languages not as *a* language, of course, but as language. In the effort of communicating with one another—at the beginning without proper understanding, then slowly by dispelling false imaginations and misconceptions—we forge a common language, we reach a mutual comprehension, we cross the boundaries. This is what I call dialogical philosophy. It is not the imposition of one philosophy or one mode of understanding, but the forging of a common universe of discourse in the very encounter, in the dialogical dialogue taking place not once for all, but in the actual encounter.

We do not assume here any hermeneutical circle. We create that circle through the existential encounter. We do not start a dialectical dialogue, which accepts a priori some rules before the dialogue takes place. The theory here cannot be severed from the praxis.

Diatopical hermeneutics is not just theory. The rules here do not precede the understanding nor the theory the praxis. At the same time, the praxis implies the theories of the meeting partners. Both are present and required.

In sum, how can we reduce to zero or at least shorten the distance between the two *topoi* of diatopical hermeneutics? The answer here is one in which theory and praxis meet. Only those persons who, for one reason or another, have existentially crossed the borders of at least two cultures and are at home in either, shall be able first to understand and then to translate. Diatopical hermeneutics are not universal. They function, generally speaking, between two different *topoi*, not between many. They bring one culture, language, philosophy into another culture, language, or religion, making it understandable. Diatopical hermeneutics is an art as much as a science, a praxis as much as a theory. It is a creative encounter, and there is no blueprint for creativity.

Diatopical hermeneutics cannot prescribe specific rules of interpretation. If we want to interpret another basically different philosophy we will have to attend the school of that philosophy and immerse ourselves in its universe of discourse as far as is possible for us. We will have to overcome our parameters and plunge into a participatory process of which we may not be able to foresee the outcome. The process may be likened to that of learning a new language. At the beginning we translate by comparing with the mother tongue, but when we become proficient we think and speak directly in that other linguistic universe. The *topoi* are connected by simply going over there and actualizing the encounter. The process could be likened to an authentic process of conversion (to the other philosophy). Mutual fecundation may take place.

It will be observed that we have not adduced formulas like "common human nature," "primitive revelation," "elementary needs," "unity of the human race," or "one Creator God," because our problem is previous to all those explanations and persists even without the mentioned hypotheses. One "nature," "revelation," "tradition," "God," or whatever unifying factor does not exonerate us from the inescapable burden of understanding those words and having our personal notion of what they mean. But our interpretation does not need to be "theirs" so that we may understand human nature very differently and cannot postulate a priori that the others have the same understanding. In a word, how do we interpret their interpretation if we do not possess a priori the key to their code? It is only in doing, the praxis, that diatopical hermeneutics functions.

RETURNING now to my point of departure, I recall my thesis that an independent discipline called comparative philosophy is not possible, strictly speaking. Yet we cannot deny the existence of a growing discipline under this apparently auspicious name. It grows while attempting precisely that impossibility. It attempts to overcome plurality.

What comparative philosophy tries to compare are the final myths on which certain cultures have constructed their worlds. Now, comparative mythology is understood as comparison of legends and sacred stories. But there cannot be a neutral comparison of myths, because we all stand in a myth and we cannot eliminate the ultimate horizon where we situate ourselves in order to understand. The moment we open our senses, mind, or spirit, or whatever name we may use, we do it within a myth in which we stand, and live and have our awareness.

In other words, comparative philosophy, qua philosophy, makes us aware of our own myth by introducing us to the myth of others and by this very fact changes our own horizon. The moment we discover our horizon it ceases to be such and immediately appears as another horizon. Comparative philosophy does not demythologize; it transmythicizes. It transforms our myth the moment we discover it as such. It saves us from falling into the fallacy of believing that all the others live in myths except us. Comparative philosophy, as philosophy, is a continuous process. If we expect definitive results, we shall be frustrated; our world would cease to exist. The very failure of the project of a truly comparative philosophy as the judgment of all philosophies discloses its real nature.

For too long philosophy in the modern West, the cradle of the new "comparative philosophy," has been convinced of its own superiority and has not even considered the plausibility of a serious philosophical reflection beyond the shores of the Mediterranean Sea and its colonies. Africa may have psychology, India religion, China ethics, and so forth, but philosophy is viewed exclusively as the genial invention of the Greek mind, set forth by the European genius and grafted later onto other parts of the world, North America especially. This naïve optimism is crumbling in our times.

Leaving aside other problems about the nature of philosophy, we are led paradoxically to a very positive conclusion about the function of comparative philosophy in the modern world.

Comparative philosophy would then be more than *compared* philosophy or *comparing* philosophy. It is contrasting and imparative philosophy. Comparative philosophy makes us acutely aware that we cannot do philosophy in a vacuum or only "among ourselves." We cannot do philosophy without contrasting and learning. We have to contrast our previous notions and learn from the opinions of others. We need, further, to be ready to contest our own conclusions. Every philosophy fulfills this triple function: it deepens our common (prephilosophical) notions, it learns from the experiences of others, and it submits to radical critique the results achieved. In this sense every philosophy is comparative philosophy.

Reversing, still paradoxically, what was hinted at the beginning, comparative philosophy boomerangs from its initial thrust. It unconsciously wanted to be the superphilosophy of the modern western critical mind, passing judgment on everything under the sun, uncritical of its own assumptions and of what philosophy is. Today we are becoming more and more aware that the true philosophical spirit cannot any longer be certain that the search for certainty is the real business of philosophy. We need to take a new step back and put on equal footing (*comparare*) the different manifestations of the human experience, beginning anew to philosophize the process of trying to understand, reflect upon, shape, transform, know reality with the help of all the means available to us. We do comparative philosophy not as an independent discipline, with adolescent urges for autonomy, but as a mature *ontonomic* activity of the human spirit, contrasting everything, learning from everywhere, and radically criticizing the enterprise itself.

HAJIME NAKAMURA

The Meaning of the Terms 'Philosophy' and 'Religion' in Various Traditions

WHAT IS MEANT by the term 'philosophy'? It is difficult, if not impossible, to give a definition of it, and it is clear that no one definition would be unanimously adopted by everybody. The fifteenth edition of the *Encyclopaedia Britannica* (the so-called *Britannica III*, published in 1974) has given up the attempt to define or formulate what philosophy is. There is no entry entitled "philosophy," so there is neither a definition nor an explanation of the term. Instead, there is a long article entitled "History of Western Philosophy." (There are also entries entitled "Chinese Philosophy," "Japanese Philosophy," "Indian Philosophy," and so forth.) At the beginning of the article on the history of western philosophy, the author sets forth various conceptions of what philosophy is, but he refrains from expressing his own view. Webster's *Twentieth Century Dictionary* sets forth, probably reluctantly, a definition of 'philosophy', namely "a study of the processes governing thought and conduct; theory or investigation of the principles or laws that regulate the universe and underlie all knowledge and reality." This account is vague, to be sure, but few would raise objections to it.

How about 'religion'? In the same edition of *Britannica III* there is no entry entitled "religion." Instead one finds entries entitled "Philosophy of Religion," "Study of Religion," and so on. Webster's *Twentieth Century Dictionary* defines religion as "belief in a divine or superhuman power or powers to be obeyed and worshiped as the creator(s) and ruler(s) or in the universe." This definition involves some vague, problematic ideas but probably represents a fair characterization of the term from the point of view of western understanding.

In any case, the terms 'religion' and 'philosophy', though difficult to define, have nevertheless been fairly sharply distinguished from each other in the West, while in eastern traditions the dividing line is often difficult to discern. Whether there has existed what is called philosophy in eastern traditions has been controversial. It is likely that countries of the Far East did not have the counterpart to 'philosophy' in the meaning of modern philosophy. When Japanese intellectuals first encountered modern western philosophy more than a century ago, they thought that philosophy was something new to them. They were surprised. Amane Nishi (1829–1897), who endeavored to introduce western philosophy into Japan, coined a new word *tetsugaku* to mean "philosophy" and used it in his work *Hyakuichi Shinron* in 1874.

In old Japan, of course, Japanese intellectuals engaged in philosophical thinking. There was no separate branch of scholarship called philosophy, however. Probably one reason was that there was no antagonism toward religion, and intellectuals saw no need to develop a separate discipline with a different name. When Amane Nishi coined the word *tetsugaku* as the Japanese translation of the term 'philosophy', he meant both the "Way of Heaven" (*Tendo*) and the "Way of Man" (*Jindo*). He included Confucianism, Buddhism, and all other ideologies within the concept of *tetsugaku*. At any rate, since Amane Nishi, the use of the term *tetsugaku* has been fixed or settled.

It was introduced into Korea, China, and Vietnam and has come to be widely used in East Asia. This fact suggests that "philosophy" was something new to intellectuals in the Far East, and that what is called philosophy in the modern West was lacking in the Far East before the term *tetsugaku* was coined.

Things were different with the people of India and South Asia generally. Indian intellectuals thought that the traditional term *darśana* was the Indian counterpart of the western term 'philosophy'. In Indian universities the department of philosophy is called *darśana-bhāga*. When the fourteenth-century philosopher Mādhava composed the *Sarvadarśanasaṁgraha*, which title is translated by E. B. Cowell and A. E. Gough as *Review of Different Systems of Hindu Philosophy*, the translators took the term *darśana* for 'philosophical system'. Much earlier, when Haribhadra, the Jain philosopher of the ninth century, composed the *Ṣaḍdarśana-samuccaya*, he called each philosophical system *darśana*. Etymologically this term is close to English 'view', as in "world view," or *Anschauung* in the German words *Weltanschauung* or *Lebensanschauung*.

The Indian tradition also has another term meaning "philosophy," namely *ānvīkṣikī*. This term first appears in the *Kauṭiliya Arthaśāstram*. The most important and representative example of the *Arthaśāstras* is the *Kauṭiliya-Arthaśāstram* traditionally ascribed to Kauṭilya (or Cāṇakya), who was the prime minister of Candragupta, the founder of the Maurya Dynasty. It is a guidebook for statesmen, concerned with politics, economics, diplomacy, conduct of life, and so forth. Not all the contents are from the pen of Kauṭilya himself, but it is supposed that it assumed its present form perhaps in the third century of the Christian era.[1]

Because this work teaches chiefly the artifices and machinations of politics with no discrimination among the various means to an end, it has frequently been compared to Machiavelli's *Il Principe*, and its central notions are very utilitarian, realistic, and materialistic. The *Kauṭiliya-Arthaśāstra* in its first chapter (*vidyāsamuddeśa*)[2] recognizes four sciences (*vidyā*): philosophy (*ānvīkṣikī*); theology or dogmatics (Vedic learning, *trayī*); economics (*vārttā*); and jurisprudence (*daṇḍanīti*). Among these sciences the first, philosophy, comprises the *Sāṁkhya*, Yoga, and *Lokāyata (Sāṁkhyaṁ Yogo Lokāyataṁ cety ānvīkṣikī)*. A most interesting point is that it makes no reference to the two schools of *Vaiśeṣika* and *Nyāya*. The later

[1] Moriz Winternitz, *Geschichte der Indischen Litteratur*, 3 vols. (Leipzig: Amelang), 3:523.

[2] Hermann Georg Jacobi has already examined this passage ("Zur Frühgeschichte der Indischen Philosophie," *Sitzungsberichte der Preussischen Akademie der Wissenschaften in Berlin* [1911]: 732ff.), reprinted in his *Kleine Schriften*, ed. Bernhard Kölver (Wiesbaden: Steiner, 1970), pp. 547ff.

Nyāya school asserts that philosophy (*ānvīkṣikī*) is nothing but the Nyāya itself. Nevertheless these two schools are not mentioned there. This may point to the fact that they had perhaps not yet been fully recognized as philosophical schools. Furthermore, neither the Mīmāṁsā nor the Vedanta schools are named. What is the reason? It is an indubitable fact that by about the third century, when the *Kauṭiliya-Arthaśāstra* was compiled in its present form, these two schools were already in existence, but the fact that they are not referred to there indicates perhaps that the author of the *Arthaśāstra* did not recognize either of them as schools of philosophy. According to the *Kauṭiliya-Arthaśāstra*, the essence of philosophy is demonstration and investigation through reasoning (*hetubhir ānvīkṣamānā*)[3] and it would be difficult to admit that the Mīmāṁsā and the Vedanta are schools that engage in purely theoretical and philosophical speculation. Both schools regard the Veda as absolute and carry out philosophical speculation only in conformity with it. For this reason the *Arthaśāstra* classifies the two schools under Vedic study (*trayī*).

If we look more closely at the historical facts, the author of the *Arthaśāstra* is expressing a new attitude in making philosophy an independent science. Other thinkers did not accept its independence but regarded it as a special field of theology ("*trayī vārttā daṇḍanītiś ceti mānavāḥ / trayīviśeṣo hy ānvīkṣikīti*").[4] The author of the *Arthaśāstra* on the contrary gives the three sciences, *Sāṁkhya*, Yoga, and *Lokāyata* an independent academic status as philosophy, distinguishing them from theology.

It is already apparent in the old law books that philosophy was distinguished from theology. For example, the *Gautama-Dharmasūtra* (11.3) says, "[The king] should be fully instructed in the threefold Veda and in philosophy" (*trayyām ānvīkṣikyāṁ cābhivinītaḥ*).[5] Accordingly, the tendency to regard philosophy

[3] Julius Jolly, trans., *Arthaśāstra of Kauṭilya* (Lahore: Punjab Sanskrit Book Depot, 1923), p. 4.

[4] Ibid.

[5] I have followed Jacobi, *Kleine Schriften*.

as an independent science has already existed from ancient times, but it is probably the *Kauṭiliya-Arthaśāstra* that particularly emphasized this point. In view of such facts it would seem reasonable that the Mīmāṁsā and the Vedanta schools, which had a close relation with the Veda, were included in theology (Vedic learning).

The same evaluation is seen in the case of the *Arthaśāstra* scholar, Kāmandaki (sixth century).[6] He also thought that the sciences of the Mīmāṁsā and Vedanta could be included in the Vedic study (*trayī*).[7] Again the view[8] that postulates simply a fourfold science—namely, philosophy, theology, economics, and jurisprudence—was accepted by the *Yājñavalkyasmṛti* (1.310) and the scholars of the Nyāya school. Further, as I shall discuss later, this placement of the Vedanta school under Vedic study was also inherited by the Nyāya school.[9] Thus, the method of classifying sciences in the *Kauṭiliya-Arthaśāstra* long remained a model for later scholars, by whom also Upaniṣadic study was not accepted as independent philosophy.

Vātsyāyana, the Nyāya scholar, accepted the fourfold learning exactly as taught in the *Kauṭiliya-Arthaśāstra*.[10] According to him, philosophy (*ānvīkṣikī*) is the fourth learning (*caturthī vidyā*), which means simply logic (*nyāyavidyā*, *nyāyaśāstra*). Philosophy was nothing but logic. An opponent asks: "Is it not meaningless to construct a philosophical system of the Nyāya school by bringing forward doubt (*saṁśaya*) and other items? For these are covered in the study of right means of knowledge (*pramāṇa*) and objects of knowledge (*prameya*) and they are not

[6] According to the study undertaken by Formichi from the astronomical point of view, Kāmandaki died at the same time as Varāhamihira, who died in A.D. 587 or a little earlier. Jacobi has confirmed Formichi's theory with the consideration of other data (see Jacobi, *Kleine Schriften*). However, Winternitz, *Geschichte*, p. 526 assigns to him the date A.D. 700–750.

[7] Kāmandaki says, "*aṅgāni vedāś catvāro mīmāṁsā nyāyavistaraḥ / dharmaśāstraṁ purāṇaṁ ca trayīdam sarvam ucyate*." Cf. *upāṅgadvitayam caitan mīmāṁsā nyāyavistararaḥ*, *Āhirbudhnyasaṁhitā* 12.12.

[8] But *Manu* 7.43 distinguishes *trayī vidyā* from *ātmavidyā*.

[9] Cf. sequel for discussion of Nyāya.

[10] *Vātsāyana ad Nyāyasūtra* 1.1.1, pp. 4–5; 10 (AnSS.).

separate things." Vātsyāyana replies that "doubt and other items should be brought forward" and argues that "If the [items] be not stated separately, this (philosophy) would become merely a study of the inner *ātman* like the Upaniṣads. Therefore, philosophy is separately established by the means of doubt and other items."[11] Commenting on this, Uddyotakara says, "If there be not such items as doubt in philosophy, it would be included in the Vedic study like the Upaniṣadic study because [it] would be merely a study of the inner *ātman*. Thus the fourfoldness [of the learning] would cease to exist."

Thus both Vātsyāyana and Uddyotakara regard the "Upaniṣadic study" (*Upaniṣadvidyā*) or a "study of the inner *ātman*" merely as theology or Vedic study and not as philosophy. According to them, it is only a certain kind of inquiry, which gives rise to doubts about every aspect of nature and life and then answers them by means of reasoning, that can really deserve the name philosophy. The Vedanta school, however, attaches importance only to the Upaniṣads and dismisses logical thinking. Considering, therefore, that the Vedanta is not philosophy in the pure sense of the term, they decline to give the name of philosophy to it. It is clear that on this point as well, these Nyāya philosophers hold the same opinion as the author of the *Arthaśāstra*. In this way the early Nyāya philosophers refused to admit the significance or *raison d'être* of the Vedanta philosophy as philosophy.

With regard to the term 'religion' things were different. When Japanese intellectuals had to introduce the concept of "religion" from the West, they equated it with the traditional Buddhist concept of *shūkyō*.[12] This equation came to be admitted by Chinese, Korean, and Vietnamese intellectuals. Thus, throughout the far eastern region the term is used nowadays to mean "religion." *Shūkyō*, however, is not necessarily identical: it was a particularly buddhistic concept. It is derived

[11] *Nyāyavārttika*, p. 12.

[12] The term *shūkyō* was fully discussed by the late Kumataro Kawata in his work, *Bukkyō to Tetsugaku* [Buddhism and Philosophy] (Kyoto: Heirakuji Shoten, 1957), pp. 25–90.

from *shū*, "the primordial, fundamental or ultimate principle" or "ultimate truth," which is ineffable; and *kyō*, "teachings," or "explanations with the aid of words." The ultimate principle is beyond verbal expressions, but in order to convey it to the mind of man, one has to have recourse to words.

Both aspects of reality or truth are implied in the term *shū-kyō*. In many cases this compound is used in the sense of "*kyō* or *shū*," so that it is almost tantamount to "religious teachings." It is understandable that Japanese intellectuals should use this word to translate 'religion'.

We can trace the origin of this word to the *Laṅkavatāra-sūtra*,[13] according to which *shū* and *kyō* are set forth in coordination. *Shū*'s Sanskrit original is *siddhānta* or *siddhāntanaya*. It is beyond conceptualization. It should be known intuitively. D. T. Suzuki translates it as 'realization'. It is called "*pratyātma*" ('self-attainment', according to Suzuki), which might be translated as 'inner intuition'. In this case the Buddhist term *siddhānta* is quite different from the Hindu concept of the same name. *Kyō*'s Sanskrit original is *deśana* or *śāsana*, or *deśananaya*.

These two concepts are explained in the *Laṅkavatāra-sūtra* as follows:

> What is the characteristic of the realization by which I and other Bodhisattva-Mahāsattvas, becoming thoroughly conversant with its meaning, may quickly attain the highest enlightenment, and, relying upon themselves, will not be led away by any speculations of philosophies [*sarva-tarkika*]? Said the Blessed One: Then listen well, and well reflect within yourself; I will tell you. There are two ways of characterizing the realization [*dvividham . . . siddhāntanayalakṣaṇam*] attained by all the Śrāvakas, the Pratyekabuddhas, and the Bodhisattvas: the realization itself [*siddhāntanaya*] and the teaching [about it: *deśananaya*]. Now, by the realization itself is meant that it is the realm of inner attainment;

[13] *The Laṅkavatāra Sūtra*, ed. Bunyiu Nanjio (Kyoto: Otani University Press, 1956), pp. 148ff., 172ff.

> its characteristic features are that it has nothing to do with words, discriminations, and letters; that it leads one up to the realm of non-outflows; that it is the state of an inner experience; that it is entirely devoid of philosophical speculations and [the doings of] evil beings; and that, destroying philosophical speculations and [the doings of] evil beings, it shines out in its own inner light of attainment. Now, what is meant by the teaching [concerning it]? It is variously given in the nine divisions of the doctrinal works; it keeps one away from the dualistic notions of being and non-being, of oneness and otherness; first making use of skillful means and expedients, it induces all beings to have a perception [of this teaching] so that whoever is inclined towards it, may be instructed in it. This is the characteristic of the teaching.
>
> (v. 15) Realization and teaching, self-attainment and doctrinal instruction—those who have an insight into the difference will not be led away by philosophical authorities.
>
> (v. 16) There is no truth in any object that is imagined by the ignorant; deliverance is where there is no objective world; why is this not sought by the speculators?

In this case the teachings of religion are admitted, but philosophical speculations by means of reasoning are repudiated.[14] Another passage also discusses these terms:[15]

> Further, the ignorant and simple-minded keep on dancing and leaping fascinated with their wrong reasoning, falsehoods, and self-discriminations, and are unable to understand the truth of self-realization [*svasiddhāntanaya*] and its discourse in words [*deśana*]; clinging to the external world which is seen of the Mind itself, they cling to the study of the discourses which are a means and do not know properly how to ascertain the truth of self-realization [*svasiddhāntanaya*] which is the truth unspoiled by the fourfold proposition.

[14] I cite from D. T. Suzuki, trans., *The Laṅkavatāra Sūtra* (London: Routledge and Kegan Paul, 1932), 127ff., 148ff.

[15] Ibid., p. 127.

> The Bodhisattva asked the Buddha: Pray tell me, Blessed One, about the characteristic features of the truth of self-realization and about the discourses on it [*deśana-siddhānta-naya*], whereby I and other Bodhisattva-Mahāsattvas in future time, understanding what they are, may keep ourselves away from the wrong logicians [*kutārkika*] such as the philosophers [*tīrthaṅkara*] and those who belong to the vehicles of the Śrāvaka and the Pratyeka-buddha.
>
> The Blessed One said this to him: There are two forms of teaching the truth attained by the Tathāgatas, Arthats, Fully-Enlightened Ones of the past, present, and future. They are: the teaching by discourses, and the teachings by the establishment of self-realization. What is meant by the studying of the discourses is this, Mahāmati: there are various materials and canonical texts and discourses by which sentient beings are taught according to their dispositions and inclinations.[16]

This is the realm of dogmatics or theology. But the realm of intuition is quite different:

> What then is the truth of self-realization [*siddhāntanaya*] by which the Yogins turn away from discriminating what is seen of the Mind itself? There is an exalted state of inner attainment which does not fall into the dualism of oneness and otherness, of bothness and of not-bothness; which goes beyond the Citta, Manas, and Manovijñāna; which has nothing to do with logic, reasoning, theorizing, and illustrating; which has never been tasted by any bad logicians, by the philosophers, Śrāvakas, and Pratyekabuddhas, who have fallen into the dualistic views [*antadvaya*] of being and non-being—this I call self-realization [*siddhānta*].

So, to summarize, there are two aspects of religion: self-realization[17] and discoursing on it.

[16] Ibid., p. 148.

[17] The Chinese word *shū* is said to mean *siddhānta* in Guṇabhadra's Chinese translation.

This is what characterizes the truth of self-realization and discoursing on it, and in this you and the other Bodhisattva-Mahāsattvas are to discipline themselves. So it is said:
61. I have two forms of teaching and truth: self-realization and discoursing. I discourse with the ignorant and [disclose] self-realization to the Yogins.

In the tradition of South Asia it is very difficult for us to find the one concept that is the counterpart to the western idea of "religion." In order to express the idea of "religion" Indian intellectuals resorted to the traditional idea of *dharma*. *Dharma* can be either ethical or legal, So it is not exactly the same as the western concept of "religion." But Buddhism is called *Buddha-dharma*, Hinduism is called *Hindu-dharma*, Christianity is called *Khristi-dharma*. A Muslim is called *Yavana-dharma-sambandhī* or *Yavana-dharma-avalambī*.[18] It is not clear why the Muslim was called *Yavana-dharma*: probably it is because anybody who came to India across the Hindu Kush was called a *Yavana*. In contemporary Hindi, Islam is called *Musalmani-dharma*.

The use of these appellations reflects the thinking of South Asians, that "religion" must be eternal and universal truth. *Dharma* does not necessarily mean "law" or "rule" alone. Already in the Upaniṣads *dharma* meant something fundamental. In the *Kaṭha-Upaniṣad* 1.21 the god of death answers Naciketas's question concerning the problem of life after death as follows:

On this problem even the gods had doubts formerly. Truly, it is not easily known. This *dharma* is subtle.
O Naciketas, select another boon. Do not make me suffer. For my sake abandon this [boon].

The *dharma* in this instance, also has a buddhistic significance. After discussing the problems concerning life after death, the well-known *sūtra* that was taught to the itinerant

[18] Monier Williams: *A Dictionary, English and Sanskrit*, 4th ed. (Delhi: Montilal Banarsidass, 1976), p. 511.

monk Vaccha teaches the same: "O Vaccha. This *dharma* truly is exceedingly deep, difficult to see and difficult to understand; it is tranquil, excellent, beyond logic; and subtle; it can be known only by the wise man. It is difficult to be known by you who have different views, who follow different faiths, who embrace different interests, who practice differently, and who act differently."

Furthermore, that the truth is subtle and extremely difficult to see, was also taught in very old *gāthā*s (stanzas) in the Buddhist scriptures. For example, there is a verse that indicates Śākyamuni's mental state, in which a hesitation to preach the *dharma* to men immediately after he had attained buddhahood is revealed:

> It is not necessary for me to teach now that which I have achieved by suffering and travail. This *dhamma* is not easily understood by those who are overcome with greed and anger [*nāyam dhammo susambuddho*]. It goes against the usual current of the world, is subtle, deep, difficult to see, and minute [*nipuṇaṁ gambhīram duddasam aṇum*]. Those who are defiled by greed and are covered by a mass of darkness cannot see [it].

The foregoing investigation reveals that *dharma* could mean "religion," but that *dharma* is beyond the differences of established religions. It should be universal to mankind, not restricted to any particular creed. When we think this way, we can say that the concept of *dharma*, as is held by South Asians to mean "religion," is quite close to the idea of *shū* or *siddhānta*, as it is understood by Buddhists of the Far East. When Amane Nishi wrote a treatise entitled *Hyakuichi Shinron*, this title represented his idea that the Hundred Teachings—including Confucianism, Buddhism, and various philosophical systems of the West—converge in one. He aimed at the eternal and universal principle.

Generally speaking, among Asians there prevails a strong antipathy to the Western use of the "ism" to represent individual religions, suggesting, in other words, that Buddhism is not an "ism" or Hinduism is not an "ism." Both are just aspects of *dharma*.

When we compare philosophy in general and religion in general, they are not always separate; they not always are distinguished as a dichotomy, but overlap at many points. Some religious practitioners engaged in subtle discussions, and some philosophers were religious. For some philosophers philosophy has meant "a search for the wisdom of life," the meaning closest to the Greek words from which the term is derived. For others it has been "an attempt to understand the universe as a whole."[19] It is only in modern times that both came to be regarded as different.

If we focus on the idea of "way of life," Greek philosophy also will be included to a great extent. Originally philosophy itself was the practical way of life. For the Orphic communities philosophy was above all a "way of life," as John Burnet has pointed out:

> In Ionia, the term 'philosophy' meant something like "curiosity," and from that use of it the common Athenian sense of "culture," as we find it in Isokrates, seems to have been derived. On the other hand, wherever we can trace the influence of Pythagoras, the word has a far deeper meaning. Philosophy is itself a "purification" and a way of escape from the "wheel." That is the idea so nobly expressed in the *Phaedo*, which is manifestly inspired by Pythagorean doctrine. This way of regarding philosophy is henceforth characteristic of the best Greek thought. Aristotle is as much influenced by it as anyone, as we may see from the Tenth Book of the *Ethics*, and we could see still more clearly if we possessed his *Protreptikos* in its entirety.[20]

Of course Burnet recognizes the possibility of philosophy's degeneration if one takes this line too far. He continues,

[19] *Encyclopaedia Britannica*, 15th ed., 14:248a.

[20] John Burnet, *Early Greek Philosophy*, 4th ed. (New York: Meridian Books, 1957), pp. 82–83.

"There was a danger that this attitude should degenerate into mere quietism and 'otherworldliness,' a danger Plato saw and sought to avert. It was he that insisted on philosophers taking their turn to descend once more into the Cave to help their former fellow-prisoners. If the other view ultimately prevailed, that was hardly the fault of the philosophers."

Democritus, the materialist, also said that philosophy was a means of delivering the soul out of suffering. "Medicine heals diseases of the body; wisdom frees the soul from passions."[21]

Plato thought that one should flee away from earthly life to become like God in heaven. Socrates says in the *Theaetetus*,

> Evils can never pass away; for there must always remain something which is antagonistic to good. Having no place among the gods in heaven, of necessity they hover around the moral nature, and this earthly sphere. Wherefore we ought to fly away from earth to heaven as quickly as we can; and to fly away is to become like God, as far as this is possible: and to become like him, is to become holy, just, and wise. But, O my friend, you cannot easily convince mankind that they should pursue virtue or avoid vice, not merely in order that man may seem to be good, which is the reason given by the world, and in my judgment is only a repetition of an old wives' fable. Whereas, the truth is that God is never in any way unrighteous—he is perfect righteousness.

Again he says:

> There are two patterns eternally set before them; the one blessed and divine, the other godless and wretched: but they do not see them, or perceive that in their utter folly and infatuation they are growing like the one and unlike the other, by reason of their evil deeds; and the penalty is, that they lead a life answering to the patterns which they are growing like. And if we tell them, that unless they depart from their

[21] Fragment 31 Diels. Kathleen Freeman, *Ancilla to the Pre-Socratic Philosophers* (Cambridge, Mass.: Harvard University Press, 1948), p. 99.

> cunning, the place of innocence will not receive them after death; and that here on earth, they will live ever in the likeness of their own evil selves, and with evil friends—when they hear this they in their superior cunning will seem to be listening to the talk of idiots.[22]

When he thinks of God in terms of righteousness, his standpoint comes quite close to the Indian *dharma*. Also, *dharma* was equated with the Greek notion of *dike* by Indo-Bactrian kings, as is evidenced on the coins issued by them. It is said that this religio-ethical tendency can be noticed throughout the history of Greek philosophy. Walter Ruben, the German Indologist, says, "Already in Xenophanes, Parmenides, Plato, and perhaps even Aristotle, one can say in a certain sense that philosophy is *ancilla theologiae* and not simply a quest for knowledge as pure *theoria*, as has sometimes been urged.[23]

For ancient Chinese and Japanese what corresponds to philosophy or religion in other traditions was called merely "way of life" (*tao*). Before the introduction of western thought Buddhism was given the appellation *Butsudo* (Buddhist Way of Life) rather than *Bukkyō* (Teachings of Buddha). When we say *Bukkyō* we are reminded of doctrinal or dogmatic tendencies, the attitude of esteeming dogmas, which are very important in some other religions but do not matter much in Buddhism.

After examining the meaning of the terms 'philosophy' and 'religion' in the West and their counterparts in other traditions, we are led to the conclusion that the common denominator seems to be "way of life." This is not to minimize the significance of various disciplines of philosophy, such as epistemology, symbolic logic, and so on, but they are subsidiary to the key subject of study, "way of life." If we insist on being too strict in emphasizing either philosophy or religion, eliminating the other from the scope of investigation, we fail to grasp

[22] *Theaetetus*, 176b, in *The Dialogues of Plato*, trans. Benjamin Jowett (Oxford: Oxford University Press, 1871).

[23] Walter Ruben, "Indische und griechische Metaphysik," *Zeitschrift für Indologie und Iranistik* 8 (1931): 155.

many important problems. It is possible that an idea or attitude held by a western philosopher finds its counterpart not in an eastern philosopher but in an eastern religious thinker, or vice versa. For example, the virtue of tolerance was stressed in the West more by enlightened philosophers than by traditional religious thinkers, while in Japan and China it was emphasized more by the religious thinkers than by modern westernized philosophers.

Thus, if we limit our scope of study to only one discipline, as they are conceived in the West, we are apt to miss some important problems. By the same token, if we investigate things on a wider, more comprehensive scope structurally, a new way of approach, which might be called tentatively "the analysis of cognitive structures," may be opened.

Terms such as 'philosophy,' 'religion,' and so forth may well turn out to be provincial clichés that need to be carefully reexamined and reinterpreted from the perspective of a broadly based cross-cultural cognitive anthropology.

FREDERICK J. STRENG

Mechanisms of Self-Deception and True Awareness According to C. G. Jung and the *Eight-Thousand-Line Perfection of Wisdom Sutra*

CROSS-CULTURAL studies in comparative philosophy are both intellectually exciting and fraught with problems. They are exciting in that they seek to locate and elucidate perennial problems in human self-awareness and in the understanding of one's social and physical environment. Comparisons can provide heuristic devices for probing different cultural imagery and definitions, and for constructing analytic tools for examining the coherence and assumptions found in general claims about human experience. By specifying similarities and differences one can clarify issues that may provide the basis for new constructive formulations of recurrent human efforts at understanding and life enhancement. At their best they help to distinguish structural elements from incidental form, the typical from the culturally accidental.

The dangers—as is well known—arise from oversimplification of important distinctions in vocabulary, assumptions, and structural approaches. The difficulties in determining "original" meanings, in assessing the relative importance of concepts in a more comprehensive structure of understanding, and in intuiting the intention of claims, especially religious or salvific ones, are legion. Without claiming that there is a single approach or hermeneutical formula that can ensure a comparison both significant and accurate, I will attempt a systematic comparison of one issue in the effort of true self-awareness according to C. G. Jung and the *Eight-Thousand-Line Perfection of Wisdom Sutra*. The goal is to balance the general interpretive structure that brings into focus the issue in the comparison with the particularity in each expression.

The general issue in this study is the nature of the transformation from self-deception to true awareness. Within this complex topic we want to focus on the understanding found in each of our sources regarding the awareness of the ego as it lets go of attachment to itself. We might phrase this differently by saying that the focus is on the experience of the nonego as a process that frees one from attachment to the ego. One of the most interesting aspects of this comparison is the different understandings of the character or nature of selfhood and that of nonego according to an early Indian Buddhist text and according to a contemporary psychoanalyst in light of two assumptions common to both. The first common assumption is that both understand the self as a dynamic process, as an expression of energy in flux. The second is that both acknowledge a deeper awareness of reality that is already inherent in existence, but which is hidden within conventional, unexamined, often compulsive personal behavior. This deeper awareness is the "true awareness," which is not simply a descriptive proposition about oneself, but a *mode* of awareness or even a deepening skill in becoming aware of oneself-in-relationship.

Nevertheless, the descriptions of the process for transforming self-deception to true awareness provide quite different definitions of selfhood and nonego. The different understandings of selfhood and nonego lead Jung to affirm the importance of an intense projection of the self in the experience of a divinity, while the *Eight-Thousand-Line Perfection of Wisdom Sutra* describes the emptying process of an empty ego in relation to an empty nonego, or empty *dharma*, or no-path. The differences, I would suggest, are intrinsically related to different assumptions about the psycho-ontological power of symbols, concepts, and the quality of consciousness. The fundamental differences, then, are not simply different notions of selfhood and nonego, but two different modes or ways of "becoming aware" at the most profound level of human experience.

When Carl Jung gave the three Terry Lectures of 1937 at

Yale University, he considered the question of the relation of religion to psychology. Interestingly, he gave two definitions of religion. One of them expresses a perspective that is common in the western theological tradition. Early in the first lecture on the anatomy of the unconscious mind, he said, "Religion . . . is the term that designates the attitude peculiar to a consciousness which has been altered by the experience of *numinosum*."[1] The other definition comes in the third lecture, entitled "The History and Psychology of a Natural Symbol," in which he discussed the mandala. Here religion is related to the unconscious dimension of the human personality. He says, "Religion is a relationship to the highest or strongest value, be it positive or negative. The relationship is voluntary as well as involuntary, that is, that you can accept, consciously, the value by which you are possessed unconsciously. That psychological fact, which is the greatest power in your system is the god, since it is always the overwhelming psychic factor which is called god."[2]

These excerpts indicate Jung's recognition of a transcendent dimension of the human condition as well as the dynamic power of consciousness in creating the world of our experience. Both aspects of his vision of the human condition make possible a comparison with the Indian Buddhist version of the human situation. The *Eight-Thousand-Line Perfection of Wisdom Sutra* (ELPW) provides a natural basis for comparison in that it also emphasizes the quality of consciousness as a basic condition for true awareness of one's self and the world. In contrast to Jung's analysis, however, it emphasizes that the basic character of the self, the deepest aspect of consciousness and all perceived things in the world, is empty. Even the *numinosum*, the divinity, is empty.

In comparing Jung's version of the human condition with that found in the ELPW, we focus on one of the most dramatic

[1] C. G. Jung, *Psychology and Religion* (New Haven: Yale University Press, 1938), p. 6.

[2] Ibid., p. 98.

claims made by Jung in his final lecture. It is that the mandala, found in the contemporary world as expressed by many of Jung's clients, had an empty center. This claim was important for Jung because he was well aware, through his study of historical sources, that traditionally the mandala had a divine figure, a god or a goddess, at the center of this great circle. He says:

> A modern mandala is an involuntary confession of a peculiar mental condition. There is no deity in the mandala, and there is also no submission or reconciliation to a deity. The place of the deity seems to be taken by the wholeness of man.
>
> When one speaks of man, everybody means his own ego personality—that is, his personality in as much as he is aware of it—and when one speaks of others one assumes that they have a very similar personality. But since modern research has acquainted us with a fact, that an individual consciousness is based upon and surrounded by an indefinite extended unconscious psyche, we must revise our somewhat old fashioned prejudice that man is his consciousness. This rather naive assumption must be confronted at once by the critical question: Whose Consciousness? Is it his consciousness or the consciousness of other people around him?[3]

Jung answers his own question by saying that the individual consciousness is partially a collective unconscious: "It is a remarkable fact that this replacement is a natural and spontaneous occurrence, and that it is always essentially unconscious. If we want to know what is going to happen in a case where the idea of God is no longer projected as an autonomous entity, this is an answer of man's unconscious mind. The unconscious produces a new idea of man *in loco dei*, of man deified (or divine), imprisoned, concealed, protected, usually dehumanized and expressed by abstract symbolism."[4]

[3] Ibid., p. 99.
[4] Ibid., p. 106.

This recognition that the religious factor is identical to one's psyche is for Jung and many other readers awe-inspiring. One's own psyche, says Jung, is the goddess:

> The gods in our time assemble in the lap of the ordinary individual and are as powerful and awe-inspiring as ever, in spite of their new disguise—the so-called physical functions. Man thinks of himself as holding the psyche in the hollow of his hand. He dreams even of making a science of her. But in reality she is the mother and the maker, the psychical subject and even the possibility of consciousness itself. The psyche reaches so far beyond the boundary line of consciousness that the latter could be easily compared to an island in the ocean.[5]

However, Jung warns that this situation is psychologically dangerous for most people. It is safer to keep the intensity and power of the beyond in an image of an external, autonomous power. He says, "The experience formulated by the mandala is typical of people who cannot project the divine image any longer. They are in actual danger of inflation and dissociation."[6] A person who denies the reality of the unconscious psychic forces, or assimilates his own ego into that psychic energy, becomes the victim of "inflation" whereby the personality is dissolved and one acts psychotically. Jung writes:

> Since the idea of God represents an important, even overwhelming psychical intensity, it is, in a way, safer to believe that such an autonomous intensity is a non-ego, perhaps an altogether different or superhuman entity, "totaliteraliter." Confronted with such a belief, man must need to feel small, just about his own size. But if he declares the tremendum to be dead, then he must find out at once where this considerable energy, which was once invested in an existence as great as God, has disappeared to.
>
> Since it is a matter of tremendous energy, the result will

[5] Ibid., p. 105.
[6] Ibid.

be an equally important psychological disturbance in the form of dissociation of personality. The disruption can produce a dual or multiple personality. It is as if one single person could not carry the total amount of energy, so that parts of the personality which were hitherto functional units instantly break asunder and assume the dignity and importance of autonomous personalities.[7]

Jung explains elsewhere the problem of being absorbed into psychic powers beyond the capacity of one's ego:

> It must be reckoned a psychic catastrophe when the ego is assimilated by the self. The image of wholeness then remains in the unconscious so that on the one hand it shares the archaic nature of the unconscious, and on the other, finds itself in the psychically relative space–time continuum that is characteristic of the unconsciousness as such. . . . Hence it is of the greatest importance that the ego should be anchored in the world of consciousness and that consciousness should be reinforced by a very precise adaptation. For this, certain virtues like attention, conscientiousness, patience, etc., are of great value on the moral side, just as accurate observation of the symptomatology of the unconscious and objective self-criticism are valuable on the intellectual side.[8]

Jung warns his readers about the danger of totally identifying the ego with its extended unconscious. We must ask, however, whether there is a way to understand the tremendous psychic power at the root of the human selfhood in an integrated manner rather than as a psychic catastrophe. Jung himself says that one can and must know the hidden, the "shadow" side of one's personality, and reconcile the conscious and unconscious aspects of the self. At the same time the autonomous

[7] Ibid., p. 104.

[8] C. G. Jung, *Collected Works*, ed. H. Read, M. Fordham, and G. Adler, 20 vols. (Princeton: Princeton University Press, 1953–1979), vol. 9, pt. 2, *Aion: Researches into the Phenomenology of the Self*, pp. 45–46.

collective unconscious always stands in tension with the ego. One's true self moves between the archetype and ego-individuality without locating oneself in either.

Another way to understand the empty center in the deepest human awareness is found in the ELPW. There it is claimed that the enlightened person knows the emptiness of both the ego and any absolute reality, whether it be termed "God," "Nirvana," the "Self," a *dharma*, or even "Buddhahood."

To be aware of oneself and the world as "empty," from the Buddhist viewpoint, required a shift in the mode of apprehending the human situation. It is a shift from the conventional or habitual way to one expressing the perfection of wisdom and compassion. True compassion, however, requires knowing that any idea, any perceived object, or oneself has to be experienced without attachment to that idea, to the object, or to the self. In chapter 9 of the ELPW, the manner of knowing emptiness in an empty manner is described as follows:

> The perfection of the bodhisattva has no mental attitude, because it is imperturbable. This perfection is unshakable, in consequence of the stability of the realm of dharma. This perfection is quieted because no sign is apprehended in all dharmas. This perfection is faultless, as the perfection of all virtues. This perfection is undefiled, because imagination is something that is not. No living being is [ultimately] found in this perfection, because of the reality limit.[9]

For the skillful perceiver of emptiness, the world, self, or interpersonal relations do not disappear into a nihilistic void.

Granted, there is a psychological danger when one pursues the empty way of knowing. The person training in the empty manner of experiencing life is warned to realize emptiness as a goal in itself or as reality in itself. This is accomplished by focusing on caring for all beings in existence. Such caring or

[9] Edward Conze, trans., *The Perfection of Wisdom in Eight Thousand Lines and its Verse Summary* (Bolinas, Calif.: Four Seasons Foundation, 1973), pp. 151–152.

compassion for all beings is understood in the profound sense that there is an intrinsic relationship between oneself and all existing beings already. The Buddha explains this concept in the twentieth chapter of the ELPW in the following words: "Since [the bodhisattva] has not abandoned all beings, he is thus able to win full enlightenment safely and securely. At the time when a Bodhisattva has made all beings into an objective support for his thought of friendliness, and with the highest of friendliness ties himself to them, at that time he rises above the factiousness of the defilements and of Mara, he arises above the level of the Disciple and Pratyekabuddha, and he abides in that concentration [on friendliness]."[10]

The topic of the emptiness of the perfection of wisdom is a very complex one. I want to make only three points regarding emptiness in the ELPW. The first is the claim that the self and its constituents are empty, or without self-existent reality. The experienced self, as an empty self, is a process of interactive energies identified as the five *skandhas*: materiality, feelings or sensations, perceptions, impulses or unconscious predispositions, and consciousness. This flow of material, sensory, mental-emotional, perceptual, and unconscious energy is without self-existent power, just as each of the constituents arises only in relation to mutually dependent conditions. In chapter 1 of the ELPW, the venerable adept of perfect wisdom, Subhūti, says that despite the talk of "a bodhisattva," there is really nothing outside the verbalizing process that corresponds on a one-to-one basis with the idea of a "bodhisattva." One who does not become fearful when hearing this is at the irreversible stage of the bodhisattva path; he stands well (*susṭhita*) while not having stood anywhere (*asthānayogena*).[11] In chapter 2 Subhūti instructs the god Śakra on the deepest value of life, perfect wisdom, and how to achieve it. He says that having abided (*tiṣṭhatā*) in emptiness (*śūnyatām*), a bodhisattva "is stayed" (*sthā-*

[10] Ibid., p. 224.

[11] P. L. Vaidya, ed. and trans., *Aṣṭasāhasrikā Prajñāpāramitā with Haribhadra's Commentary Called Āloka* (Darbhanga: Mithila Institute of Post-Graduate Studies and Research in Sanskrit Learning, 1960), p. 4.

tavyam) in the perfection of wisdom. Then he continues by contrasting "abiding in emptiness" with other possibilities, which one should avoid. For example, the bodhisattva should "not be stayed" (*na sthātavyam*) in form and the other four *skandhas*, not in any of the five senses or minds (*manas*), not in sensory or mental objects, not in the elements, not on "the pillars of mindfulness, right efforts, roads to psychic power, faculties, powers, limbs of enlightenment and limbs of the path,"[12] nor on the fruits of different levels of spiritual attainment, even arhatship.

The second point is that the experienced world has various dimensions or levels of quality. One of the most important variations is between the compulsive personal identification with projected images of oneself and the world, on the one hand, and the freeing, spontaneous (or empty) manner of interaction of self and one's environment, on the other. A person's awareness includes thoughts and images; but more fundamental than the directional and organizing power of symbols for determining either self-deception or true awareness is the mode or quality of becoming conscious. The ELPW speaks of the freeing, or empty, manner of awareness as "not being stayed" (*na sthātavyam*) in things or ideas. In two subsequent sections of chapter 1, the text delineates several possibilities of what one should not be stayed in, for example, the idea that form is empty, that it is to be apprehended as something, not even in the idea that "this is Buddhahood."

Further, a bodhisattva should not "be stayed" in the notion "that the fruits of the holy life derive their dignity from the Unconditioned," nor "be stayed" in the stage of a Buddha, nor in the recognition that he has done a Buddha's work.[13] This list of negations by Subhūti leaves another disciple, Śāriputra, with a question to himself: if one should "not be stayed" even in the highest level of enlightenment, *how* then should one abide in emptiness and train oneself (*śikṣitavyam*)?[14] Subhūti re-

[12] Conze, *Perfection of Wisdom*, p. 97.

[13] Ibid.

[14] Vaidya, *Astasahasrika Pranjnaparamita*, p. 19.

sponds with a question: Where did the Buddha abide (*sthita*)? Śāriputra answers: The Tathāgata, the completely enlightened one's (*samyaksambuddha*) abode (*sthita*) is nowhere. On what ground is this claim made? That the completely enlightened one has "not stationed" (*apratiṣṭhita*) his mind anywhere.[15]

The third point regarding emptiness in the ELPW is the claim that to live in an empty manner is enlightenment. Enlightenment is the freeing of one's thoughts, emotions, or psychic energy from inappropriate restrictions due to attachment or compulsive identification with them. In the conversation between Subhūti and Śāriputra mentioned previously, regarding where did the Buddha "abide" in his attainment of perfect enlightenment, Śāriputra correctly says that the Tathāgata did not abide in the conditioned realm or in the nonconditioned realm, nor did he abandon (*vyutthita*) them both. Subhūti then affirms Śāriputra's statement and summarizes the view of the ELPW by saying:

> Even so, Śāriputra, a bodhisattva, a great being, is stayed (*sthātavyam*), is trained. [He thinks:] As the Tathāgata, the highest (completely) enlightened one, so I am not anywhere stayed (*sthātaḥ*), not non-abiding (*nāsthitaḥ*), not fixed (*viṣṭhitaḥ*), not non-fixed (*naviṣṭhitaḥ*). Being stayed in this way, one is trained (*śikṣitavyam*, i.e., trained correctly). As the Tathāgata, so I "stand" (*sthāsyāmi*); thus I am trained. As the Tathāgata has stood (*sthānam*), thus, I stand; thus I train . . . well placed, not having stood anywhere (*asthānayogena*). Even so a bodhisattva, a great being, is stayed (*sthātavyam*), is trained. Thus trained the bodhisattva, a great being, abides (*viharati*) in the perfection of wisdom and does not lose his attentiveness to it.[16]

Thus to train, or to stay in the course of perfect wisdom, a person should avoid being "fixed" or "stayed" in any object of perception or mental ideal.

Our language and the way we use language in a habitual

[15] Ibid.
[16] Ibid.

symbolic way disposes us to think that there are units of reality that exist in themselves. Insight shows that such a view is not true. The point of meditating on the perfection of wisdom is not simply to construct a new system or image for understanding, but to allow insights into the kind of verbal fallacies and emotional afflictions that human beings easily slip into. The formulations and imagery are, at best, expedient means. According to this perspective neither the ego nor the archetype is a final determinate. They are determinates of selfhood only to the degree that a person gives them power.

The attachment to the concept or image of the "I" can be called a type of narcissism; however, it is a narcissism that pervades all existence and is based on the habitual division between oneself and others. It can be eliminated only by actualizing a sense of myself-in-relation-to-others; selfhood is a complex of interaction even before there is an "I" specified. Narcissism, as a precognitive tendency to define reality from the standpoint of the ego, is—from the perspective of the ELPW advocates—based on a dualistic mode of perception. It is a fabrication looming into a fantasy because it misappropriates the experience of becoming.

From the perspective found in the ELPW, any talk of a self, ego, or archetype is a mental construction. If one wants to talk about them, one should do so with the recognition that they are simply concepts that direct one's perception but do not represent (or re-present) entities outside the language system in a one-to-one relationship. Indeed, there are some notions that are said to be more useful than others for actualizing true awareness. To say that things are empty is more useful than to say that they refer to an essential self-existent entity; but one should not get caught in thinking that therefore there must be something that is essentially empty and something that is essentially self-existent. This would exemplify a dualistic orientation. The thought process about oneself and others that is conventional and symbolically powerful tends to keep one bound to one's own projections and obstructions. Symbolic image-construction participates in the same reality of dependent co-arising as the freeing actualizing of emptiness, but it is without awareness of the empty character of that in which one is actually participating.

How do these two visions of the condition of the human situation contribute to an understanding of the emptiness at the center of the deepest human self-consciousness? The answer, I suggest, is related to an understanding of the way people know the truth about themselves. This understanding, in turn, is related to the way one finds one's own deepest values—that is, the way one valorizes experience. The Jungian approach places an emphasis on the symbolic power of images and dispositions for constructing an experienced world, called archetypes, which is derived from a transpersonal unconscious. The bodhisattva in the ELPW places emphasis on shifting from a symbolic mode of consciousness to a different quality of consciousness, which we might call here an "emptying consciousness." Despite many overlapping concerns a difference is reflected in the way that each orientation understands the possibility and danger of identifying the conscious individual or the conventional self with the deepest or most comprehensive dimension of that self.

From the Buddhist perspective in the ELPW, letting go of a mythic consciousness as a valorizing process is the highest goal in the most radical form of emptiness meditation. By contrast, Carl Jung warns that inflation of ego necessarily attends the identification of oneself with an archetypal motif. The fears of identifying oneself with an archetypal motif arise, to a significant degree, because of a common western assumption, suggested in his first definition of religion: he follows the advocates of main-line Christianity who are trained to perceive ultimate values and to give ultimate value to things by locating them outside human awareness. The manner or process by which ultimate values are identified begins with an assumption of a radical distinction between the sacred and the secular, between the holy and the profane. The sacred is the incomprehensible, the wholly other source of everything, the creator who is never to be confused with the creature.

According to Jung, people need to maintain a balance between the archetype and the ego by avoiding the integration of all possible archetypes into the ego. If the ego is absorbed into the archetype, it loses contact with the conditioned world. This model depends on the assumption that there is an ultimate value expressed in the archetype and the ego, and that there is some autonomy in each, such that each must stand opposed to the other in a mutually dependent tension. God is an autonomous psychic complex. Thus, for Jung, a mandala is an expression of the way one views one's awareness through a symbol, a psychic construct, or a constructed world of experience. A mandala is a true image of an experienced world. An empty center is dangerous because total absorption into the nonego requires the loss of the conditioned ego.

The Buddhist view in the ELPW suggests that the mandala, as any symbol, may function not only as a way of constructing a world with order and meaning. It may, at a more profound level, be a tool or expedient for shifting one's mode of consciousness from a concern to construct a meaningful world as a process of self-realization to a concern to dissipate attachment to an empty self-image as a process of self-realization. In the latter process of self-realization, the value given to a particular symbolic form is transcended by a process that recognizes all symbolic forms as conditioned mental-emotional processes. It is a process of letting go of a mythologizing process of valorization.

ELIOT DEUTSCH

Knowledge and the Tradition Text in Indian Philosophy

IT IS NOT uncommon, among western philosophers who are not at the same time Indologists, Sinologists, or Buddhologists but who nevertheless have some interest in Asian thought, to engage that thought as if it had been put forward by contemporaries in their own cultural milieu. Arguments are lifted out of the forms in which they are (presumed only to have been) presented, not embedded, and are then dealt with in straightforward truth-value terms. The unspoken assumption is that philosophers everywhere have addressed the same basic problems, adhere (or at least ought to adhere) to the same standards of what constitutes a good argument, and employ similar conceptions about the nature of truth and knowledge. Philosophical universality, itself conceived according to prevailing contemporary notions, becomes then what is simply assumed to be, rather than something that may or may not be worth striving to attain.

Now of course there are many of us who have been trained in western philosophy and who do recognize the extraordinary naïveté in this easy (imperialistic) universality. We acknowledge that one must first understand the set of philosophic problems at work during the period in which the particular philosophical ideas are developed; that one must know with what alternative positions a particular argument is contending, the various linguistic and stylistic conventions that might govern modes of thoughts, and so on. In short, one must first have insight into context before one can have access to text.

I would like to take that recognition one step forward by showing that before one can engage a philosophical argument, idea, or theory in Asian thought in truth-value terms one must first appreciate (with that appreciation subsequently influencing one's engagement) what it is that constitutes a text in Asian thought and how this relates to its understanding of the nature of human knowledge. I will concentrate on Indian (namely, Vedantic) philosophy, though I strongly suspect that this discussion will apply, mutatis mutandis, to East Asian traditions as well. I will concentrate, then, on the form of philosophical thought in India as this has bearing on its content. In the broadest sense, I am concerned here with the problem of philosophical style.[1]

SOME philosophers of language believe that the meaning of what is said can never be utterly divorced from the manner of the saying. It is not only with poetry that the "what" and "how" of language are inseparably united. In all forms of speech meaning is affected by stylistic factors and by the form in which it is articulated and embedded, but especially in philosophical discourse. Something important and essential is lost when we study (and teach) philosophy—as has unfortunately become typical in many contemporary analytic circles—as if it were made up of a series or set of alternative arguments, ideas, or isms capable of being abstracted from the concrete forms in which these arguments, ideas, and theories were presented and shaped. Plato without his dialogue, Nietzsche without his

[1] For present purposes I am not considering the question of how the nature of the (natural) language used in various traditions might affect the style in which philosophical thinking is expressed, important as the contribution of the natural language to philosophical meaning might be. I concentrate instead on philosophical *form*, isolating this dimension to see if it might not disclose something of importance about comparative philosophy. Although the linguistic and the structural clearly belong together in any articulation of a philosophical idea, it is seldom the case that there is any necessary connection between them. The use of a *sūtra* form in Indian (Hindu/Brahmanic) philosophy is clearly not dependent on the fact that Sanskrit was the language in which they were composed, albeit Sanskrit might lend itself nicely to this compact form.

aphorism might in some ways be interesting; but assuredly it is not Plato or Nietzsche as the philosophers they were.

And philosophical style, especially in this formal aspect, is not just an individual matter; for it has pervasive cultural dimensions. I do not mean that which constitutes period styles in the art-history sense (Romanesque; Gothic), but those shared values, expectations, understandings which inform the thinking-expressive process of an individual within his culture in a fundamental way. The cultural dimensions of style are no doubt made up of many elements, some derived from the nature of the natural language employed, others from various social and political factors, and so on. Whatever these elements are, they form the basis for the accepted philosophic possibilities and limits of any historical time or place: everything from the accepted length of a philosophical work to the kinds of imagery and metaphor that are considered appropriate.

Arthur Danto has gone so far as to argue that there is an intimate connection between the culturally developed form in which philosophy is expressed and its conception of truth. He writes, "The concept of philosophical truth and the form of philosophical expression are internally enough related that we may want to recognize that when we turn to other forms we may also be turning to other conceptions of philosophical truth."[2] I want to follow out this idea somewhat and ask what is the basic attitude toward knowledge that is involved with the special form of philosophical thought in India. Let us first examine that special form.

It has often been pointed out that Indian philosophy developed historically (and especially the dominant Vedantic schools) as a commentarial tradition, the major philosophers having written commentaries and subcommentaries on basic *sūtras* and (again especially with Vedanta) on what is taken to be other authoritative sources (such as Upaniṣads). Karl Potter, for example, writes: "Much of the Vedānta literature is

[2] Arthur C. Danto, "Philosophy as/and/of Literature," in *Proceedings and Addresses of the American Philosophical Association* 58 (1984): 7.

composed following the tradition of *sūtra* and commentary that reflects the oral tradition in which it was born. *Sūtra*s are aphoristic phrases designed to remind their memorizer of the elements of the literature so summarized."[3] And J.A.B. van Buitenen has also noted that the original *sūtras* were summaries that were "as concise as possible to facilitate their being remembered."[4] The compact, sometimes laconic series of statements making up the *sūtra* were then more like minutes of a committee meeting than an independently structured argument; and like committee-meeting minutes they were often open to very different readings, depending on the predilections—and the memories—of their readers, especially when there was an occasion for dispute. Gerald Larson, however, has pointed out that "Most modern interpreters or translators deal with the problem of the traditional format of Indian thought by simply dismantling or ignoring it. The laconic, formulaic shorthand of traditional Indian philosophizing is explained away as a mnemonic device for preserving the oral tradition."[5]

Larson seems to suggest here—and he develops this idea considerably in the rest of his article—that the *sūtra* (or *kārikā*) is in fact a carefully structured argument that has a unity and coherence, at least once we have the map, as it were, to traverse

[3] Karl Potter, ed., "*Advaita Vedānta* up to Śaṁkara and his Pupils," *Encyclopedia of Indian Philosophies* (Princeton: Princeton University Press, 1981), p. 4.

[4] In *A Source Book of Advaita Vedānta*, ed. Eliot Deutsch and J.A.B. van Buitenen (Honolulu: University of Hawaii Press, 1981), p. 4.

[5] Gerald James Larson, "The Format of Technical Philosophical Writing in Ancient India: Inadequacies of Conventional Translation," *Philosophy East and West* 30 (1980): 376. Larson argues (p. 375) that "In many instances, unfortunately, the commentaries, subcommentaries, and glosses on the various collections of *sūtra*-s or *kārikā*-s are from periods that postdate the compilation of *sūtra*-s and *kārikā*-s by several centuries, and it is frequently impossible to judge if a given commentator (*bhāṣyakāra*) is a reliable interpreter of the *sūtra* or *kārikā*. Moreover, because of this unusual format for philosophical writing, it is often difficult to sort out what is a legitimate explicating of a *sūtra* or *kārikā*, on the one hand, from what is a creative innovation by a commentator on the other." This assumes, of course, an opposition between a "legitimate explication" and a "creative innovation"—an opposition that, as one of the purposes of this paper will be to show, is basically nonexistent in Indian thought.

its passageways.[6] I do not think we have to go that far. Van Buitenen, in the context from which I quoted earlier, does go on to say,

> It is one of the distinctive peculiarities of Indian learned traditions that is is taken for granted, in a formal way, that the fundamentals of each of them are given at the very outset of the history of the discipline and hence that it is the task of successive generations simply to restate them and to explicate them. The textual history of the discipline thus takes on the form of a basic text with generations of commentaries written on this basic text and on the preceding commentary.[7]

My argument will be that this idea of philosophy as "recovery" rather than "discovery" is central to the traditional Indian understanding of a philosophical text. In making this argument I am not claiming that we have some completed original text as such on which diverse commentaries were written, but rather that what constitutes the text in Indian thought is precisely the *sūtra* (or *kārikā*) and/or other authoritative sources, together with the ongoing exegetical work. In Indian philosophy we have as the basic unit what we might call the "tradition text": the philosophical content of a "school," in the best sense of the word.[8]

A tradition text has, as indicated, its authoritative sources grounded in the oral transmission, its summaries, its ongoing written elaborations. The basic commentary (*bhāṣya*), or the

[6] Larson develops his own positive view about the *sūtra* form with the *Tattvayāthārthyadīpana*, a Sāṁkhyan text of "twenty-five utterances." He argues that "the *sūtra*-s provide a network of symbolic notations that permit a systematic 'seeing' (*darśana*) of a certain way of interpreting some aspect of human experience or some aspect of the world" (ibid., p. 376).

[7] *Source Book of Advaita Vedānta*, p. 65.

[8] With respect to Vedanta, then, it would follow that there is no "original" Vedanta to which various and diverse interpretations were given (or were superadded to); there are rather several Vedantas consisting of the tradition text of the different schools (Advaita, Viśiṣṭādvaita, etc.), each text incorporating the *sūtra*in its own way.

shorter commentaries (*vṛttis*), with the subcommentaries (*ṭīkās*) and glosses (*vārttikas*), form, hermeneutically, integral parts of a continuing argument or text. They are not so much appendages to an otherwise fixed and completed work (the *sūtra*)—as though the writers, the philosophers, were involved simply as scholars wrestling with the meaning of what was said and believed by others—as they contribute to a larger, developing work. The exegetical material expands, refines, modifies arguments and ideas, and presents new ones, usually with increasing precision (oftentimes, somewhat unfortunately, in terms of a multiplication of distinctions reminiscent of scholasticism), seeking to bring greater systematic coherence to its body of ideas. The philosopher-commentator, in other words, seeks to remain faithful to his authoritative sources, but in his own creative terms. It is thus that we can speak of his work, together with its authoritative sources, as constituting a "tradition text."

Hans-Georg Gadamer has written that "If the prestige of authority takes the place of one's own judgment, then authority is in fact a source of prejudices. But this does not exclude the possibility that it can also be a source of truth. . . . It [tradition] is, essentially, preservation, such as is active in all historical change. But preservation is an act of reason, though an inconspicuous one."[9] This "act of reason" for Gadamer and for Vedanta is a creative undertaking. A tradition text becomes a repository of knowledge, at once eternal and temporal. Defying the usual opposition between the two, the tradition text simultaneously *is* a kind of authorless truth (as embodying *śruti*) and *becomes* something new with each vital engagement with it. From the philosopher-commentator's point of view, he is not remarking on a finished product, as a literary critic might do; he is contributing something to it through his creative appropriation of its very life and being.

This appropriation takes many forms, some of which are

[9] Hans Georg Gadamer, *Truth and Method* (New York: Seabury Press, 1975), pp. 247, 250.

quite puzzling to the western reader. In Indian philosophy generally one finds a tendency to incorporate and repeat arguments from highly diverse sources (often using those of one's opponent against another of one's opponents), as though a philosophical argument were a kind of public property, which anyone could use for his or her own purpose. The opponent (*pūrvapakṣin*) in the debate-discussion is himself sometimes purely formal, insofar as his "school" is no longer at the time a living force with which to contend. This peculiar temporality of a work of philosophy reflects its being as part of a tradition text. Arguments—old ones, those of one's erstwhile opponent, as well as novel ones—are intended to refine a certain position, develop a certain idea, expand a particular viewpoint. Also, because of their being part of a tradition text, individual philosophical works in Indian thought seldom have an independent, integral form, an architectonic structure (of the kind associated with, say, Spinoza's *Ethics* or Kant's *Critiques*), for they are not intended to be self-sufficient, completed wholes. They are not intended to be isolated from their "school" context.

J. N. Mohanty has rightly stated,

> There is, apparently, an underlying assumption that no one individual can claim to have seen the truth for the first time and, therefore, that an individual can only explicate, state, and defend in a new form a truth that had been seen, stated, and defended by countless others before him; hence the tradition of expounding one's thoughts by affiliating oneself to one of the *darśanas* [schools]. If one is to be counted as a great master (*ācārya*) one has to write a commentary (*bhāṣya*) on the *sūtras* of the *darśana* concerned.[10]

I have said that from the philosopher-commentator's point of view he is not so much remarking on an already finished text as he is himself contributing to that text through his appropriation of its content. The key term here is "appropriation." If

[10] J. N. Mohanty, "Indian Philosophy," in *Encyclopaedia Britannica*, 3:314.

knowledge is something that is basically recovered rather than discovered, then it is incumbent upon the philosopher to be committed to the truth of his "school," to be entirely open to its teachings as he makes it his own. This commitment, this openness, this engagement is then a kind of self-making. To appropriate something means to take it on as part of one's own being. The content of appropriation is the stuff of personal identity. My person as a historical being is constituted in part by what I have appropriated from human history. Appropriation is a creative retaining and shaping of a content that is made one's own. It is not a passive receptivity, but a dynamic engagement: what is appropriated gets changed in the act of changing the bearer of it.

Knowledge, then, is something made; it is a genuine action (*karman*), in this "existentialist" sense: it is not so much that which is contained in a (justified, true) belief or statement, as that which becomes wholly real in one's life. Although Indian philosophers in their technical epistemological analyses make the usual distinctions among knower (*pramatṛ*), knowledge (*pramā*), and object of knowledge (*prameya*)—as well as between a valid means of knowledge (*pramāṇa*) and truth (*prāmāṇya*)—there is the underlying assumption that the only knowledge really worth having is that involved with *mokṣa*, liberation: in short, self-knowledge.

Self-knowledge is not knowledge *about* a self, as though *ātman* were an object, a thing to be known by a subject standing apart from it. Self-knowledge, for Vedanta at any rate, is a form of realization—it is the recognition of that which already is. And if one already is the truth of being, then self-realization does not involve some radical remaking of oneself; some conversion into a new being; some finding of one's true character or personality. Knowledge rather involves the removing of ignorance, of the sources of bewilderment, and the accepting recognition of the timeless ground of being. "Truth" finally is what conduces to this knowledge.

It should not be surprising, then, that there is in Indian thought a close connection between its conception of self-knowledge and what is taken to be the nature of a tradition text. Both assume the timeless presence of that which possesses supreme value (*ātman/brahman*) and the authoritative sources; both assume that individual persons (qua *jīvas*) must realize that value and make it their own in a creative way. Self-knowledge, as realization and appropriation, in fact becomes the content of the tradition text in its essential form. Although language is recognized (in some teachings of Vedanta) to be inherently inadequate to render the truth of being, nevertheless—as the tradition text—it becomes at once the embodiment of knowledge and the means to its acquisition.

If the western philosopher is to engage classical Indian thought in truth-value terms, as indeed (being a philosopher) he should and must, it becomes clear that he must first listen carefully to what that tradition is saying, and what alternative understandings about the nature of truth and knowledge it might be opening up for others; for it is precisely in that opening—in that "clearing," if we may appropriate Heidegger's expression—that the most meaningful truth-value engagement can then occur.

NINIAN SMART

The Analogy of Meaning and the Tasks of Comparative Philosophy

ONE OF THE convenient aspects of the Indian, or more generally South Asian, philosophical tradition is that it is typically organized into systems. These are, of course, often referred to as the *darśanas*. But it is important here for us not to be misled by some older and some more modern classifications—to which point I shall return in a moment. The systematic character of South Asian viewpoints gives us a clear view of the way that key terms are embedded in contexts. As so embedded the terms acquire systematic ambiguity. Consider that so prominent and widely emphasized expression, *mokṣa*, and its cognates and surrogates, *mukti*, Nirvana, *kevala*, and so on. It is an obvious point that the term means different things according to the variety of contexts in which it is used. Consider for instance the role played here by the concept of heavenly existence. Only in some cases does rebirth in heaven count as liberation: thus it is the longed-for goal of Viśiṣṭādvaita and is the aim of Mīmāṁsā; but it is not final salvation described in the Theravāda or Advaita, or for that matter in Sāṁkhya or Jainism. These examples make us ask what, if anything clear, counts as a transcendent state of being in the Indian tradition, seeing that *mokṣa* can be tied both to heavenly (that is, subtle spatial) existence and to transspatial existence. The examples also lead us to question how we can compare *mokṣa* to the rather different ideas (it seems) in the western tradition. To complicate matters, India also distinguished between final *mukti* and *jīvanmukti* or living liberation, as in the Yoga and Buddhist traditions.

Certain morals, which I want to sketch out in greater detail, already emerge from these brief remarks. They can be stated as follows. First of all, the Indian philosophical tradition contains among other things a stock of key terms that have systematic ambiguity insofar as they appear embedded in differing systems. By and large these key terms are shared between *āstika* and *nāstika* schools alike, though some regional belief-systems may have an idiosyncratic stock of key expressions—for example Śaiva Siddhānta.

Second, despite the variations according to systematic context, there emerge from the tradition broad patterns that indicate ways in which the tradition differs from that in the West: so there is a double ambiguity in our translations and modes of grasping Indian ideas ("we" here means westerners: I write as a westerner approaching India cross-culturally).

Lastly, the notion of "living liberation" reminds us that there are experimental and behavioral and indeed institutional ways in which the systems themselves not only embedded key concepts but in their turn are embedded in life. If being embedded in a system can be called horizontal contextuality, being embedded in a form of life can be called vertical contextuality. In particular the major systems, with two possible exceptions, make no sense unless we take seriously their embedment in religious and spiritual practice. Although some writers, in part under the influence of modern western ideas about the autonomy of philosophy, are hesitant or hostile about the claim that Indian philosophy is rooted for the most part in religion, it seems to me reasonable to note the close relations. Indeed, as there is no word that univocally corresponds to 'philosophy', it is important to think about the underlying reasons for this state of affairs. There is no lack of analytic insight in the Indian tradition, and religion is more rationally presented in many ways than it has been in the West: so the issue is not about intellectual credentials. It is just that we must be realistic about the ambience, the vertical context, of Indian reflection.

Moreover, I think it would be inept for us to start with the imperial assumption that somehow there is a clearly and well-defined place in our intellectual firmament for what is called philosophy. It seems to me that modern western philosophy has been the product of a number of cultural accidents, one of which is institutionalization of universities into a departmental structure. Another is the retrospective adoption of a canonical list of philosophers (and sometimes important thinkers have been on the whole ignored in the canon at certain periods: for example, Schopenhauer, Nietzsche). Such retrospection involves projecting into the past the perceived important themes of present vogues and trends. It is worth noting that modern conceptions of Indian philosophy are the product of a synthesis of western and Indian thinking in the period since the second half of the nineteenth century. In certain ways modern ideas of Indian philosophy do not fit with elements in the tradition itself—that is, the South Asian tradition dominated primarily by emerging Buddhist and Hindu religious and social structures and world views. Let me sketch briefly some of the problems about talking about "Indian philosophy" at all.

First, in premodern times there was a complex civilization in the Indian subcontinent in which various world views were held and practiced, ranging from the six official *darśana*s of the *āstika* variety through to the various and multiplying world views or schools of thought through which Buddhism was expressed, via Jainism, the Ājīvikas, materialism, and other unorthodox positions. And this is not to mention emerging regional viewpoints such as Kashmiri Śavisim, Śaiva Siddhānta, the Lingāyatas, and so on. Modern histories of Indian philosophy tend to stick to the six official *āstika* schools plus some reference to the principal *nāstika* schools. The perspective is very much the projection of modern Indian (predominantly Hindu) self-awareness onto a much more chaotic past. The six *darśana*s are not exhaustive or logically arranged, and though they all have some philosophical or ratiocinative interest, they differ radically in scope, from the strange hermeneutical world view of Mīmāṁsā to the logical slant of Nyāya and the protoscientific shape of Vaiśeṣika. Moreover, the most important philosophical division within the *āstika* tradition, found in the varieties of Vedanta, are lumped together under a single head. And the very concept of *āstika* does not comprehensively cover the Hindu tradition itself: it is a Brahmin classification, and so otherwise fascinating and ingeniously worked out theologies, such as that of Śaiva Siddhānta, are left on one side.

The explanation of all this messy lack of fit with some unitary view of philosophy from a western perspective has, of course, to do with the vertical context. The way knowledge is classified in the Indian tradition has to do with social and spiritual attitudes and behavior. Thus the fact that the idea of *āstika* figures so prominently in classifications of philosophical systems reflects a social fabric in which only upper-class Hindus had access to Brahmin administered knowledge.

Moreover, the *āstika*ness of the *darśana*s actually varies widely. Sāṁkhya owes little in fact to the Vedas, and Sāṁkhya ideas where they occur in later scriptures have a different horizontal context from that in which they find themselves in systematic Sāṁkhya. Mīmāṁsā is rather flagrant in its repudiation of much in the Upaniṣads and of the whole concept of the Lord. Frankly, the classification *āstika* versus *nāstika* is rather misleading. Its main interest is that it was taken seriously for some purposes: and those purposes philosophically involved mainly the special role of the *pramāṇa* of *śabda*. Incidentally, if one wanted a rough equivalent of most English-speaking philosophy of today it would be *pramāṇavidyā*—the science of the sources of knowledge.

Also incidentally: if the categorization of Indian philosophy is traditionally a bit of a mess, so is it in western philosophy: putting Aquinas, Thales, Pico della Mirandola, Nietzsche, A. J. Ayer, Wittgenstein, Russell, Heidegger, Schopenhauer, Kant, and Habermas in the same basket is bound to cause trouble.

I have said that the *darśana* categorization owes itself to social and spiritual facts: its chaos in part reflects too the anarchic nature of the evolution of the so-called Hindu tradition. Hinduism is a rather recent invention; but for a new religion it has remarkably ancient roots. It is a matter of creating the consciousness of synthesis, and in this regard the proponents of the modern Hindu ideology turned out to be remarkably eloquent spokespeople. We are now held in the grip of this vision of a tradition flowering pluralistically but in its own way coherently, from the *Ṛg Veda* through to the great Vedantins and beyond. But I ask: What was Hinduism before the *Gītā*? Or before temples? Or before Śaṅkara and Rāmānuja? Were the typical features of the Hindu tradition present in nuce in the Vedas: reincarnation, Śiva, Viṣṇu, the *smārta*s, caste, images, bathing tanks, pilgrimages, the *Manu-smṛti*, the bathing ghats along the Ganges, the various practices of Yoga, the cat and monkey schools? Of course not: but as in other religions hermeneutics did its best to turn scraps and ambiguities into scriptural proofs. I do not want to be thought to be undervaluing the modern Hindu synthesis of such men as Vivekananda and Radhakrishnan. It was a creative and noble vision, and it did much both for the Indian national struggle, a new Hindu self-awareness, and tolerant and pluralistic attitudes.

Actually, this modern Hindu ideology is itself a forecast of what one aspect of comparative philosophy is likely to yield—namely, a reflective synthesis of the outlooks of differing past civilizations, in the interests of a new global reflection on the history of the human race. The ideology may also remind us that the past is precious, because it can act as a treasure house of resources for us in our thinking through present and future problems.

I have remarked that we need to look to the vertical contexts of the various schools; and the general vertical context was predominantly religious; but those who wish to emphasize the secular features of ancient and medieval India are of course entitled to do so. The *Lokāyata* for example was a long and rich tradition of thinking, and many critical styles of thinking in any event entered into the more religious paths. To select among these aspects of the past is one mode of resource selectivity. Maybe, though, it would be more realistic and comprehensive to take one strand of Indian thinking about the tradition and generalize it. The term *darśana* can be appropriately enough translated viewpoint or "world view" in English. Generally speaking, what we mean by Indian philosophy is the process and results of various attempts to articulate and argue for world views—ranging from Rāmānuja's devotional theism to forms of materialism. Logic and linguistics were brought in as technical adjuncts to such world-view construction or world view articulation, though they can have an independent existence (as today: separate programs of linguistics and logic in our universities are a sign of the independence of these disciplines, which have been raised in part by their adoptive parents in philosophy). So if we wanted a way of characterizing Indian philosophy in general it would be as world-view articulation. And, by the way, what would be wrong with that characterization for western and other kinds of philosophy? At one time many philosophers dreaded the thought that metaphysics might be the scope of philosophy: but they still held to some form of (antimetaphysical) world view, so even they might have been satisfied. Moreover, this formula covers more than philosophy as often narrowly institutionalized: it would cover theologies (and rightly so, for are they not in competition with other world views?) and political ideologies such as Marxism. It would be educationally logical to group together the exploration of alternative world views, both historically and evaluatively. Philosophy, parts of politics, history, religious studies, and so on would coalesce into a *darśanavidyā*.

Such a *darśanavidyā* is in part analytic and in part argumentative. By analytic I mean that practitioners try to understand rather than defend or attack world views. It is directed to description instead of construing a better articulation or creating arguments for a position. Religious studies as historical, sociological, and phenomenological inquiry is world-view analysis and, if stretched to cover nonreligious ideologies, would comprehend the descriptive aspect of the total field. Similarly we can think of comparative *darśanavidyā* as having an analytic side and a constructive side. This essay began with some analytic problems: the need to see the ambiguity of key terms in Indian *darśana*s because of their horizontal contextuality. When we come to cross-cultural *darśanavidyā* the systematic ambiguity becomes stretched: salvation or liberation includes the varieties of *mokṣa* plus much more. Can such ambiguity, such analogy of meanings, be turned to our advantage?

From what standpoint? I think that the analysis is important in the present *philosophical* context because it can suggest new ways of thinking: it calls into question some of the forms of thought with which we may approach the world. Let me list a few cases in which the Indian tradition displays an analogy of meaning that stimulates new reflection from a western standpoint.

First, there is the strangely (that is, from a western viewpoint) conceived distinction between *prakṛti* (materiality) and *puruṣa* (consciousness): strangely conceived in that what we might classify as mental—such as *buddhi* and *manas*, and the like—here falls under the the heading of matter. Similarly in the case of Buddhism the description of human psychology does not include a self, for it all falls, so to say, on the hither side—on the side of impermanence. So the soul–body distinction is drawn differently. Second, the very act of thinking that India typically draws the line between soul and matter in a different place causes us to question whether matter or even nature is in any way a proper translation of *prakṛti*, especially *prakṛti* as conceived in the Sāṁkhya system. If it has an inherent teleology, is it not a very different conception from our (currently dissolving) concept of matter? Third, and connectedly, the Buddhist nonself doctrine, which might at first sight seem puzzling, becomes intelligible when we see that Buddhism among other things aims to delineate a world composed of events (*dharma*s). But the consequence is a quite new view of transcendence, which is like "this world" desubstantialized. The various notions, incidentally, of *loka* or universe and the various concepts of the ultimate stimulate a quite new debate in regard to what is meant by "transcendence." Fourth, the Indian *pramāṇavidyā* has something surprising from a western point of view: the inclusion of testimony. Much depends on this, for on it turns the whole question of the acceptability of *śruti* (scriptural authority). This raises some important questions in the philosophy of religion, but at the same time obliquely raises an issue about the communal character of knowledge. These, then, are a few ways in which the manner of carving the joints of the world differs in the Indian and western milieus.

If we look on the various philosophical heritages as resources, then we may hope that ideas drawn from them might help to resolve some of the major world-view problems of the new intellectual world taking shape through the meeting of cultures. I have mentioned ways in which the Indian heritage, by its very carving of the categories, may act as a stimulus to western thinking. Let me try out some ideas in the opposite direction.

A pervasive feature of much of Indian thinking is the distinguishing of differing levels of truth: we find it of course in classical Mādhyamika and in Vasubandhu and Śaṅkara. If one looks to the vertical context, it is evident that the pursuit of the contemplative path to a "higher" kind of consciousness is crucial. The experience of *nirguṇa brahman* makes sense of the two-level theory: in the light of the nondual consciousness the ordinary world is indeed like a dream. This echoes a concern rather differently expressed in the West: namely, a way of thinking of differing modes of experiencing reality, either by religious experience or through ordinary perception, scientific investigation, and so on. In different ways this synthetic way of combining religious and nonreligious apprehensions can be seen in Otto, Buber, Stace, Hick, and Capra. Can the Indian scheme then be picked up and placed in a different context, where it is not a matter of higher or lower, but rather of alternative modes of experiencing? Again: can the notion of *śabda* (verbal authority) be put in a new context, namely of communication? For the process of scientific knowledge is a community exercise in which concepts of falsification, verification, testing hypotheses, degrees of confirmation, and so forth all presuppose a community of communicators. This presupposition may take us away from the solitarian preoccupations of so much western epistemology: Descartes in solitary doubt, Russell squinting at elliptical pennies by himself, and so on.

It also raises some questions about the teacher: do we pay any credence to the claim that some people have a higher religious insight in which we simply "have to take their word" for it? The appeal to *śabda* brings into sharper focus a major issue in global world-view construction: the issue whether anyone is entitled to appeal to transcendental testimony. Some of the major traditional religions rest on revelations, and a major question is whether eventually such revelations themselves do not rest upon experience. If so, then the central issue of a transcendent-oriented world view is whether we are justified in claiming at all that some experiences can give insight into what lies beyond. And in what sense of beyond? For one thing, if we maintain the Kantian distinction between a noumenal reality and the phenomenal world presented by it, how does this distinction relate to the parallel but quite different distinction between the nondual and duality-drenched realms of experience and truth? There is the strange, but persuasive, thought that there is something noumenal behind the nondual experience, which suggests a tripartite God: the noumenal *X*, the nondual Brahman, and the duality-drenched Creator.

These thoughts are mere hints about ways in which a religious philosophy may be excogitated combining both Indian and western resources. In an important sense this type of speculation is not comparative philosophy but cross-cultural world-view construction. Unless of course that is what comparative philosophy really is.

In the process, key terms will take on new meanings. Although it is vital that we recognize the contextuality, both horizontal and vertical, of key terms, we can note too that by suggestively transplanting some of them into the new context of the interactive global situation we are helping to impart to them a new dynamism. If systems can argue with one another sensibly within the Indian tradition, despite the perils of systematic ambiguity, it is possible for them to do so creatively in a cross-cultural context.

In summary, the *darśanavidyā* that I propose has differing levels and compartments. One compartment is the study of Indian philosophy as such. Descriptive or analytic *darśanavidyā* describes the systems and movements of thought in context and helps to elucidate both the inner horizontal dynamic and the vertical contextual correlates of systems. At another level *darśanavidyā* is decompartmentalized, because it is global in character. We are now in a period of cross-cultural interaction on a total global scale. If we sometimes forget this it is partly because western philosophy itself remains rather compartmentalized. In the global context we can practice a new kind of *pramāṇavidyā*, that is, examining the consequences of alternative world views and the way they regard each other. It may also prove irresistible beyond this stage to indulge in more than analytical global *darśanavidyā*: in a word, *sarvadarśanavidyā*. There may be the call to begin to fashion world views that arise from the situation of today and the suggestive resources from various cultures now at our disposal. And now who would *we* be? No longer adherents of one tradition, but human intellectuals in a pregnant sense: belonging to the new paratribe, Humanity.

SENGAKU MAYEDA

Śaṅkara and Nārāyaṇa Guru

THE VEDANTA school of philosophy, which has historically produced so many branches, is still quite viable in India today. Among active branches, the Advaita Vedanta school founded by Śaṅkara in the eighth century constitutes the main current of Indian philosophy.

It is well known that Śaṅkara's philosophy, which is rooted in the purely orthodox Brahmanic tradition of thought, exercised a strong influence on Ramakrishna, Ramaṇa Maharṣi, and Vivekananda in modern India. It is, however, surprising that Śaṅkara's philosophy also played an important role in religious and social reform among the scheduled castes or untouchables during the nineteenth and twentieth centuries. This historical fact seems to have been heretofore nearly unknown or neglected.

The movement alluded to is that initiated and led by Nārāyaṇa Guru (1854–1928), who was an untouchable thinker and religious reformer and yet has been regarded as "a direct successor of Śaṅkara" by his followers.[1] It is reported that he himself said to a follower that "What we have to say is [just] what Śaṅkara said."[2] By contrast, Nārāyaṇa's younger contemporary B. A. Ambedkar (1891–1956), who was also from an untouchable caste (Mahar), found it necessary to convert from Hinduism to Buddhism, a religion advocating the equality of mankind, so that he might carry out his religious and social reform known as the Neobuddhist movement.

In this article, by comparing Nārāyaṇa with Śaṅkara, I would like to try to clarify whether Nārāyaṇa was really a fol-

[1] Nataraja Guru, *The Word of the Guru: An Outline of the Life and Teachings of the Guru Narayana* (Cochin: PAICO, House, 1968), p. 61.

[2] Ibid.; cf. p. 192.

lower of Śaṅkara and how Śaṅkara's purely Brahmanic philosophy could come to be Nārāyaṇa's philosophical background for religious and social reform for the depressed classes. As the analysis develops it will become clear how great religious leaders cross various boundaries.

TODAY there are no extant materials from which to reconstruct Śaṅkara's life with certainty. But tradition says that he was born into a family that belonged to the celebrated Nambudiri Brahmin caste in a quiet village called Kālaḍi in the northern part of Kerala state, southern India, in the eighth century. Nārāyaṇa was born into a family of the Ezhava untouchable caste in a village called Chempazhanthi, about ten miles northeast of Trivandrum in the southern part of Kerala state on August 20, 1854.[3] Although his father was a farmer, he is said to have been a noted teacher as well as a Sanskrit scholar, versed in astronomy and in *āyurveda*.

At the age of thirty-four in 1888, Nārāyaṇa reached the turning point of his life. Renouncing the wandering, ascetic life, he started on his new life to save people of lower castes by means of social and religious reform. His first achievement was to consecrate a Śiva temple at Aruvippuram, twelve miles south of Trivandrum. This act amounted to an open revolt against the traditional orthodox notion that only a Brahmin priest could perform such religious acts.

Near the Śiva temple he founded a *maṭha* or monastery and established a small organization for the protection of the tem-

[3] There are differing opinions concerning his date of birth. I have followed here Nataraja Guru (*Word of the Guru*, p. 387). A. Aiyappan also supports this date in his article "Narayana Guru," in T.M.P. Mahadevan, ed., *A Seminar on Saints* (Madras: Ganesh, 1960), p. 284. Nataraja Guru remarks in his note in the aforementioned book, "Actual date is still under dispute" (p. 254). Nārāyaṇa Guru's date of birth is August 26, 1854, according to Nitya Chaitanya Yati, *Sri Narayana Guru: A Brief Bibliographical Sketch* (Srinivasapuram: East–West University of Brahmavidya, n.d.), p. 2. It is "the day of Chatayam (Satabhisha) star in the month of Chingam (August–September) of 1032 M.E. corresponding to 1856 A.D.," according to M. K. Sanoo, *Nārāyaṇa Guru*, trans. Madhavan Ayyappath (Bombay: Bharatiya Vidya Bhavan, 1978), p. 2.

ple property and the welfare of the worshipers. This organization later developed into the Sree Narayana Dharma Paripalana Yogam, or SNDP Yogam, in 1903.

In 1904, Nārāyaṇa founded the Śivagiri Maṭha on the hill of Śivagiri at Varkala in southern Travancore, about twenty miles north of Trivandrum. Nārāyaṇa's construction of the *maṭha* is reminiscent of the well-known tradition that Śaṅkara founded four *maṭhas* at Śriṅgeri, Purī, Dvārakā, and Badarinātha. It is also interesting to note that in 1922, Nārāyaṇa consecrated a figure of Śāradā, the goddess of wisdom, in Śivagiri; Śāradā is the presiding goddess of the Śriṅgeri Śaṅkara Maṭha, which is also called the Śāradā Pīṭha.[4] When Nārāyaṇa named the hill Śivagiri, he must have taken into consideration the name of Śriṅgeri derived from Ṛṣyaśṛṅgagiri.

In 1913, Nārāyaṇa founded the Advaita Āshrama in Alwaye near Śaṅkara's birthplace, Kālaḍi, for the purpose of teaching and propagating the Advaita philosophy, and in 1914 he built a Sanskrit school adjacent to the Āshrama in order to restore the sanctity of Sanskrit. In his lifetime he founded more than sixty temples in India and carried out various religious and social reforms. In 1928, he passed away, and his body now lies in state in the Mahā Samādhi Mandir on the beautiful peak of Śivagiri.

[4] At present the Śāradā temple is central to the Śriṅgeri Maṭha, but it is said that "originally it was an unpretentious shrine with the *mūrti* of Śāradā made of sandalwood installed over the Śrī Chakra that Śrī Ādi Śaṁkara carved on a rock," *Sri Abhinava Vidyatheertha Nahaswamigal Pattabhisheke Silver Jubille Souvenir* (Śriṅgeri, 1979), p. 39. In Śriṅgeri Śrī Śāradā within the sanctum and Śrī Rāja Rajeśvari and Śrī Durgā in the *maṇḍapa* are three modes of conceiving the absolute in a *saguṇa* form. Śrī Śāradā represents the *samaṣṭi* (collective) aspect and the other two *devis* represent the *vyaṣṭi* aspects (K. R. Venkataraman, *The Throne of Transcendental Wisdom: Śrī Śamkarācārya's Śāradā Pīṭha in Śringeri* [Madras: Higginbothams, 1959], p. 145). It is to be noted here that the Maṭha at Kāñcīpuram, which is very influential especially in Tamil Nadu today, claims its authenticity as the one where Śaṅkara spent his last days and that it is called the Śāradā Maṭha, while its *pīṭha* is called the Kāmakoṭi Pīṭha. Cf. Pologam Sri Rama Sastrigal, *The Mutts Founded by Sri Sankara Bhagavatpada* (Madras, 1973).

The essence of Nārāyaṇa's philosophy is condensed in his famous maxim: "One Caste, One Religion, and One God for Man." Nārāyaṇa called it *Sanātana Dharma*, or "Eternal Law."[5] Therefore, it is useful for present purposes to compare Nārāyaṇa with Śaṅkara concerning those three concepts (caste, religion, and God). First of all, I would like to take up caste (*jāti*) for comparison.

The main caste groups in Nārāyaṇa's native region were Brahmins, Nayars, Ezhavas, Pulayas, and Parayas. Among the Brahmins, the Nambudiri Brahmins ranked highest socially and economically.[6] The Nayars, who were in fact Śūdras, served as warriors at wartime in Kerala, where Kṣatriyas were actually lacking; so the Nayars were powerful[7] and constituted 15 percent of the total population there. The Pulayas and the Parayas were untouchables and belonged to the lowest classes of Hindu society.

The Ezhavas, of whom Nārāyaṇa was one, because they ranked higher than the Pulayas and the Parayas, constituted nearly one-fifth of the population of Kerala and were numerically the largest community there. There caste occupations were officially limited to the cultivation of palm trees and the preparation of toddy and arrack. The majority of the Ezhavas were tenant farmers or free agricultural laborers. A small per-

[5] Sanoo, *Nārāyaṇa Guru*, p. 199. J. Dharmatheerthan, Nārāyaṇa's early associate and disciple, once tried to interpret this maxim in the light of the teaching of Christ and came to the conclusion that "Nārāyaṇa Guru's message looks like another version of Christ's teaching" (quoted in V. Thomas Samuel, *One Caste, One Religion, One God: A Study of Sree Narayana Guru* [New Delhi: Sterling, 1977], p. 113, from J. Dharmatheerthan, *Hinduism and Christianity and the Religion of the Free People* [Trivandrum, 1958], p. 91, which is not available to me).

[6] It is said that during the medieval period they established cultural dominance in Kerala, freezing "the pattern of communities into an extremely rigid and complicated form" (Samuel, *One Caste*, p. 22).

[7] The Nayars had the custom of the sambandham form of morganatic marriage peculiar to Kerala, according to which the younger sons of Nambudiri families married Nayar women, though their eldest son married a Nambudiri Brahmin wife (J. H. Hutton, *Caste in India*, 3d ed. [Bombay: Oxford University Press, 1961], p. 14; Samuel, *One Caste*, p. 24).

centage were small businessmen or *āyurvedic* medical practitioners.[8]

The Ezhavas were at the top of the caste group known as *tindal jāti* or polluting caste. They were regarded as polluting by proximity, and were not allowed to come near the houses of Nambudiris or Nayars, their temples, tanks, or wells.[9] The Hindu society of the nineteenth century in Kerala was so tightly tied up by the caste system and the fear of pollution that Swami Vivekananda called it "a veritable lunatic asylum of India."[10]

"One Caste," the first slogan proclaimed by Nārāyaṇa, was like a cry from the very foundation of his existence, representing the general feelings not only of the Ezhavas but of the depressed classes generally. Nārāyaṇa wrote the following inscription on the wall of the Śiva temple that he first consecrated at Aruvippuram in 1888:

> Without differences of Caste,
> Nor enmities of creed,
> All live like brothers at heart
> Here in this ideal place.[11]

As I have already mentioned, this temple at Aruvippuram is the first monument of his struggle for liberation from the caste system and for religious freedom. Vivekananda and Gandhi, who were both contemporaries of Nārāyaṇa, criticized the caste system but, while rejecting untouchability, they regarded the *varṇāśramadharma* as ideal, and adhered to the *varṇa* system.[12]

[8] Hutton, *Caste in India*.

[9] In Kerala the fear of "distance pollution" or "touch pollution" was incomparably intense. An Ezhava had to remain thirty-six paces from a Nambudiri Brahmin and was not allowed to come within twelve paces of a Nayar (Hutton, *Caste in India*, p. 79; Samuel, *One Caste*, pp. 26–27).

[10] Swami Vivekananda, *The Complete Works of Swami Vivekananda*, 8 vols. (Calcutta: Advaia Ashrama, 1955–1960), 3:294; Samuel, *One Caste*, p. 23.

[11] Nataraja Guru, *Word of the Guru*, p. 24; Samuel, *One Caste*, p. 54; Sanoo, *Nārāyaṇa Guru*, p. 60.

[12] Cf. "Competition—cruel, cold, and heartless—is the law of Europe. Our

Regarding Nārāyaṇa's concept of "One Caste," the best material is probably his *Jātimīmāṁsa (The Critique of Caste).*[13] The first stanza of this short poem on caste reads as follows:

> Man's manhood [*manuṣyatva*] is his *jāti* [caste = species],
> just as is the cowhood [*gotva*] of a cow.
> Brahminhood and the like are not so for him.
> Nobody knows this truth, alas!

Here in this first verse, utilizing the double meanings of the Sanskrit word *jāti,* which can be both caste and species, Nārāyaṇa evidently shows that caste has no basis in actuality on the ground of the empirical and biological truth that there is only one *jāti* for man, namely personhood, just as there is only one *jāti* for cow, namely cowhood. Brahminhood and other caste

---

law is caste—the breaking of competition, checking its forces, mitigating its cruelties, smoothing the passage of the human soul through this mystery of life" (Vivekananda, *Complete Works*, 3:205).

[13] It is reported that Nārāyaṇa was always reticent in speech and that he was not an eloquent orator at mass religious meetings, but his mere presence on such occasions meant more than words. He was not a prolific writer, but there do exist a number of devotional and philosophical poems meant for the ordinary people, which are mostly very short. Although we do not know the exact number of his works, forty-three—either in full or in part, written in Malayalam, Sanskrit, and Tamil—have been collected by the Sree Narayana Dharma Sangham trust (Samuel, *One Caste*, p. 65). His works, most of which are written in verse, can be classified into three groups: hymns, short essays, and philosophical works. The first two groups comprise his earlier works, which "abound in references to Indian myth and legend and generally speak the language of iconography" (Nataraja Guru, *Word of the Guru*, pp. 172–173). *Guha Aṣṭakam, Bhadrakali Aṣṭakam*, and others belong to the first group. The second group comprises the *Cidjaḍacintanam*, the *Daivacintanam*, and the *Jātimīmāṁsā*. The first two essays are written in Malayalam prose. The *Jātimīmāṁsā* is very important in order to understand his idea of caste. The third group includes works written during his mature years such as the *Ātmopadeśaśatakam* and the *Darśanamālā*, which are held to be the major works of his philosophy. The *Ātmopadeśaśatakam*, one hundred verses in Malayalam, and the *Darśanamālā*, one hundred verses in Sanskrit, are brief but systematic expositions of his Advaita. In addition to these two important works, the *Brahmavidyāpañcakam, Advaitadīpikā, Daivadaśakam, Janani Navaratna Mañjari*, and *Arivu* may be mentioned as elucidating his Advaita teachings.

or racial distinctions are only external and superficial factors and have not the fundamental biological importance to constitute another *jāti*.

The second and third verses again stress the homogeneity and equality of mankind as follows:

> One caste [*jāti*], one religion, one God for man
> Of the same blood and form, there is no difference.
>
> Animals of the same species [caste, *jāti*] alone procreate,
> Viewed thus all humanity belongs to one caste.

The first line of the second verse is the famous slogan of Nārāyaṇa. In the third verse, he applies the biological law of interspecific sterility[14] to the proof of the oneness of all people, an idea amplified in the fourth verse.[15] Then, in order to strengthen his arguments, Nārāyaṇa concludes his discussion of caste by showing the instances of two sages of indisputable status who came from the pariah line, namely, the stage Parāśara of an untouchable girl and the sage Vyāsa of a fisher maiden.[16]

As is clear from these stanzas, Nārāyaṇa's slogan "One Caste for Man" means that personhood is unique and indivisible in any way. No distinctions are possible in personhood,

[14] Cf. Nataraja Guru, *Word of the Guru*, p. 285.

[15] Of the human species even a Brahmn born
As is the pariah too,
Where is the difference then in caste as between man and man?

Both Nataraja Guru and V. Thomas Samuel take this stanza as showing the inevitable dialectical counterparts of the problem of caste; without the Brahmin, the concept of pariah would be meaningless, and vice versa. But as far as I can see, this passage does not intend such a dialectic but simply elucidates the previous point.

[16] In bygone days, of a pariah woman
The great sage Parāśara was born.
As even he of Vedic-aphorism fame, of a
Virgin of the fisher folk.

Parāśara is traditionally said to be the father of Vyāsa, who is regarded as the author of the *Brahmasūtra*, *Mahābhārata*, and others.

socially or religiously. Any divisions based on heredity and ancestry are false. Criticizing the conventional notion of caste which was the dividing principle and the basis of inequality and hierarchy, Nārāyaṇa reinterpreted its time-honored conception and transformed it into a principle of solidarity and equality for mankind.[17]

For his part, Śaṅkara did not actively take up the problem of caste for philosophical discussion, though he sometimes referred to it in his works. In his commentary on *Brahmasūtra* 1.3.38, Śaṅkara states that although *Smṛti* regards all the four classes as qualified for acquiring knowledge of the *Itihāsas* and *Purāṇas*, the Śūdras do not possess such qualifications with regard to the Veda.[18] Although the *Smṛtis* are not in agreement as to whether the ascetic life (*saṁnyāsa*) is open to all the three upper classes or only to the Brahmins, Śaṅkara definitely says in his commentary on the *Bṛhadāraṇyaka Upaniṣad* (3.5.1, p. 454; 4.5.15, p. 725) that only a Brahmin can be a *saṁnyāsin.*[19] In his work *Upadeśasāhasrī* (2.1.2), Śaṅkara accepts as qualified for his teaching a Brahmin who follows the life of a *paramhaṁsa* or wandering ascetic. These passages, show Śaṅkara to be rather rigid and strict with respect to caste.[20] He must have taken caste or class distinctions for granted.[21]

[17] Cf. Samuel, *One Caste*, pp. 101–102.

[18] Cf. P. V. Kane, *History of Dharmaśāstra*, 5 vols. (Poona: Bhandarkas Oriental Research Institute, 1930–1962), 5.2:1642.

[19] It is to be noted here that in his *Vārttika* (verse 1,651, p. 758) on his teacher's commentary of *Bṛh. Up.* 3.5.1, Sureśvara, one of Śaṅkara's direct disciples, rejects Śaṅkara's view; and that Ānandajñāna, in his commentary on Sureśvara's *Vārttika* (p. 759) quotes a passage from the *Mahābhārata* to support the position that Kṣatriyas can enter the ascetic life. Cf. Kane, *History of Dharmaśāstra*, 2.2:942–944.

[20] Śaṅkara is stricter than his followers (see n. 19) and the author of the *Brahmasūtra*. According to the *Brahmasūtra* (1.3.34–39) the upper three classes of people, excluding the Śūdras, are entitled to the knowledge of Brahman. Moreover, not only the *saṁnyāsin* but also the householder is accepted as qualified for it; even a person who does not belong to any state of life because of lack of means or some other cause is regarded as qualified for knowledge of Brahman (*Brahmasūtra* 3.4.36–39). It is not out of place for me to refer to the small work, *Manīṣāpañcaka*, traditionally attributed to Śaṅkara. Among its

Turning now to the second part of Nārāyaṇa's maxim—religion—although the Ezhavas were Hindus, they had to suffer various forms of extreme social injustice simply because of being untouchables. Therefore, by the time of Nārāyaṇa many Ezhavas had accepted Christianity, Buddhism, or Islam, which gave them a higher degree of social equality.[22] Thus, there were great tensions among the Ezhavas at the time as to whether they should continue to be Hindus or should convert to other religions that promised them greater opportunities. Christian missionaries, Sikhs, and Muslims were making efforts to convert them. Besides, the influence of the Āryasamāj was penetrating into Kerala, as was the Ramakrishna mission.[23]

Facing a religious situation in Kerala packed with rivalries and tensions, Nārāyaṇa advocated the notion that there is only "one religion" for man. Nārāyaṇa did not stick to the assumption, then popular in India, that all religions are the same, leading to the same goal. Instead he recognized not only the existence of various religious traditions[24] but also their specific *raisons d'être*. He nevertheless pointed out the oneness of their essence in verses 44–46 of his *Ātmopadeśaśatakam*, written in Malayalam—a text that has been praised as "The *Bhagavadgītā* of the Malayalees"[25]—as follows:

five verses the first two end with the line: "*cāṇḍālo 'stu sa tu dvijo 'stu gurur ity eṣā manīṣā mama*." Its authenticity is very doubtful and it is certain that its author had no intention to refute untouchability or the caste system.

[21] Cf. Nataraja Guru, *Word of the Guru*, pp. 191, 274; Samuel, *One Caste*, p. 96. However, though Śaṅkara did refer to the matter, his discussion seems to be concerned only with the fourfold *varṇa* system and not with what is known as the caste system (*jāti*) today.

[22] It is reported that even some of the admirers and close associates of Nārāyaṇa were either Buddhists or leaning toward Buddhism (Samuel, *One Caste*, p. 87).

[23] The real work of this mission, however, is said to have started in Kerala only in 1911 (Ibid., p. 115).

[24] Ibid., p. 123.

[25] For the English translation of *Ātmopadeśaśatakam* I depend upon Nitya Chaitanya Yati, *Neither This nor That but . . . Aum* (New Delhi: Vikas, 1982).

> The many faiths have but one essence; not seeing this, in this world, like the blind men and the elephant, many kinds of reasoning are used by the unenlightened who become distressed; having seen this, without being disturbed, remain steadfast.
>
> Any religion is despicable to the man of another faith; the Absolute described in one religion is defective from the perspective of another. However, the essence of various religions is the same. Nobody can be free from confusion without knowing this.
>
> Realizing it, one may avoid futile religious rivalry. As the historical survey of religions clearly shows, even if one wants to conquer another faith by fighting, it is impossible to do so.

What, then, is the essence of the many religions? Nārāyaṇa asserts that it is "spiritual happiness" (*ātmasukha*).[26] According to him, this spiritual happiness is what all people of different religions always strive for with great effort. In this sense spiritual happiness is the supreme goal common to all religions. It is on the ground of this spiritual happiness that "one religion" is possible. Nārāyaṇa comments that "Conflicts between countries and peoples end when one party defeats the other. The fight between religions is never ending, because one cannot finally vanquish another. If there should be an end to religious quarrels, all religions should be studied with a free mind; and then it will be discovered that in essentials they do not differ considerably. The discovery so made is the 'one religion.' "[27]

There is a dialogue between Nārāyaṇa and C. V. Kunjuraman, a noted literary critic and journalist, concerning "One Caste, One Religion, and One God for Man." In the course of

[26] Nitya Chaitanya Yati translates this word as "the happiness of the Self," but Samuel and others take it to mean "happiness their own." It seems to me that Nitya Chaitanya Yati sees here too much Advaitic philosophy.

[27] Samuel, *One Caste*, p. 127.

their conversation Kunjuraman pointed out that there was an increasing tendency toward religious conversion in their society and that those who wanted to remain in Hinduism said that modern Hinduism did not meet their needs. Nārāyaṇa answered as follows:

> Then what they say is that both they and Hinduism need a change. There is no such religion as Hinduism. The residents of Hindustan were named Hindus by foreigners. If the inhabitants of India are Hindus, then what about the native Christians and Muslims? No one would agree to it. Present day "Hinduism" is a common designation for the religions which originated in India, except foreign religions like Christianity and Islam. That is why Buddhism and Jainism are also included in Hinduism by certain scholars. If Hinduism is a common name describing *Vedism, Sanātana Dharma*, and the religion of *Sāṁkhya, Vaiśeṣika, Mīmāṁsā, Dvaita, Viśiṣṭādvaita, Śaivism, Bhakti, Śakti* and *Vaiṣṇavism*, it is not unreasonable if all religions that advocate the ultimate goal of salvation are called "one religion." Why should one doubt its rationality?[28]

From this passage it is clear that Nārāyaṇa's "one religion" is a common designation including all religions that advocate the ultimate goal of salvation or spiritual happiness. This goal will not be established by fighting one another but only through the discovery of the essential identity of all religions by means of the open-minded study of them.

By contrast, Śaṅkara is, in his various works, found busily engaged in refuting the other schools of philosophy such as the Lokāyata, Buddhist schools, Jainism, Sāṁkhya, Vaiśeṣika, Mīmāṁsā, and even some philosophers of the Vedanta. It is, thus, quite probably that Śaṅkara had no idea of "one religion." He engaged in extensive polemics to establish his own Advaita Vedanta.[29]

[28] Ibid., p. 184.

[29] Explaining the fact of Śaṅkara's criticism of other doctrines in his works,

Nārāyaṇa seldom mentioned the names of the existing religions or philosophies such as Hinduism, Vedanta, and Advaita Vedanta as the culmination of all religious sects and philosophical schools or the salvation of all mankind. In this respect Nārāyaṇa is in contrast with Śaṅkara, who is traditionally regarded as the author of the *Sarvasiddhāntasaṁgraha*, or *Epitome of the Accepted Conclusions of all the Systems of Philosophy*, which explicitly claims that all systems of philosophy culminate in the system of the Vedanta. Nārāyaṇa also differs from Swami Vivekananda, who advocated Advaita as the religion that could save both East and West.[30]

Nārāyaṇa did not attempt to form a syncretistic religion by "taking all good value from diverse creeds,"[31] because he recognized the specific contributions of each. Furthermore, in his opinion, "the function of religion is to turn the ears of men upward, onward,"[32] and religions serve as the signposts[33] for the seekers after truth; but religion is no longer authoritative for the one who has already attained truth, for he himself is the author of religion. His metaphor of religion as a signpost perhaps reminds the reader that, in Buddhism, religion is compared to a raft that is regarded only as a means by which to take people from this shore to the other.[34]

T.M.P. Mahadevan writes: "The answer is very simple. When Śaṅkara points out the defects and inconsistencies in the various schools and cults, he does so not in the spirit of a partisan, but with a view to making them whole. . . . partisanship is incompatible with Advaita. The remark that the Advaitin has no position of his own is quite pertinent. . . . The function of criticism performed by Advaita teachers should be viewed, not as destructive, but as a constructive help" (*Ramaṇa Maharshi: The Sage of Aruṇācala* [London: Allen & Unwin, 1977], p. 126).

[30] Samuel, *One Caste*, p. 127.

[31] Ibid., p. 126.

[32] Dharmatheerthan, *Prophet of Peace*, pp. 106–107; Samuel, *One Caste*, p. 125.

[33] Religion is also compared to "guide" in the voyage of discovery (Sanoo, *Nārāyaṇa Guru*, p. 203).

[34] It is certain that Nārāyaṇa was acquainted with Buddhism to some extent. When he visited a Buddhist *vihāra* in Śrī Laṅkā, he is reported to have re-

When Nārāyaṇa said "one God," the original Malayalam was *Oru Daivam*. Nārāyaṇa used the term *Daivam* in the same sense as the term Brahman. But *Daivam* was more familiar to Nārāyaṇa's followers and free from the Advaitic connotation. Therefore, it is possible that he could communicate more directly to them by using the term *Daivam*.[35]

Nārāyaṇa states in his main work, *Darśanamālā*, written in Sanskrit, that in the beginning before creation this world was nonexistent (1.1); it consisted of residual impressions (*vāsanā*, 1.2); it was latent within the Lord himself (1.3); it was merely in the mind like a painting in the mind of an artist (1.5).

According to the *Darśanamālā*, who is identical with Brahman, Brahma, Viṣṇu, and Śiva (1.10), created the whole world by means of *Māyā* (1.12) or by his power (*śakti* 1.13). Brahman itself is free from origination and dissolution, though people wrongly understand, owing to *Māyā*, that it has origination and dissolution (2.3). Brahman is Being (*sat*), Consciousness (*cit*), and Bliss (*ānanda*, 2.5–9).

However, this world consists of mind (*manas*) only, which does not exist anywhere (3.1); it is falsely supposed to be real by reason of ignorance (*avidyā*), or darkness (*tamas*, 3.4).

Nārāyaṇa's above-described concepts of Brahman and the world are evidently in line with the Advaita Vedanta advocated by Śaṅkara. His concept of *Ātman* also seems to agree with Śaṅkara's. Nārāyaṇa says in his *Darśanamālā* that as the eye does not see itself, the *Ātman* does not see itself and is never the object of seeing (5.9); the object of seeing is what is superimposed, and what is superimposed is unreal (5.10). "I"-consciousness, which is also the object of seeing—is what is superimposed upon *Ātman*. *Ātman* is only one and remains above all things eternally.

It is the supreme knowledge that Brahman is identical with *Ātman (brahmātmaikya)*, free from false construction (7.10).

marked, "It is my opinion that several parts in the books of Buddhism were actually written by Brahmins" (Ibid., p. 160).

[35] Samuel, *One Caste*, pp. 136, 143.

Ātman is Brahman; the knower of *Ātman* meditates on the *Ātman* (8.4).

I have so far briefly outlined Nārāyaṇa's philosophy on the basis of his *Darśanamālā*, and it is obvious that Nārāyaṇa was really an Advaitin and follower of Śaṅkara. This is also true of his philosophy in his *Brahmavidyāpañcaka*, written in Sanskrit. Its first stanza reads as follows:

> Having attained detachment completely, even through the discrimination between things eternal and noneternal, the truly well-informed one will be duly adorned with the six [means] such as tranquility and seek after final release here on earth: thereafter, he should ask the highest Brahman-knower that is pleased with salutation, services and the like: "O Master, Who am I? From where has this world come? Please tell [me] this."

This first stanza is reminiscent of the four requirements for the study of the Vedanta which Śaṅkara first stated in his *Brahmasūtrabhāṣya* 1.1.1. According to Śaṅkara, the four requirements are: discrimination between things eternal and things noneternal (*nityānityaviveka*); dispassion toward the enjoyment of things here and in the other world (*ihamutrārthabhogavirāga*); attainment of the means such as tranquility and self-control (*samadamādisādhanasaṁpad*); and being a seeker after final release (*mumukṣutva*). Furthermore, the style of the dialogue between teacher and pupil and the topics discussed also remind us of the prose portion of Śaṅkara's *Upadeśasāhasrī* and the first part of the *Vivekacūdāmaṇi* traditionally ascribed to Śaṅkara.[36]

In the next verse the teacher gives the following reply to his pupil:

> You are really Brahman. And you are neither senses nor mind [*manas*] nor intellect nor intelligence [*citta*] nor body nor vital airs nor "I"-consciousness. [Everything] else is also unreal, being superimposed on your own *Ātman*. Every-

[36] Cf. *Upadeśasāhasrī* 2.1.2; *Vivekacūdāmaṇi* 17–26.

> thing, being the object of perception, is material; this world, being different from you, is neither originated from anything else [than you] nor from itself; it appears like a mirage.[37]

As is clear from the preceding discussion, Nārāyaṇa's concept of "one God" follows the tradition of the Advaita Vedanta advocated by Śaṅkara. But Nārāyaṇa departed considerably from Śaṅkara in his two other concepts, "one caste" and "one religion," which are both of vital importance for his thought. There is no place appropriate for accommodating these two concepts in Śaṅkara's philosophy. It is reported that Nārāyaṇa himself explicitly said to a pupil that Śaṅkara had been wrong about caste.[38] So when Nārāyaṇa said to his pupil, "What we have to say is what Śaṅkara said," just what did Nārāyaṇa consider to be "what Śaṅkara said?" It is certain that what Nārāyaṇa had to say was at the least "One Caste, One Religion, and One God for Man." If so, what is caste and what is religion from Śaṅkara's point of view? It may be necessary for us to consider these concepts a little further.

Śaṅkara regards caste merely as one of the *upādhis* or limiting adjuncts of *Ātman*, like family, *āśrama* (stage of life), and purifying ceremonies, and not as the nature or *Ātman* of man. In his *Upadeśasāhasrī* (2.1.9–10) there is an interesting dialogue between a teacher and his pupil, which reads as follows:

> Teacher: "Who are you, my dear?"
> Pupil: "I am a Brahmin's son belonging to such and such a family. I was a student . . . [but] now I am a *paramahaṁsa* or wandering ascetic. I wish to get out of the ocean of trans-

[37] *Brahmavidyāpañcaka*, stanza 2.

[38] In his conversation with his pupil Sahodaran, Nārāyaṇa said, "Caste has established its sway over men. Śaṅkarācārya himself erred on this. Even Vyāsa who wrote the *Gītā* and the *Brahmasūtra* has spoken of the four *varṇas* differently in two places. Caste has to be eschewed. Otherwise there is no salvation" (Sanoo, *Nārāyaṇa Guru*, p. 152).

migratory existence infested with great sharks of birth and death."[39]

The teacher is not at all satisfied with this answer of his pupil, and in the course of their dialogue the guru points out how his pupil has answered wrongly: "Through such statements as 'I am a Brahmin's son belonging to such and such a family,' you have identified the *Ātman* with the body; *Ātman* is free from caste, family, and purifying ceremonies while the body has a distinct caste, family, and purifying ceremonies" (*Upadeśasāharsī* 2.1.15).[40]

Thus Śaṅkara was theoretically well aware that *Ātman* has nothing to do with distinctions in caste, family, and purifying ceremonies, which belong to the body only, and he asserted that identification of the *Ātman* with the body is only due to ignorance (*avidyā: Upadeśasāharsī* 1.1.6). However, we have seen that in practice he adhered to distinctions in caste. Śaṅkara's teachings were meant only for selected *samnyāsins*, and it is quite probable that Śaṅkara himself was not aware of any inconsistency.

It was Nārāyaṇa who actually and boldly put into practice what Śaṅkara said about caste.[41] It is reported that one Nārāyaṇa said to his followers, "Some of you still think that I belong to this community or that creed. It is now years since I gave up such distinctions. I have also arranged that those who join the order at my Āshrama shall have no such limitations."[42] All the distinctions in caste, religion, sect, or god appear as real. But from the Advaitic point of view they are all false, because they are merely superimpositions upon the one *Ātman* made due to ignorance (*avidyā*). Nārāyaṇa clearly asserted, in his *Darśanamālā* 3.10, "The One alone is real without second. The unreal seems to be real. Śivaliṅga is stone itself, not a sec-

[39] *Śaṅkara's Upadeśasāhasrī*, ed. Sengaku Mayeda (Tokyo: Hokuseido, 1973), p. 193.

[40] Ibid., p. 194.

[41] Cf. Samuel, *One Caste*, p. 152.

[42] Dharmatheerthan, *Prophet of Peace*, p. 67; Samuel, *One Caste*, p. 94.

ond made by a mason." According to Nārāyaṇa, the Śivaliṅga, which the Hindus worship, is merely a stone. After raising the temple at Aruvippuram, he built temples at various places. When he was requested to build a temple at Meluveli, he remarked that future temples should be schools. In a temple he is said to have installed the words "Satyam-Dayā-Dharmam" at the altar instead of placing the image of any Hindu god. In another temple he placed only a burning lamp at the altar. At the Alwaye Advaita Āśrama he preferred to have no image at all.[43]

Nārāyaṇa mainly depends on empirical and biological truth and does not use the term Brahman or *Ātman* when he interprets the term *jāti* in the sense of species, probably because he intended to avoid an Advaitic interpretation as far as possible in view of the principle of "one religion." It is, however, quite probable that he saw Brahman or *Ātman* through *jāti* since *jāti*, which is also falsely superimposed upon Brahman or *Ātman* owing to ignorance (*avidyā*), is not essential to man at all whereas Brahman or *Ātman* is really the nature of man. Man cannot reach the ultimate goal by discriminating between person and person, between religion and religion, and between god and god, but only by discriminating clearly between the real and the unreal, in other words, between *Ātman* and non-*Ātman*. *Jāti* is, of course, non-*Ātman*. Nārāyaṇa concludes his *Darśanamālā* (10.10) with the following lines: "There is no doubt that Brahman exists, One without a second, and nothing else. Knowing thus, one shall attain liberation from duality and not again return to it."

BOTH caste and religion are problems at the level of daily experience, while God is at the level of highest truth as well as of daily experience. To be sure, Nārāyaṇa did not himself use Śaṅkara's doctrine of two truths; Nārāyaṇa used neither the term *avidyāvasthā* (the state of ignorance) nor *paramārthavasthā* (the state of highest truth) which Śaṅkara used in his works.

[43] Yati, *Sri Narayana Guru*, pp. 20–21.

But if we apply these terms here, caste and religion are problems of *avidyāvasthā* and God is that of *paramārthāvasthā* as well as *avidyāvasthā*. Therefore, caste and religion cannot originally be the traditional and proper problems of Advaita Vedanta.

When Nārāyaṇa wanted to speak to his audience of the Ezhavas and other depressed classes, however, he did so in their language, Malayalam, and he positively dealt with the *vyavahārika* problems such as caste and religion in addition to *paramārtha* problems—namely, God, Brahman, or *Ātman*—as, for example, in the *Jātimīmāṁsā* and *Atmopadeśaśatakam*, especially the *Jātimīmāṁsā*. It is to be noted here that in the *Jātimīmāṁsā* the first verse only is composed in Sanskrit, and the remaining verses, the second of which contains his famous maxim, are all composed in Malayalam. Nataraja Guru, one of Nārāyaṇa's direct disciples, remarks about this fact that "there is a kind of poetic justice in crowning this set of verses with a summary in the classical language," because the concept of caste first appeared in Sanskrit and because Sanskrit and Malayalam represent the Brahmins and the untouchables, respectively.[44]

By contrast, when Nārāyaṇa wanted to appeal to the world of Advaitins as well, he expressed himself in Sanskrit. For example, in the *Darśanamālā*, written in Sanskrit, caste and religion are not taken up at all and the problems proper to the traditional Advaita Vedanta only are discussed, for example, *adhyāropa* (superimposition), *apavāda* (removal), *māyā* (illusion), and the like. Without prior knowledge to the contrary, it is quite impossible for us to imagine the author of the *Dar-*

[44] Nataraja Guru gives the following explanation: "Sanskrit is the language in which the idea of caste in the hereditary social sense came about: hence there is a kind of poetic justice in crowning this set of verses with a summary in the classical language. Malayalam itself has a large proportion of Sanskrit in its composition, grafted on to an early Tamil framework, but Malayalam belongs structurally to the non-Vedic Dravidian context. So here in this poem there is an implied ambivalence in putting the inquiry in the two languages which belong, as it were, to the group representing the Brahmin and the group representing the Pariah respectively, out of whose interactions the false notion of caste has arisen" (Nataraja Guru, *Word of the Guru*, p. 276).

śanamālā as being an untouchable religious and social reformer or *karmayogin*. The text leads us to imagine him only as an Advaitin and *paramahaṁsa* or wandering ascetic.

In all probability Nārāyaṇa was not a religious and social reformer as much as he was an Advaitin *samnyāsin*. This can be ascertained not only from his writings and his wearing a *samnyāsin*'s clothes but also from the fact that, apart from the SNDP Yogam, which he felt to be moving away from his teachings and which has today come to be an exclusively Ezhava social and political organization, he founded an organization of *samnyāsin*s called the Sree Narayana Dharma Sangham in 1928, the last year of his life, the headquarters of which is the Śivagiri Maṭha. This organization was created so that he might carry out his ideal of "One Caste, One Religion, One God for Man" and protect the interests of the various religious institutions established by him.[45]

It is said that Nārāyaṇa's area of influence was mostly limited to the area around Kerala.[46] His life and philosophy, however, serve as an interesting illustration of the manner in which intracultural boundaries are reinterpreted and crossed in a modern South Asian context.

[45] Cf. Samuel *One Caste*, p. 168.

[46] See Ibid., pp. 162–163. But it is also reported that Nārāyaṇa was consulted regarding Vedanta philosophy by Brahmins from Kāñcīpuram (Sanoo, *Nārāyaṇa Guru*, p. 136).

FRITS STAAL

Is There Philosophy in Asia?

MOST OF THE contributors to this volume are not only members of the Society for Asian and Comparative Philosophy, but also authors and teachers in the area of Asian philosophy. We are the last people, therefore, to have an unbiased opinion on the question, "Is there philosophy in Asia?" For if the answer is negative, we ought to change our society and professions, or at least their names. One might even go farther and claim that posing this question has a paradoxical twist to it. For our work exists because there is such a thing as Asian philosophy; if there were not, there would be no comparative philosophy—between East and West, that is—and we would not be doing what we are. A parallel with Descartes highlights this paradox. For "there is philosophy in Asia, therefore we are here" is like "I think, therefore I am." The contrapositives of these statements must be equally true: "We are not here, therefore there is no philosophy in Asia," and "I am not, therefore I don't think." But these statements are either senseless, or true simply because I am using material implication; and their antecedents are false. Either position would be supported by Śaṅkara, who declared at the end of his comments on the first sutra of Bādarayaṇa: "*sarvo hy ātmāstitvam pratyeti na nāham asmīti*" ("everyone assumes that he exists and no one says 'I am not' ").

These being our existential and logical predicaments, you might assume that I will answer our question in the positive. But if I made that assumption, there would be no point in asking it. I shall therefore make no such assumption, but instead two general remarks. The first is that it is easy to answer such questions in any way we wish by defining our terms appropriately. For example, if we define philosophy in terms of thinking, our conceptual machinery can make it happen that every thinking Asian contributes to Asian philosophy. Since we will grant that Asians think, there will be such a thing as philosophy in Asia. Or else we might define philosophy in terms of the legacy of the ancient Greeks. Then, there will be philosophy in the West, including the Arab world, but India and China will be left out.

My second remark is related to this issue. One should not hold forth on things one does not know about, and my field is supposed to be India; then why does "Asia" figure in the title of my paper? So I must make some simplifying assumptions. I shall assume that what is called philosophy in Asia has mainly developed in India and China. I apologize for making this assumption, especially to the Arabs, the Japanese, and others I hold in high esteem. Furthermore, I shall mainly deal with India, but I hope to offer some observations on China on the strength of the recent good fortune that put me in the proximity of an eminent Sinologist who collaborated with me in an area on the periphery of philosophy.

As for India, I shall be inspired by Viṣṇu and take three large steps. At the first, I shall consider philosophy as *ancilla theologiae*, that handmaid of theology which some western philosophy was considered to have been during the Middle Ages. At the second step I shall consider philosophy as analysis, and at the third, as an interpretation of ritual. As for China, I shall confine my remarks to topics dealt with during my third step in India.

THE idea that philosophy is a handmaid of theology can only be applicable to India if there is such a thing as theology there. If we take theology in the etymological sense as a "discourse on God," we must also require that there be a God in India. Although India may seem to be teeming with gods, we know that several of the so-called philosophical systems did not recognize anything like a god, and certainly not a personal God. Then why can we not say that theology is the same as *brahmavidyā*—a venerable term as ancient as the Brahmanic literature? In that case *brahmavid* and *brahmavādin*, terms that are even older, could be translated as 'theologian'. A. B. Keith adopted that rendering in his translation of the *Taittirīya Saṃhitā* of the Black Yajurveda. There are difficulties, however. *Brahmavādin* in the Yajurveda means "ritual expert." In Advaita Vedanta, it means the same as *vedāntin*, namely, a person who regards all things as identical with Brahman. If there is theology in India, we may have to look elsewhere.

When Thomas Aquinas distinguished philosophy from theology he did not think of theology as a discourse about God. For philosophy, according to him, can also be a discourse about God, and then the distinction would be between philosophy as a whole and one of its parts.[1] The distinction he had in mind is between philosophy—including what is now called "natural theology"—and theology based on the Christian revelation. To Aquinas, theology in that sense is more important than philosophy because philosophy is based on reason alone. Where would man be, he asks, if he had to rely on his reason only? *In maximis ignorantiae tenebris* (in the greatest darknesses of ignorance). Reason and demonstrations are limited because many would remain in doubt "about those things even which are most truly demonstrated, through ignoring the force of the demonstration: especially when they perceive that different things are taught by various men who are called wise." He concludes: "Therefore it was necessary that definite certainty and pure truth about divine things should be offered to man by the way of faith." Étienne Gilson comments on this passage from the *Summa Contra Gentiles* that "the spectacle of these contradictions between philosophers contributes not a little to the scepticism of those who are looking in from the outside."[2]

Such expressions seem to be echoes from Bhartṛhari or Śaṅkara. In the *Vākyapadīya* (1.34) we read: "*yatnenānumito'py arthaḥ kuśalair anumātṛbhiḥ / abhiyuktatarair anyair anyathaivopapadyate*" ("whenever something is inferred with great pains by

[1] F. C. Copleston, *Aquinas* (Harmondsworth: Penguin, 1955), p. 52.

[2] Étienne Gilson, *L'Esprit de la philosophie médiévale*, 2 vols. (Paris: Vrin, 1932), 1:42.

people who are expert at inference, it is established differently by others who are still more ingenious"). And Śaṅkara says in *Brahmasūtrabhāṣya* 1.3.28: "*kaiścid abhiyuktair yatnenotprekṣitās tarkā abhiyuktatarair anyair ābhāṣyamānā dṛśyante*" ("whenever arguments are excogitated with great pains by ingenious people, they are seen to be refuted by others who are still more ingenious"). In both cases, the ingenious people referred to or thought of are founders of systems such as Kapila.

Śaṅkara holds that Brahman cannot be known by inference (*anumāna*) or by other means of right knowledge (*pramāṇa*). He admits these only "in as far as they do not contradict the Upaniṣads" (*vedāntavākyāvirodhi: Brahmasūtrabhāṣya* 1.1.2). So philosophy, to the extent that it is confined to these means of knowledge, is a handmaid of something else that may be called theology. Christian theologians like De Smet who have written knowledgeably about Śaṅkara[3] have in fact referred to his method as theological.

The *ancilla* idea of philosophy seems to apply very well to the Vedanta, both in the sense of the Upaniṣads and in that of the later systems based on the sutras of Bādarāyaṇa, and also to most schools of Buddhism, which are very similar in doctrine to the Vedanta though they do not recognize the authority of the Vedas.[4] The traditional opening of many Buddhist sutras: *"evam mayā śrutam ekasmin samaye bhagavān Śrāvastyām viharati sma" (Pali: evaṃ me sutaṃ ekaṃ samayaṃ bhagavā Sāvatthiyaṃ viharati")*—"Thus heard I on one occasion: the Blessed One was staying at Śrāvasti . . ."[5]—is very similar to quotes from the *śruti* in the Vedanta, not only in concept but also in function. The *ancilla* idea is also in accordance with the widespread popular notion that Indian philosophy is not based on reason, interested in theories, or seeking intellectual satisfac-

[3] Richardo de Smet, *The Theological Method of Saṃkara* (Louvain: Pontificia Universatatis Gregorianae, 1954).

[4] See Frits Staal, "Substitutions de paradigmes et religions d'Asie," *Cahiers d'Extrême Asie* (Kyoto) 1 (1985): 21–57.

[5] Cf. J. Brough, " 'Thus Have I Heard . . .'," *Bulletin of the School of Oriental and African Studies* 13 (1950): 416–426.

tion like western philosophy, but is concerned with practical aims such as *mokṣa* or Nirvana. The same seems to hold for Chinese philosophy, if we accept its general characterization by Fung Yu-Lan: "Chinese philosophers for the most part have not regarded knowledge as something valuable in itself, and so have not sought knowledge for the sake of knowledge; and even in the case of knowledge of a practical sort that might have a direct bearing upon human happiness, Chinese philosophers have preferred to apply this knowledge to actual conduct that would lead directly to this happiness, rather than to hold what they considered to be empty discussions about it."[6]

These views on philosophy in Asia, whether correct or not, can be formulated in a variety of ways. Franklin Edgerton, for example, writes about the Upaniṣads: they "seek to know the real truth about the universe, not for its own sake; not for the mere joy of knowledge; not as an abstract speculation; but simply because they conceive such knowledge as a short cut to the control of every cosmic power."[7] P. T. Raju expresses similar ideas in different terms when he argues that philosophy in India is subordinate to religion: "In order to be religious, man has to believe that the basis or origin of the world is spiritual and that his goal is to realize it in his own being, not merely in his thought. Understood as such, religion includes a philosophical theory of reality and also a plan to guide man's life towards such a realization."[8] What corresponds most nearly to religion in India is, according to Raju, "*yoga*, which means 'uniting'. The word *yoga* and the English word 'yoke' have the same Indo-Germanic root (*yuj*) meaning 'to join'." Actually, commentators on the Yogasūtra derive *yoga* from the root *yuj*-

[6] Fung Yu-Lan, *A History of Chinese Philosophy*, trans. Derk Bodde, 2 vols. (Princeton: Princeton University Press, 1952–1953), 1:2.

[7] Franklin Edgerton, *The Beginnings of Indian Philosophy* (Cambridge, Mass.: Harvard University Press, 1965), p. 28; cf. idem, "The Upaniṣads: What Do They Seek and Why?" *Journal of the American Oriental Society* 49 (1929): 97–121, exp. p. 118.

[8] P. T. Raju, *The Philosophical Traditions of India* (Pittsburgh: University of Pittsburgh Press, 1972), p. 26.

a (*Dhātupāṭha* 4.68) in the sense of 'concentration, attention' (*samādhau*), not from the root *yuj-i* (*Dhātupāṭha* 7.7) in the sense of 'uniting' (*yoge*).

Is it correct to characterize western philosophy in general, excluding its *ancilla* episodes, as interested in theories and based on reason? Of course, philosophers hold widely divergent views on these matters. Yet many would agree with what Edmund Husserl said in his lectures on the crisis of European humanity about classical Greece: it was there that man first conceived of the world (the world as a whole) as a question to answer. The Greeks questioned the world not in order to satisfy this or that practical need, but because "the passion of knowing had seized mankind." Husserl was careful not to claim (like many others) that *only* the Greeks possessed such a passion. I have quoted him for that reason, and also because his views on this matter may be acceptable to philosophers of various backgrounds and persuasions.

General characteristics of philosophy, such as we are looking for in Asia, are not easily found in the West. Even were Husserl's characterizations valid in general, there are exceptions, and they are not confined to the western Middle Ages. I am not thinking of the uniquely western forms of irrationalism that one finds in existentialism, which are tinged with theology,[9] or even more extreme positions such as those affected by people like Jacques Derrida, which are best regarded as simple aberrations. I am thinking of the ancient Greeks themselves, who were very much concerned with practical aims such as human happiness. This is clearly set forth, for example, by Michel Foucault in his last two books.

General perspectives change with the times and are often misleading. This may be true of our general perspective on philosophy in Asia as practical or religious. Nowadays, popular culture and fads in most parts of the western world and even in Asia hail Asian philosophy as a spiritual wonderland

[9] Cf. Frits Staal, *Exploring Mysticism* (Berkeley: University of California Press, 1975), pt. 1.

and universal remedy for western ills. But similar views were held, a century ago, with respect to the Greek philosophy itself. This is demonstrated by a passage in *Morgenröte* (number 544), in which Nietzsche takes his contemporaries to task: "I know only too well that our philosophising youths, women and artists expect from philosophy the exact opposite of what the Greeks derived from it. He who does not hear the constant jubilation resounding in every speech and rejoinder of a Platonic dialogue, the jubilation over the new discovery of rational thinking, what does he understand of Plato or ancient philosophy?" Nietzsche continues with an evocation of the Greek love for dialectics, concepts, ideas, argumentation, generalizations, and refutations, which he compares with the enthusiasm of the masters of counterpoint for their musical creations. But our contemporaries, says Nietzsche, do not like to think of themselves as rational beings, but rather as "intuitive beings," "artistic natures," endowed with "inner sense" or "intellectual intuition." "And such people are pursuing philosophy today! I am afraid they may one day discover that they have made a mistake—that what they are looking for is religion."[10]

THE idea that philosophy is solely practical or spiritual, an *ancilla* of something else, calls for a reaction. In the study of Indian philosophy, that reaction has not failed to appear. Its starting point is simple, straightforward, and ethnocentric: we define philosophy in western terms and then try to find what the Indians, or Asians generally, have got that resembles it. Starting with what for lack of a better term I shall call contemporary western analytical philosophy, the results are not disappointing.

Contemporary analytical philosophy contains at least three strands. The first is a traditional feature of western philosophy to which I have already referred: it emphasizes reason, argu-

[10] Friedrich Nietzsche, *Morgenröte* no. 544, in *Werke in Drei bänden*, ed. K. Schlechta (Munich: Carl Hanser, 1954), 1:1265–1266.

ment, and conceptual analysis. This strand provides the background for the other two, which may be regarded as more specialized developments. The first of these two is logic, conceived either as a part of philosophy or as a separate discipline; it goes back at least as far as Aristotle, but in its modern forms it has developed close links with mathematics. The other strand is a more original contemporary development: the ordinary language analysis that began to flourish with J. L. Austin and which continues to play an important role in British and American universities.

What does India have to offer when looked at in this light? If we start with the third trend—ordinary language analysis—we can find examples, though the methodology does not seem to have been pursued for its own sake. I offer three illustrations. First, in *Bṛhadāraṇyaka Upaniṣad* 1.5.3 it is argued that we see and hear with our mind (*manasā*) because we say: "*anyatramanā abhūvaṃ nādarśam anyatramanā abhūvaṃ nāśrauṣam iti*" ("because my mind was elsewhere, I did not see; because my mind was elsewhere, I did not hear"). A literal translation is possible here because the argument from ordinary language is applicable to English as well as to Sanskrit.

Second, Śaṅkara tries to refute the Buddhist *śūnyavāda* in *Brahmasūtrabhāṣya* 2.2.25 by arguing that the fact that we remember things can only be accounted for if we assume that we have a continuous personality. This is obvious because we say: "*aham ado'drākṣam idam paśyāmīti*" ("I have seen it and now I am seeing it [again]"), but we never say: "*ahaṃ smarāmy adrākṣīd anya iti*" ("I remember but someone else has seen it").

Third, the followers of the Mīmāṁsā school of Prabhākara Guru support the *anvitābhidhāna* view—according to which the meaning of a sentence arises directly from the collection of its words, so that words convey no meaning except in the context of a sentence—by arguing that children learn language in this manner: for a child who hears the sentences "*gām ānaya*" ("bring the cow") and "*aśvam ānaya*" ("bring the horse") understands in each case the meaning of the entire expression from the context or situation and arrives at the meaning of individual words only by distributional analysis (*anvayavyatireka*).[11]

In the area of logic it has long been known that India has much to offer. It is remarkable, however, that the earliest work of the so-called logical system of the Nyāya, the *Nyāyasūtra*, and its earliest commentaries, are inferior in logical insight and acumen not only to Aristotle, but also to the Indian grammarian Patañjali, who was certainly earlier.[12] Interesting logical distinctions such as between *paryudāsa* and *prasajya* negations, were developed by the grammarians and philosophers of the Mīmāṁsā before the Naiyāyikas had even considered the problem.[13] Indian logic began to flourish with the Buddhist logicians before it finally culminated and became codified in the Hindu system of "modern logic" (*navya-nyāya*), which ruled for almost eight hundred years in the Sanskrit colleges of northeastern India with ramifications to the west and the south. Unlike western logic, Indian logic was never close to mathematics; it was closer to grammar, but this is a general characteristic of the traditional sciences in India.[14]

The main features of analytical philosophy—the emphasis on arguments and conceptual analysis—are relatively widespread in India; they seem to have developed through centuries of debate and controversy between the traditional systems, especially Nyāya, Mīmāṁsā, Vedanta, and the Buddhist schools. Key concepts such as *vidhi*, *vivarta*, *apoha*, and *vyāpti* have been endlessly discussed, analyzed, and refined. There re-

[11] K. Kunjunni Raja, *Indian Theories of Meaning* (Madras: Adyar, 1963), pp. 188–196; cf. Frits Staal, "Sanskrit Philosophy of Language," *Current Trends in Linguistics* 5 (1969): 499–531, esp. pp. 512–513, reprinted in Herman Parret, ed., *History of Linguistic Thought and Contemporary Linguistics* (Berlin: de Gruyter, 1976), pp. 102–136, esp. p. 116.

[12] Cf. Frits Staal, review of Hartmut Scharfe, *Die Logik im Mahabhāṣya* (Berlin: Deutsche Academie der Wissenschaften, Institute für Orientforschung, 1961), in *Journal of the American Oriental Society* 83 (1963): 252–256.

[13] Frits Staal, "Negation and the Law of Contradiction in Indian Thought," *Bulletin of the School of Oriental and African Studies* 25 (1962): 52–71.

[14] Cf. Frits Staal, "Euclid and Pāṇini," *Philosophy East and West* 15 (1965): 99–116.

mains a difference, however, with modern western philosophy and even with its Greek predecessors. If we retain Husserl's terminology, we can say that the Indians, like the Greeks, conceived of the world as a whole as a question to answer. The answer, however, was generally in the negative, or otherwise unflattering to the world itself. B. K. Matilal is right when he writes: "Whatever might have been the motive or driving force behind this refutation of [the] external/material world, it was received with all philosophic seriousness in India."[15] But it is difficult to approach the world as a whole, even if it is not denied, with that "passion of knowing" mentioned by Husserl. That passion is in a position to appear when the world is analyzed, which can only be done when it is neither denied, nor left as a whole. Of course, philosophy must always lag behind the sciences when it comes to an analysis of the world. But while in the West the natural sciences developed in relatively close cooperation with philosophy, in India they developed very largely by themselves. This holds for astronomy, chemistry, botany, and medicine, but not for the more characteristically Indian sciences such as ritual and grammar: for the latter inspire philosophy, for example in the two systems of the Mīmāṁsā or in Bhartṛhari's *Śabdādvaita*. The situation in China may be different, if Joseph Needham is right that the sciences in China were inspired by Taoism.

The distinction between practical or spiritual philosophy on the one hand, and theoretical or analytical philosophy on the other, can to some extent be formulated in Indian terms. It has been done by Matilal:

> There is a very well established philosophic tradition in India, which tries to maintain that reality lies beyond the reach of language and construction (i.e., discursive thinking). In other words, the real world is inexpressible in terms of concepts. There is also the opposite philosophic thesis which

[15] B. K. Matilal, "A Critique of Buddhist Idealism," in L. Cousins, A. Kunst, and K. R. Norman, eds., *Buddhist Studies in Honour of I. B. Horner* (Dordrecht: Reidel, 1974), pp. 139–169, at p. 155.

> tries to show that reality is knowable and hence expressible in language. The structure of our knowledge reflects the structure of the real world. One side in the philosophic debate of these two opposing views is represented by the various forms of Buddhism, while the other side is represented by the non-Buddhist schools, chiefly by the *Nyāya-Vaiśeṣika.*[16]

This view, which may be generalized (for example, by adding the Vedanta to the one side, and the Mīmāṁsā to the other) is clearly based on Nyāya terms and concepts. According to the Nyāya, everything is knowable: technically, *jñeyatvam* (knowability) is *kevalānvayin* (universally positive). Everything is therefore expressible in language because of Nyāya inferences such as "*abhidheyam prameyatvāt*" ("it is namable because it is known") and "*vācyaṃ jñeyatvāt*" ("it is expressible because it is known"). In Buddhism, by contrast, we have *avyākṛtavastūni* (inexpressible things), and in the Advaita Vedanta, Brahman is *sadasadbhyām anirvacanīya* (indeterminable as to whether it is or is not). The locus classicus of this inexpressibility is in the *Taittirīya Upaniṣad*: "*yato vāco nivartante aprāpya manasā saha*" ("that from which all words return, which is not within reach of the mind").

In western philosophy, the distinction is similar but not the same: it emphasizes rational versus irrational, whereas the Indian distinction is between expressible and inexpressible. The latter distinction reflects not only the emphasis on language which is a feature of Indian culture, but also the emphasis on ritual which is a feature of all Asian culture. The distinction between "expressible" and "inexpressible" as *nírukta* and *anírukta*, respectively, goes back to Vedic ritual.[17] Before we look into this subject more closely, however, we may provisionally

[16] Idem, *Epistemology, Logic, and Grammar in Indian Philosophical Analysis* (The Hague and Paris: Mouton, 1971), p. 14.

[17] See, e.g., Louis Renou and Lilian Silburn, "Nírukta and Anírukta in Vedic," in *Sarūpa Bhāratī: Lakshmana Sarup Memorial Volume* (Hoshiarpur, 1954), pp. 68–79.

conclude that, in spite of these differences and unless appearances are misleading, there is such a thing as philosophy in India.

Traditionally, the beginnings of western philosophy have been sought in the Milesian school of natural philosophy. In these speculations, the unity of the world, tacitly presupposed, was sought in a single cosmic and elementary matter, which Thales declared to be water, and Anaximenes, air.

Traditionally, the beginnings of Indian philosophy have been sought in the Upaniṣads. In these speculations, the unity of the world, tacitly presupposed, was sought in identifications such as "*tat tvam asi*" ("you are that": *Chāndogya Upaniṣad* 6.8–16) and "*aham brahmāsmi*" ("I am Brahman": *Bṛhadāraṇyaka Upaniṣad* 1.4.10).

The origins of the traditional story of the origins of western philosophy lie in Aristotle, the Greek doxographers, Hermann Diels's "Fragmente der Vorsokratiker," and the German Kantian idealism of historians of philosophy such as Windelband. But research into these origins has not come to a stop, and if one consults the works of contemporary classical scholars such as Walter Burkert, Marcel Detienne, E. R. Dodds, Jean-Pierre Vernant, or Paul Veyne, one gets a different story.

The origins of the traditional story of the origins of Indian philosophy lie in Śaṅkara and his followers, Mādhava's fourteenth-century *Sarvadarśanasaṃgraha (Compendium of All Systems)*, Schopenhauer, and Paul Deussen. Before we take a fresh look at these origins themselves it will be helpful to review briefly the traditional story.

According to Śaṅkara, the essence of the Vedic tradition is expressed in the "great statements" (*mahāvākya*) of the Upaniṣads. This view is a reaction to the Mīmāṁsā view that the Vedic tradition consists of injunctions (*vidhi*), mantras, names (*nāmadheya*), prohibitions (*niṣedha*), and explanations (*arthavāda*), of which the injunctions are the most important. While Śaṅkara is saturated with Mīmāṁsā,[18] the Mīmāṁsā view it-

[18] ". . . tout pénétré de Mīmāṃsā": Louis Renou, *Prolégomènes au Védānta*

self is a development of the Vedic view, expressed especially in the Yajurveda, that the primary distinction in the Vedic corpus is between *mantra* and *brāhmaṇa*.

Beginning with Sureśvara, Śaṅkara's followers spent a great deal of time on the semantic analysis of these "great statements." In the later Advaita Vedanta, statements such as "*tat tvam asi*" are interpreted semimetaphorically in terms of what is technically called *jahadajahallakṣaṇā* (secondary meaning which is exclusive and inclusive of primary meaning).[19] The "great statements" are partly *jahallakṣaṇā* (exclusive of primary meaning), as in "gaṅgāyāṃ ghoṣaḥ" ("the village is on the Ganges"), where the village is not on the Ganges itself, but on the banks of the Ganges; and partly *ajahallakṣaṇā* (nonexclusive of primary meaning), as in "kuntāḥ praviśanti" ("the lances enter"), where the lances enter along with the men who carry them. In "*tat tvam asi*," the apparent addressee, *tvam*, excludes the individual Śvetaketu, son of Uddālaka, through *jahallakṣaṇā*, but includes pure consciousness and other general features through *ajahallakṣaṇā*. These features are identical with similarly general features of *tat* (that), from which all ordinary and imperfect features have also been excluded by a similar procedure. Of course, by thus turning a statement into a tautology, its truth is guaranteed but its meaning is reduced to the point of nothingness. This semantic procedure is similar to the argument that *A* equals *B* because both are letters, or Paris equals London because both are capitals.

Let us now take a closer look at "*tat tvam asi*" in its proper context. The *Chāndogya Upaniṣad* is a Upaniṣad of the *chandogas* that is, people who sing *(ga)sāmans* of the *Sāmaveda* composed on *mantras* (*chandas*) of the *Ṛg Veda*. The term *chandoga* is sometimes used for one of the *Sāmaveda* priests in particular, namely, the Udgātṛ. The importance of the *Sāmaveda* for Śaṅkara's Advaita Vedanta[20] is in fact largely due to the importance of the *Chāndogya Upaniṣad*. (This Upaniṣad is also im-

(Paris: Imprimerie Nationale, 1951), p. iii; see also Otto Strauss, *Udgīthavidyā* (Berlin: de Gruyter, 1931).

19 Cf. de Smet, *Theological Method*; and Raja, *Indian Theories*, pp. 251ff.

20 Cf. Renou, *Prolégomènes*, p. iii.

portant for the *Bhagavad Gītā*: see 10.22, where Kṛṣṇa says "*vedānāṃ sāmavedo'smi*" ["among the Vedas I am the *Sāmaveda*"].)

The primary purpose of a *Sāmaveda* Upaniṣad is to provide an explanation or interpretation (*upavyākhyānam*) of the chant of the Udgātṛ, the *udgītha*. We shall see that this *udgītha* is *om*. At the beginning of the *Chāndogya Upaniṣad* it says, "With that [*om*] they perform the ritual, he who knows [that explanation] and he who does not know [it]. But knowing and not knowing are not the same. Only ritual performed with knowing, trust [in its efficacy][21] and 'upaniṣad' is most efficacious. That indeed is the explanation of that syllable" (1.1.10).

The Upaniṣad takes it for granted that the ritual continues to be performed, that it will be done by people who know and by people who do not. But the ritual is only efficacious if it is executed by people "who know." This was already stated in the *Brāhmaṇas*, which often refer to the person "who knows thus" (*ya evaṃ veda*) and who "knowing thus" (*evaṃ vidvān*) performed the rites; and even earlier, in the *Atharvaveda*.[22] Such knowledge means knowledge of the interpretation, not knowledge of the ritual: for the latter is common to both groups. In order to understand this adequately we therefore have to know first what both groups know, and then what the Upaniṣad proposed to add to that knowledge as "special knowledge."

What both groups know, first of all, is that the *udgītha* is not just any chant. It is a specific portion of a specific chant. It is the second portion (*bhakti*) of the ritual chants called *stotra* or *stuti* that are sung during Soma rituals. Each of these consists of five portions, and is followed by a *śāstra* recitation from the *Ṛg Veda*, which consists in part of the same verse as what underlies the chant. The chants from the *Sāmaveda* and the recitations from the *Ṛg Veda* are therefore closely related. The

[21] M. Hara, "Note on Two Sanskrit Religious Terms: *bhakti* and *śraddhā*," *Indo-Iranian Journal* 7 (1963–1964): 124–145.

[22] See Edgerton, *Beginnings*, p. 23 n.3.

Adhvaryu priest recites the following formula before the beginning of the chant, when he hands two blades of *darbha* grass (also called *stotra*) to the Udgātṛ: "*ṛksāmayor upastaraṇam asi mithunasya prajātyai*" ("you are the bed for the coupling of chant and recitation, for the sake of procreation"). The Upaniṣad says accordingly: "Laughing, eating, and making love—that is what is done with chants and recitations" ("*atha yadd hasati yaj jakṣiti yan maithunaṃ carati stutaśastrair eva tad eti*": CU 3.17.3).

Chant and recitation are the first two elements of a sequence of four called "Soma sequence," of which the third element is a Soma libation, and the fourth, the drinking of Soma by the ritual's celebrants. Each of the Soma rituals is characterized by a specific set of Soma sequences. The prototype of the Soma rituals, the Agniṣṭoma, for example, is defined by twelve Soma sequences: five at the morning pressing, five at the midday pressing, and two at the third pressing. The twelve chants that are sung during these twelve episodes are composed on different melodies, such as *gāyatra, rathantara, vāmadevya, naudhasa, kāleya*, and so on. Many of them are discussed and interpreted in the *Chāndogya Upaniṣad* 2.11–21.

To illustrate the structure of these chants I shall treat a relatively simple example, the fourth Soma sequence of the morning pressing as it occurs in an Atirātra Soma ritual.[23] The underlying mantras are *Ṛg Veda* 1.7.1:

> *indram id gāthino bṛhad*
> *indram arkebhir arkiṇaḥ*
> *indram vāṇīr anūṣata*
>
> "The chanters have loudly chanted to Indra,
> the singers have sung with their songs to Indra,
> the musicians have resounded to Indra."

The meter (*chandas*) of this verse is *gayatrī*, in other words, it consists of three octosyllabic "feet" (*pada*), with the long and short syllables distributed as follows:

[23] Frits Staal, ed, *AGNI: The Vedic Ritual of the Fire Altar*, 2 vols. (Berkeley: University of California Press, 1983), 1:631.

– ⏑ – – / ⏑ – ⏑ ⏑
– ⏑ – – / ⏑ – ⏑ ⏑
– – – – / ⏑ – ⏑ ⏑

This verse will be recited by the Brāhmaṇacchaṃśin priest after the chant is over. He will not pay any attention to the original meter or accents (which I have not marked), but take breath at special places (which I shall indicate by the solidus "/"), repeat the first verse (which is all I have quoted) thrice, and make certain insertions of long vowels, including *o*. He will also recite the formula "śoṃsāvo" ("let us both recite!") at the beginning. The result is as follows:

śoṃsāvo—indram id gāthino bṛhad indram arkebhir arkiṇa-a-a
indram vāṇīr anūṣato-o-o indram id gāthino bṛhad indram arkebhir arkiṇa-a-a
indram vāṇīr anūṣato-o-o indram id gāthino bṛhad indram arkebhir arkiṇa-a-a
indram vāṇīr anūṣato-o-o . . .

This same verse was used in the preceding *stuti* chant, which consists of five portions (*bhakti*) that are sung by three of the four *Sāmaveda* priests:

(1) *prastāva*, prelude, sung by the Prastotṛ;
(2) *udgītha*, sung by the Udgātṛ;
(3) *pratihāra*, response, sung by the Pratihartṛ;
(4) *upadrava*, accessory (optional), sung by the Udgātṛ;
(5) *nidhana*, finale, sung by all three.

Under certain conditions, to which I shall return, these portions are preceded by the sound *hṃ*, and the *udgītha* by the sound *om*, called the *ādi* part of the chant. Since the original meter of the underlying verse from the *Ṛg Veda* was *gāyatrī*, the chant is composed on the melody called *gāyatra*, which results in a composition in five parts, of which all but the first words are hidden by syllabification or "unexpressed":

(1) *prastāva: indram id gāthino bṛho-o-om*
(2) *udgītha: o vā o vā o-o-o vā*

(3) *pratihāra: hṃ bhā*
(4) *upadrava: o*
(5) *nidhana: vā*

The entire chant consists of three such melodies, which I shall refer to as I, II, and III; I have only explained the first. Each of them is repeated five times, and other sounds are added, so that the resulting structure consists of fifteen chants, in accordance with the following pattern:

o hṃ. I I I II III
hṃ. I II II II III
hṃ. I II III III III

Thus the *udgītha*, which is sung in each of these fifteen chants, is an *aniruktagāna*, an "unexpressed chant," consisting of "*o vā o vā o-o-o vā*"—sounds that also occur elsewhere in the chants and recitations. It is this mysterious sequence of sounds that the Upaniṣads of the *Sāmaveda* try to understand and interpret.

The *Chāndogya Upaniṣad* spends a great deal of time speculating about these sounds. The first two chapters are almost entirely devoted to these speculations, and the numbers, 3, 5, and 7 play an important role in them. It is obvious that most of these interpretations have nothing to do with the ritual itself and are entirely arbitrary and ad hoc. But some are more than that; they are also fantastic and incorrect. The pseudoetymological idea that *sāman* (chant) is connected with *sama* (equal), for example, leads to the following statements in *Chāndogya Upaniṣad* 2.10: *hṃ* has three syllables, the *prastāva* has three syllables, therefore there is equality (2.10.1); 2 = 4 therefore there is equality, provided one is taken from 4 and added to 2 (2.10.2); 3 = 4, therefore there is equality, since 3 = 3 and one remains (2.10.3); another 3, therefore another equality (2.10.4); and so on.

Apart from absurdities, there is also a great deal of confusion: terms enter into various identity statements, but they are not regarded as identical in other contexts. There are also amusing, or apparently amusing episodes, for example the chant of the dogs in 1.12: "*Om*! let us eat! *Om*! let us drink!" And there are erotic interpretations, such as in 2.13, about the *vāmadevya* chant: "*hṃ* is calling her; *prastāva* is making his proposition; *udgītha* is lying down with her; *pratihāra* is lying upon her" (the Upaniṣads mention only the missionary position); and "*nidhana* is coming." We also find interesting narrations, some with social overtones, such as those in 4.3 and 4.4 about the boy who did not know his father's name because his mother had told him, "When I was young I moved around a lot before I conceived you, and so I don't know what your family *gotra* is." The boy went in search of a teacher whom he told what his mother had told him. The teacher said to him: "Only a Brahmin will speak like that. Bring the firewood sticks, I shall initiate you. You have not deviated from the truth."

Numerical identifications play an important role in these interpretations. I shall not repeat what was said about these by Barend Faddegon[24] and more recently by G. Gren-Eklund,[25] but I cannot fail to refer to the identifications in which the *udgītha* plays a part. This "essence of the chant" is identified with many things, especially quintuples, and including breath, speech, eye, ear, mind, sun, the ultimate, space, atmosphere, rain, waters flowing to the east, rainy season, cows, fire blazing from the firewood sticks, midday, sky, flesh, Agni, Vāyu, Āditya, the universe, everything. Much of this applies also to the *gāyatrī*, this universe, the world, the body, the heart, inner and outer space. The same will be said again of Brahman, of *Ātman*, and virtually of everything that is or is not identical with anything. It need cause no surprise that we also come across a teacher who tells his pupil, who is in search of Brahman and *Ātman*, "you are that."

Am I suggesting, then, that we should not take this "great

[24] B. Faddegon, "Ritualistic Dadaism," *Acta Orientalia* 5 (1926–1927): 177–195.

[25] G. Gren-Eklund, "An Upaniṣad of Sāman," *Orientalia Suecana* 27–28 (1978–1979): 148–158.

statement" seriously? I am afraid that that is what I am suggesting. For if we take it literally, we should do the same with the others: it makes no more sense than they do. Such expressions are good to chant, and to muse about when musing about chant. But they should not be taken more seriously than a real estate agent who offers a house for a hundred-hundred-thousand million dollars, a million dollars, a thousand dollars, a hundred dollars, one dollar—just as the Yajamāna, when the Agnicayana altar has been completed, wishes that the bricks be turned into one cow, a hundred cows, a thousand cows, a million cows, a hundred-hundred-thousand million cows.[26] Śaṅkara's followers understood this quite well when they made the attempt to turn the "great statements" into tautologies.

That the Upaniṣads are full of absurdities and contradictions is not something we did not know before. What I have said about the *Chāndagya Upaniṣad* is applicable, mutatis mutandis, to the *Bṛhadāraṇyaka*, which also contains many sections on the *udgītha*, not to mention a long passage on sex left untranslated, but which starts out with lengthy ritual identifications and interpretations concerned with the horse sacrifice. Nor is this rambling proclivity confined to the older Upaniṣads. *Maitrāyaṇīya* or *Maitri Upaniṣad* 6.22, for example, invokes the same *udgītha om*, which is identified with the Brahman of sound (*śabda*), but which also refers to a Brahman of nonsound (*aśabda*), which is attained when one immerses oneself in the Brahman of sound. This can be done by placing one's thumbs against one's ears and listening to the sound that emerges from the space inside the heart. As I have indicated already, there is nothing new about "nonsound": in Vedic ritual there had always been a tendency to stress "unexpressed" sounds, muttering and silence.[27] The *Chāndogya* itself had identified *om* with the sound that the sun makes when running its course—not so different, after all, from the harmony of the spheres, which

[26] Staal, ed., *AGNI*, 1:508.

[27] Cf. L. Renou, "La Valeur du silence dans le culte védique," *Journal of the American Oriental Society* 69 (1949): 11–18; Renou and Silburn, "Nírukta and Anírukta."

Pythagoras could hear, according to his biographer Porphyrius, although others are prevented from hearing it because of the mediocrity of their natures.

The thesis that the Upaniṣads are full of absurdities and contradictions calls for three general comments. The first is that this tradition of fanciful interpretations did not start with the Upaniṣads, but is characteristic of the entire literature of the Brāhmaṇas, to which the Āraṇyakas and the Upaniṣads are merely the appendixes. Weber, Eggeling, Keith, and many others have drawn attention to this fact. The Brāhmaṇas swarm with interpretations of rites and rituals that are contradictory and have nothing to do with the ritual itself.[28] Even generally accepted theories are often arbitrary and ad hoc, for example, the idea that the prototype of Vedic sacrifice is the dismemberment of a primeval male as described in the *Puruṣasūkta* of *Ṛg Veda* 10.90—an idea that has appeals to western scholars with a penchant for religious interpretation.

My second general comment is related to this largely negative observation, but it is positive. For although this entire tradition of Brāhmaṇa–Āraṇyaka–Upaniṣad is significant for the origins of what is generally called Indian philosophy, there exists another tradition in India—equally ancient, venerable, and attached to ritual—that is not at all contradictory or absurd: the science of ritual that is constructed and developed in the *Śrauta Sūtras*. This tradition is not the precursor of "philosophy" but the precursor of grammar (*vyākaraṇa*). Here there are no absurdities, no contradictions, no arbitrariness: everything is carefully formulated and subjected to detailed and logical analysis. Indian grammar is in many ways comparable and quite possibly superior to contemporary western linguistics. "This grammar," wrote Leonard Bloomfield about Pāṇini's grammar of Sanskrit, "is one of the greatest monuments of

[28] See Frits Staal, "The Meainglessness of Ritual," *Numen: International Journal of the History of Religion* 26 (1979): 2–22; idem, "Ritual, Mantras and the Origin of Language," in *Amrtadhara: Festschrift F. N. Dandekar* (Poona: Oriental Book Agency, 1984); idem, "The Search for Meaning: Mathematics, Music and Ritual," *American Journal of Semiotics* 2.4 (1984): 1–57.

human intelligence."[29] The Indian science of ritual is naturally superior to its western counterparts because there is no western science of ritual, and no other culture seems to have produced anything similar.[30]

My third general comment is directly relevant to the problems under consideration. For if our characterization of the Upaniṣads is correct, Śaṅkara was wrong, or at any rate unfair, when he isolated a few so-called "great statements" from all the others that are equally great—and arbitrary. His attitude is simply anachronistic and has little to do with the Upaniṣads themselves. What is remarkable is that Śaṅkara's perspective has determined the approach of almost all students of Indian philosophy. Most handbooks treat the Upaniṣads as if their doctrines were identical with those of the later Vedanta. Some scholars have recognized this problem: for example, Edgerton says about the Upaniṣads, "The dry bones of the Vedic ritual cult frequently rattle about in them in quite a noisy fashion, and seriously strain our patience and our charity."[31] Well put, but alas it is a purely subjective expression of a sentiment that has nothing to do with a scientific account of what it is we are trying to study. Who would believe a physicist who exclaims that atoms consist of photons, though "protons and electrons frequently rattle about in them in quite a noisy fashion, and seriously strain our patience and our charity"?

I have tried to give you a glimpse of what was in the minds of the authors of the Upaniṣads. Their universe of discourse may not look like what we call philosophy, but anyone is free to call it that. What is important is that this background explains many features of Indian thought that would be unintelligible without it, for example, the emphasis on Karma,

[29] Leonard Bloomfield, *Language* (New York: Henry Holt, 1933), p. 11. For illustrations see, e.g., Paul Kiparsky and Frits Staal, "Syntactic and Semantic Relations in Pāṇini," *Foundations of Language* 5 (1969): 83–117; and Paul Kiparsky, *Pāṇini as a Variationist*, ed. S. D. Joshi (Poona: University of Poona, and Cambridge, Mass.: M.I.T. Press, 1979).

[30] Frits Staal, *The Science of Ritual* (Poona: Oriental Book Agency, 1982).

[31] Edgerton, *Beginnings*, p. 28.

dharma, and *śabda* that pervades much of Indian speculation. Karma, after all, is ritual; *dharma* what the Vedas teach and what cannot be obtained by other means of knowledge, namely by ritual; and *śabda* refers to the *mantras* that are recited during the performance of ritual. Karma is the object par excellence, "the most desired" (*īpsitatamam*: Pāṇini 1.4.49). We find it among the categories of the Vaiśeṣika, but not among the categories of Aristotle, which are quite similar in other respects. Similarly, there are long and often puzzling discussions on *śabda* in all branches of what has been called "Indian epistemology."

If Indian philosophy originated in speculations about the meaning and significance of ritual, it is certainly rather different from western philosophy. To ancient Greece, ritual was also important, and it was connected with science through the geometry of altar construction. In both India and Greece, ritual marks the origin of geometry. One of the three great classical problems of Greek mathematics, the so-called duplication of the cube, was inspired by ritual geometry because it was the altar at Delos that had to be doubled.[32] What is more striking and significant, however, is that in India, as in Asia generally, ritual is a permanent feature of civilization. It is more widespread than "religion."[33] There is no need to interpret rituals across boundaries, because the remarkable fact about them is that their interpretations vary already beyond our wildest dreams while they themselves remain invariant, or almost invariant, across religious and geographical boundaries. The same rites and *mantras* move from Vedic to Hindu and Buddhist contexts, and from India to Southeast Asia, China, Korea, and Japan. Thus we find Buddhist laymen all over Asia become monks through an initiation ceremony, *upasampadā*, that is similar to the Vedic *upanayanam* initiation ritual through

[32] A. Seidenberg, "The Geometry of the Vedic Rituals," in Staal, ed., *AGNI*, 2:95–126, esp. p. 101.

[33] Cf. Staal, "Substitutions de paradigmes."

which a high-caste Hindu enters the twice-born state. Once initiated, these monks perform all kinds of rites, including not only rites for pacifying (*śānti*), for gaining prosperity (*puṣṭi*), for subjugation (*vaśya*), for destroying (*abhicāra*), but also funeral and Vedic fire rites—as if the Buddha had not intervened.[34] This is the situation to which *Chāndogya Upaniṣad* 1.1.10 refers, when it declares that rituals are performed in any case whether the performers know or do not know. This is the context we have to consider if we wish to account for the origins of philosophy in India. But philosophy is only one of the varying interpretations given to this ongoing ritual activity, which strikes participants and observers alike as puzzling and mysterious.

I am now in a position to say the little I have to say on ritual speculation as a source of philosophy in China. We find such speculation in both Confucian and Taoist contexts. In Confucianism, the relevant classic is the *Li Chi* or *Book of Rites*, which has been translated into French by Séraphim Couvreur and into English by James Legge. Other works dealing with ritual speculation were composed by the Confucian scholar Hsün Tzu. Excerpts from both works are discussed by Fung Yu-Lan in his *History of Chinese Philosophy*.[35] According to these Confucian sources, rites are used to determine proper limits, and thus restrain desires; but they are also used to refine desires. Music is in these respects similar to ritual: but whereas music comes from within, ritual acts from without. From its very beginning, the universe has possessed a natural order or harmony, of which ritual and music are the concrete exemplifications.

As in India, interpretations of individual rites vary enormously. Some are straightforward and commonsensical. For example, why should the corpse of a dead person not be dressed until three days after death?

[34] See C. Hooykaas, "Agni Offerings in Java and Bali," in Staal, ed., *AGNI*, 2:382–402; T. Skorupski, "Tibetan Homa Rites," ibid., 2:403–417; and M. Strickmann, "Homa in East Asia," ibid., 2:418–455.

[35] Fung, *History*, vol. 1, chap. 14.

> When his parent is dead, the filial son is sad and sorrowful, and his mind is full of trouble. He crawls about and bewails his loss, as if the dead might come back to life. How could the dead be taken away from him and be dressed? Therefore, when it is said that the dressing does not begin till after three days, the meaning is that he is waiting during that time to see if [his parent] will come back to life. When after three days there is no such return, there is indeed no life, and the heart of the filial son is still more downcast. Moreover [during this time] the means of the family can be calculated, and the necessary clothes can be provided and made accordingly; the relatives who live afar can also arrive. Therefore the Sages have decided in this case that three days should be allowed, and the rule has been made accordingly.[36]

Other interpretations are less convincing, or acknowledge their limitations or failure:

> Divination, finding the lucky days, fasting, cleaning the temple, spreading out tables and mats, offering animals and grain, praying for blessings [from the deceased] as if the deceased enjoyed the sacrifice; selecting the offerings and sacrificing them as if the deceased tasted them; offering the three-legged winecup without washing it; for the one who sacrifices to have a wine-flask ready as if the deceased drank from his goblet; when the guests leave, for the host to bow them off, changing into his mourning clothes and take up his position and cry, as if the spirit of the departed had left: with such sorrow and reverence one serves the dead as one serves the living, and serves the departed as one serves those who are present. What is served has neither substance nor shadow, yet this is the completion of refinement.[37]

The most extraordinary interpretations are offered to the varieties of music and chant. For example:

[36] Ibid., 1:347.
[37] Ibid., 1:351.

> An intimate relationship exists between the first note of the scale and the prince, between the second and the officers, between the third and the people, between the fourth and the acts, between the fifth and the resources. When the five notes of the scale sound correct, the skies are harmonious. When the first note is defective, the sound is rough; the prince is haughty. When the second note is defective, the sound exhibits a deviation; public duties are badly executed. When the third note is defective, the sound is sad; people are dissatisfied. When the fourth note is defective, the sound is sorrowful; public works overwhelm the people. When the fifth note is defective, the sound is abrupt; resources are lacking. When all five notes are defective, they encroach upon one another; that is called public contempt for authority and the rights of others. When that is the case, the state is two digits away from total loss.[38]

Other arbitrary interpretations are given to chants (I retain French transliterations):

> Tseu kuong asked his music master I: "I heard that there are specific chants appropriate to each person; can you tell me what are the chants that are appropriate to a person of my character?" Master I answered: "I am a clumsy musician; why ask me what is most appropriate? However, I can tell you what I have heard, and you may decide for yourself. Those who are generous and calm, sweet and correct, should chant the songs of the Cheu king called *soung*. Those who are magnanimous and calm, very intelligent and sincere, should chant the songs of the Cheu king called *ta ia*. Those who are respectful, reserved, and friends of ritual, should chant the songs of the Cheu king called *siao ia*. Those who are correct, simply, and calm, friends of duty and very humble, should chant the songs of the Cheu king called *foung*. Those who are straight, good, and beneficent, should

[38] Séraphin Couvreur, *Mémoires sur les bienséances et les cérémonies*, 2 vols. (Leiden and Paris: Cathasia, 1950), 2:48–49; my translation.

chant the songs of the Chang dynasty. Those who are sweet, good, and resourceful, should chant the songs of Ts'i. Man corrects himself and exhibits virtue by means of chants. He prompts himself to act, and heaven and earth respond to his action: the four seasons are tempered, the stars follow their regular courses, all beings develop."[39]

In Taoism, many of the ancient rites of China seem to have been combined and preserved. The resulting ceremonies resemble Vedic ritual in respect to their complexity and structure.[40] The following brief remarks are from a comparative study on Taoist and Vedic ritual.[41] All Taoist sources assume that without ritual activity, nature would lose its perfect harmony: the seasons would not appear in regular succession and the crops would not ripen. Most Taoaist ritual manuals do not provide explicit meaning or interpretations, but they may display talismanic diagrams and mandalalike structures. Some of the recitations and chants that accompany the rites are closely related to the ritual action, in others the relationship is more remote, and often there appears to be no link at all. Sometimes the reverse holds: the words may seem appropriate, but not the action. K. M. Schipper writes:

> When investigating the meaning of Taoist ritual, it soon becomes clear that there is not one general value system, but a number of different and overlapping ones. They no doubt reflect different stages and moments in the continuous quest for meaning and periodically renewed adjustments and additions to cope with the preoccupations of the time. Yet at the same time the core of ritual was preserved and subsequent transformations in meaning did not touch fundamental ritual actions like singing, the burning of incense, and the disposal of sacred, be it often unintelligible writings.

[39] Ibid., 2:111–112.

[40] See K. M. Schipper, *Le Fen-teng: Rituel taoiste* (Paris: École Française d'Extrême Orient, 1975); idem, *Le Corps taoïste* (Paris: Fayard, 1982).

[41] K. M. Schipper and Frits Staal, *Vedic and Taoist Ritual: A Comparative Study*, forthcoming.

I believe that more wide-ranging conclusions could be derived from these varied data, though it would take more time to derive them than I have at my disposal. For although philosophy is on the one hand a fickle attempt at making sense of ritual, it can also have close links with the sciences. There is no such thing as conceptual analysis that is confined to philosophers and from which others are excluded; in fact, the best pieces of conceptual analysis with which we are familiar can be found in mathematics, logic, linguistics, the science of ritual, and a score of other fields. This fact is related to the untenability of the distinction between the analytic and the synthetic. To say that the Upaniṣads are full of extravagant absurdities, while such Indian scientists of ritual and grammar as Baudhāyana, Pāṇini, Āpastamba, Kātyāyana, or Patañjali have contributed great insights, is not so different from the observation that, in our own time, Marx, Freud, Darwin, Einstein, or Chomsky have made more important contributions toward the understanding of the world than any philosopher. Some philosophers have contributed more than others because they abandoned conventional distinctions, in particular the distinction between philosophy and the sciences. Others have contributed less, or next to nothing, because instead of studying the world they confined themselves to reading other philosophers. 'Philosophy', however, is an extremely loose term that covers a great variety of concepts. We may very well make a parade of that term in Asia as we have long been doing in the West; but it is not the same kind of thing in both, and it cannot be isolated from other things in either.

WING-TSIT CHAN

Chu Hsi and World Philosophy

LET ME BEGIN by recalling the first East–West Philosophers' Conference in 1939. It was a very small beginning. There were only five of us: Charles A. Moore, the organizer, and Filmore S. C. Northrop from Yale representing the West, George P. Conger of Minnesota representing India, Takakusu Junjirō, the eminent Buddhist scholar, representing Japan, and I, representing China. We dealt with generalities and superficialities and lumped Brahman, Tao, and Buddhist Thusness together. We hardly went beyond Spinoza in western philosophy and confined Chinese thought largely to the pre-Christian era. We saw the world as two halves, East and West.[1] In his book, which resulted from the conference, Northrop neatly but sharply contrasted the entire East, as using doctrines out of concepts by intuition, to the West, as constructing its doctrines out of concepts by postulation.[2] Contrast that conference in 1939 with the International Conference on Chu Hsi, held in Honolulu, two years ago, and you will see the tremendous progress made in the past several decades. Eighty-six members participated instead of twenty or so. Almost all of the top-notch Neoconfucian scholars from China and Japan attended, along with authorities from other parts of the world. Thirty-three young scholars from Asia and the United States were recruited as fellows. Topics were discussed on a highly philosophical level, including some novel to the West, such as Chu Hsi's *Treatise on Jen* (humanity), his theory of the standard and the expedient, his system of thought regarding Changes, his discipline of propriety or system of rites, his literary criticism,

[1] For results of the conference, see Charles A. Moore, ed., *Philosophy East and West* (Princeton: Princeton University Press, 1944).

[2] F.S.C. Northrop, *The Meeting of East and West* (New York: Macmillan, 1946), p. 448.

and his interpretation of wisdom as hidden and stored. The last has not been studied even in China or Japan, let alone in the West.

In the intervening years, many international conferences have been held in America and Europe on Asian philosophy, often on a comparative basis. These meetings were largely initiated and directed by Professor Wm. Theodore de Bary. The frontier of Chinese, Japanese, and Korean thought was thereby greatly broadened, and the horizon on Asian thought, as far as the West is concerned, has been greatly lifted.

While conferences were being held in the West, international symposia have also been conducted in Asia during the past several years. The most notable are the Hangchow conference on Neoconfucianism in 1981 and the series of conferences of the T'oegye Institute at Seoul, Cambridge, Massachusetts, and Germany. To me the most interesting thing about the T'oegye series is that a comparative study shows how Chu Hsi's philosophy developed differently in the two different cultures. T'oegye (Yi Hwang, 1501–1570, honored as Master of T'oegye) was, of course, the most prominent follower of Chu Hsi in Korea. He carried on a long debate at first with his pupil Ki Kobong (Ki Taesung, 1527–1572) and later with Yi I (honored as Master Yulgok, 1536–1584) over the question of whether the Four Beginnings[3]—namely, humanity, righteousness, propriety, and wisdom—and the Seven Feelings—joy, anger, love, pleasure, sorrow, hate and dislike, and desire—proceeded from principle (*li*) or from material force (*ch'i*). T'oegye contended that the Four Beginnings issued from principle and that material force follows it, while the Seven Feelings issue from material force and principle rides on it. Kobong and Yulgok, however, refused to separate material force from principle or the Seven Feelings from the Four Beginnings. This is the famous Four–Seven debate, which lasted for more than a century.[4] I shall not deal here with the question of

[3] *Book of Mencius*, 2A.6.

[4] For a story of this debate, see Youn Sa-soon, *A Study on Toegye's Philoso-*

li and *ch'i*. My interest lies rather in the numbers four and seven. Whenever Neoconfucianists in China talk about feelings, they always refer to the four mentioned in the opening chapter of the *Doctrine of the Mean*—joy, anger, sorrow, and pleasure—instead of the seven mentioned in the *Book of Rites*.[5] Why this difference? My suspicion is that it is due to the difference in the development of Chu Hsi's philosophy in the two cultures. The *Book of Rites*, being one of the Five Classics,[6] exerted a great influence in the first millennium of the Christian era in China. For decades Chu Hsi was intensely interested in this and in allied texts on rites. In 1190, however, he grouped the *Great Learning*, the *Analects*, the *Book of Mencius*, and the *Doctrine of the Mean* as the Four Books. Ever since, this set, instead of the Five Classics, has served as the main source of Chinese thought, the basic texts in school education, and the official texts for civil-service examinations. Chu Hsi considered the Five Classics less important than the Four Books, for he contended that the Classics were not the direct words of Confucius (551–479 B.C.) and Mencius (ca. 372–ca. 289 B.C.).[7] As a result, the *Doctrine of Mean* became the main source, instead of the *Book of Rites*, as far as feelings are concerned. Hence feelings have been referred to as four, the remaining three being regarded as functions of the four, while joy is sometimes replaced by apprehension. My question is: Since Korean Neoconfucianists talked about the Seven Feelings instead of the four, has the tradition of the *Book or Rites* been stronger than the *Doctrine of the Mean* in Korea? The latter is of course a chapter in the *Book of Rites*, but it has been singled out

---

phy (Seoul: Korean University Press, 1980), and Tu Wei-ming, "Yi Hwang's Perception of the Mind," *Toegye Hakbo* [The journal of Toegye study] 19 (1978).

[5] *Book of Rites*, "The Evolution of Rites," sect. 23.

[6] *Book of Odes*, *Book of History*, *Book of Changes*, *Book of Rites*, and the *Annals of Spring and Autumn*.

[7] Chu Hsi, *Chu Tzu yü-lei* [Classified Conversations of Master Chu] 104.12 (Taipei: Cheng-chung, 1970), p. 4156.

to be a Classic itself, and it has been very strong in the Chinese tradition.

In the 140-chapter *Chu Tzu yü-lei* (Classified Conversations of Master Chu), there are only two brief conversations on the relation between the Four Beginnings and the Seven Feelings. In one, a student expressed the opinion that the Seven Feelings seem to issue from nature, that only anger issues from the sense of shame and dislike (which is the Beginning of Righteousness), and that joy, anger, sorrow, and desire all issue from the sense of commiseration (which is the Beginning of Humanity).[8] Chu Hsi replied, "Where do sorrow and apprehension issue from? As we come to think about it, they both issue from the sense of commiseration, for apprehension is caution to the highest degree. But the Seven Feelings cannot be matched with the Four Beginnings. The former cut across the latter."[9] When another pupil asked about the match, he answered, "Joy, anger, love, and dislike are matters of humanity and righteousness, sorrow and apprehension are based on propriety, and desire belongs to water and hence is wisdom. We roughly say so, but it is difficult to match."[10] In other words, it is not feasible to match the Four Beginnings with the Seven Feelings. What the Chinese Neoconfucianists wanted was a four-to-four correspondence.

This type of correspondence has prevailed in China since the third or fourth century B.C. For example, *wu-hsing*—the Five Agents or Five Operations of water, fire, wood, metal, and earth—were equated with the five tones, the five colors, the five stars, the five emperors of antiquity, and more. Chu Hsi faithfully followed this tradition. He equated the Four Qualities of Changes—origination, flourishing, advantage, and firmness—with wood, fire, metal, and water, earth being the basis of the four.[11] In speaking about the human person, he said that "its material force is spring, summer, autumn, and

[8] *Book of Mencius*, 2A.6.

[9] Chu Hsi, *Chu Tzu yü-lei*, 87.85 (p. 3558).

[10] Ibid., 87.87 (p. 3559).

[11] Ibid., 94.61 (p. 3776), and the *Book of Changes*, hexagram no. 1.

winter, its stuff is metal, wood, water, fire, and earth, and its principle [the Five Constant Virtues of] humanity, righteousness, propriety, wisdom, and faithfulness."[12] He perpetuated the age-old correspondence of the Five Agents with the Five Constant Virtues.[13] Metal, wood, water, and fire, he said, not only correspond with humanity, righteousness, propriety, and wisdom; they are never separated.[14] Can we say that the tradition of correspondence was weaker or absent in Korea? If so, what factors were responsible? These are intriguing questions in comparative study.

In the case of the Hangchow conference on Neoconfucianism, to which Professor de Bary and I were the two foreign guests invited from the United States along with eight others from various countries, its chief significance was the belated recognition of Chu Hsi's importance in Chinese history. For the first three decades of the People's Republic, he was simply ignored. Of the 213 books published there between 1949 and 1963, only one was about him and that dealt with his school in Japan; and of the 756 articles published in the same period, the four on him were generally derogatory.[15] In the conference in 1981, however, which was attended by 262 Chinese scholars, the section on Chu Hsi was marked by highly scholarly discussions and fairly objective evaluation. There was very little comparative study. His philosophy has usually been described as objective idealism, but the western term is applied to him with practically no analysis. In the plenary sessions, Chu Hsi was criticized as a defender of feudalism, but his ideas were judged transformable to support Marxism. If mainland scholars do more comparative study, they will find that Chu Hsi was used to support the regimes in China, Korea, and Japan, but those regimes could not escape from his influence.

Modern Japanese promotion of Chu Hsi studies has taken a

[12] Ibid., 94.62 (p. 3777).

[13] Ibid., 94.66 (p. 3777).

[14] Ibid., 1.11 (p. 4).

[15] See Wing-tsit Chan, *Chinese Philosophy, 1949–1963* (Honolulu: East-West Center Press, 1967), pp. 38, 193–194.

different route. Instead of conferences as in Korea and China, Neoconfucian scholars in Japan have devoted their energies chiefly to publication. Vast volumes of indexes have been published on Chu Hsi's work. Beginning in 1974, a huge series of fifteen volumes on Chu Hsi began to appear.[16] This series is in addition to several others that include many Neoconfucian works by Chu Hsi and others. A great number have been reprinted in Taiwan. Of these I shall mention only one, which has yet to attract the attention of western, mainland, or even Taiwanese scholars: the *Chu Tzu nien-p'u* (Chronological Biography of Master Chu), compiled by Yeh Kung-hui in 1431. It is the oldest extant chronological biography of Chu Hsi. There is no doubt that it drew largely from the first chronological biography of the Master by his pupil Li Fang-tzu, compiled before 1237. Li's work has long been lost. In the last two hundred years, the standard chronological biography is the one by Wang Mao-hung (1668–1741), which was completed in 1741, the year he died, but was not published until ten years later. Wang had to depend on Li Mo's chronological biography of 1552 and Hung Ch'ü-wu's of 1700. We are very fortunate, therefore, to have an account several hundred years older. The wonder is that it generally confirms the account given by Wang, which implies that the several accounts over the centuries are generally reliable. As has been said, the first chronological biography was lost in China. So was Yeh's, though it was fortunately preserved in Korea. From Korea it went into Japan, and now from Japan it has returned to China. The copy preserved in the Cabinet Library of Tokyo was printed in both Japan and Taiwan in 1972.[17]

FROM the foregoing, it is clear that the comparative study of Chu Hsi has taken a giant step forward. In spite of this encouraging picture, however, there are still a couple of hurdles

[16] *Shushigaku daikei*, ed. Morohashi Tetsuji et al. [Great Chu Hsi Studies Series] (Tokyo: Meitoku shuppansha, 1974).

[17] In *Chin-shih Han-chi ts'ung-k'an* [Recent Chinese Work Series] (Taipei: Kuang-wen, 1972), vol. 21.

to overcome. The first is to appraise Chinese philosophy by western standards. In my opinion, western study of Chu Hsi is still conducted very much from the western point of view. That is to say, Chu Hsi is still looked at from the outside, especially from the Christian standpoint. This is not bias, not by any means. It is simply that Christian thought is so closely linked with western philosophy that a western philosopher is bound to view Chu Hsi with a Christian eye. Let me illustrate this with just one example of the western idea of Chu Hsi's concept of God.

In the late seventeenth and early eighteenth centuries, there was a heated controversy among Catholic fathers over Chu Hsi's belief in God. Father Niccolò Longobardi (1565–1655) held that neither Confucius nor the Neoconfucians believed in an anthropomorphic God.[18] In this he was supported by Father Antonio de Santa María (1602–1669).[19] Nicolas Malebranche (1638–1715) even set up an imaginary debate between a Chinese philosopher and a Christian philosopher. By the Chinese philosopher, he meant a pupil of Chu Hsi, who was arguing for materialism, for in his view, Chu Hsi did not believe in God and was a materialist.[20] This line of thought was continued at the end of the nineteenth century by Stanislas Le Gall, who insisted that Chu Hsi was a materialist and an atheist.[21] On the other side, following the lead of Father Matteo Ricci (1552–1610), who believed that the Confucian *Shang-ti* (Lord-on-High) and *T'ien* (Heaven) were identical with the Catholic *T'ien-chu* (Heavenly Lord), Leibniz (1646–1716) maintained in 1710 that although the foundation of Chu Hsi's philosophy is

[18] Niccolò Longobardi, *Traité sur quelques points de la religion des Chinois* (Paris: Josse, 1701).

[19] Antonio de Santa María, *Traité sur quelques points importans de la mission de la Chine* (Paris, 1710).

[20] Nicolas Malebranche, *Entretien d'un philosophe chrétien et d'un philosophe chinois dur l'existence et la nature de Dieu* (Paris: M. David, 1708).

[21] Stanislas Le Gall, *Le Philosophe Tchou Hi; sa doctrine, son influence* (Shanghai: Imprimerie de la Mission Catholique, 1894): also *T'oung Pao* n.s. 6 (1895): 111.

principle and nature, and principle is abstract without any anthropomorphic character, still principle can be interpreted as an anthropomorphic God, as Ricci had believed, for it is a moral principle and can therefore be equated with God and is not a materialistic reality as Longobardi had supposed.[22] Le Gall's interpretation was strongly attacked by Charles de Harlez, who pointed out that in one of Chu Hsi's conversations, which Le Gall had translated himself, he said that *t'ien* sometimes means the blue sky, sometimes means the Lord, and sometimes means principle. To de Harlez, there was no doubt that Chu Hsi believed in the Lord.[23]

The Catholic position was reaffirmed by a Protestant, J. P. Bruce of Oxford. In 1918, he published an article in which he said that *li* has a religious character because it includes benevolence and wisdom and *T'ien* is the Lord.[24] When he published his book *Chu Hsi and His Masters*,[25] he used the title of the article for the fourth part of the book, thus reemphasizing Chu Hsi's theistic position. His main point is that Chu Hsi regarded Heaven as the Divine Immanence and the Supreme Ruler, and thus anthropomorphic. Several decades later, in *History of Scientific Thought*, the second volume of his monumental work *Science and Civilisation in China*, Joseph Needham did not discuss Chu Hsi's concept of God specifically. But he did mention that Chu Hsi did not approve of the conception of a personal God, and this point was appreciated much better by Le Gall than by Bruce, who read into it his Protestant theology.[26]

[22] In a letter to M. Nicolas de Remond in Baron Gottfried Wilhelm von Leibniz, *Opera omnia*, ed. Ludovici Dutens (Geneva: Fratres de Tournes, 1710).

[23] Charles de Harlez, "Tschou Hi était-il athée?—Tschou Hi et le Peȓe Le Gall," *Le Muséon* 14 (1895): 411–414. Le Gall translated Chu Hsi's conversation about *T'ien* from chap. 49 of the *Chu Tzu ch'üan-shu* [Complete Works of Master Chu]. The original source of the conversation is the *Chu Tzu yü-lei* 1.22 (p. 8).

[24] J. P. Bruce, "The Theistic Import of the Sung Philosophy," *Journal of the North China Branch of the Royal Asiatic Society* 49 (1918): 111–127.

[25] (London: Probsthain, 1923).

[26] (Cambridge: Cambridge University Press, 1956), p. 492.

I have reported on the controversy elsewhere and need not go into detail here.[27] My point is that Chu Hsi's philosophy was entirely viewed from the western perspective. Father Longobardi and Father Sainte-Marie, for example, contended that the spiritual beings or cosmic forces (*kuei-shen*) of the Neoconfucians were different from Christian angels and that *hun* (the spirit of man's vital force expressed in his intelligence and his power of breathing) and *p'o* (the spirit of man's physical nature expressed in bodily movements) were not the Christian soul, and as such they were not acceptable. Even Needham was not free from his western perspective. In explaining why science did not develop in China in the past several centuries, he maintains that science flourishes in Europe because there was the belief in God as personal lawgiver, but since the Chinese do not believe in a personal God, there was no personal lawgiver and the concept of natural laws failed to evolve.[28] To him, Chu Hsi's *li* was order or pattern and as such excluded the notion of Law.[29] He has never explained why it was possible for Taoism to have natural law without a lawgiver; why, if it was indeed true that a lawgiver was required for science to develop in Europe (a point yet to be proved), it automatically follows that one will be required in other cultures; and why science did not develop in Europe two millennia ago when the concept of a personal God emerged. I cannot help feeling that all these contentions, right or wrong, are from the western point of view. Besides, to say that the Neoconfucians did not believe in a personal God simply means that their conception of *T'ien* differs from the Christian God not in being personal but in personal

[27] Wing-tsit Chan, "The Study of Chu Hsi in the West," *Journal of Asian Studies* 35 (1976): 555–577; Japanese translation, "Ō-Bei no Shushigakku," by Takata Hiroshige, in *Shushigaku daikei*, vol. 1, *Shushigaku nyūmon* [Introduction to the Study of Chu Hsi], pp. 491–529; Chinese translation, "Hsi-feng tui Chu Hsi ti yen-chiu," by Liu K'un-i, *Chung-kuo che hsüeh* [Chinese philosophy] 5 (1981): 191–217; Original Chinese version, "Ou-mei chih Chu Tzu hsüeh," *Sinological Monthly* 31 (July 1974): 1–23.

[28] Needham, *History of Scientific Thought*, pp. 518, 562–564, 567, 582.

[29] Ibid., p. 572.

expression. I am glad to say that the western perspective is fast fading, as more and more western scholars have closer contacts with Chinese scholars, travel more, and use a greater number of original sources. They are beginning to look at Asian thought from within.

At this point I may be excused if I say a few words about Chu Hsi's religious life. His ideas about *T'ien* and *kuei-shen* are well known. Many western scholars still think he is too rationalistic. By that they mean that Chu Hsi lacked an intuitive insight necessary for religious belief and behavior. They never allow that rationality and intuition can go together. Others require that Chu Hsi's *T'ien* must be personal in the same way as their own God. Still others think that Chu Hsi was not a diligent practitioner of religion.

Recently, when I wanted to look into the matter, I was surprised to find that there is practically no account of his religious practice in any language. In the biographical account (*hsing-chuang*) written by his pupil Huang Kan (1152–1221), there are sentences about his sincerity and devotion in religious sacrifices in the family temple and before Confucius.[30] These sentences have been repeated in chronological biographies and similar works. But there is hardly anything more. The record is scanty partly because the Chinese consider religious life to be a private matter and not something for public discussion and partly because material on the subject is scattered and obscure. But the more I investigated, the more I found that he was an extremely religious person. Not only did he rise before dawn to perform religious sacrifice, he cared for his ancestors' graves in Anhui enough to make two long trips to visit them. When his mother died, he built a cottage by the side of her grave and stayed there for years. He reported to Confucius in a religious ceremony at every stage of his professional development, such as building a study or a library, reconstructing

[30] Chu Hsi, *Chu Tzu wen-chi* [Collection of Literary Works by Master Chu] (*Ssu-pu pei-yao* [Essentials of the Four Libraries], ed. entitled *Chu Tzu ta-ch'üan* [Complete Literary Works of Master Chu], Shanghai: Chung-hua shu chü, 1927–1935), 86.1a–12a.

an academy, or publishing a set of classics. As a government official, aside from practical measures to prevent drought, he prayed to deities for help.[31] During most of his life he was devoted to revising social and religious ceremonies. He was so insistent on certain points about imperial temples and imperial graves that he offended the court and was finally dismissed from office as lecturer to the emperor. As the persecution of his school as "false learning" became increasingly severe, he was urged to send his pupils home instead of continuing teaching, but he said that blessing and catastrophe depend on one's *ming*, that is, one's destiny or fate, or Heaven's mandate.[32] Even on his deathbed, he wrote letters to pupils to complete his compilation of books on rites. When pupils came to see him the day before he died, he was already seriously ill, but he told them, "This is how principle operates. We must all make strong efforts. Only then can progress be achieved."[33] To him the mandate of Heaven was extremely real and personal. It was not that the Lord on High came, like the Jade Emperor in the Taoist religion, to declare that his days of life were now up. Rather in his view, the mandate of Heaven is like the law of gravity, which operates automatically. But the law itself originates in heaven. As the beginning sentence of the *Doctrine of the Mean* says, "What Heaven imparts [*ming*, commands] to man is his nature."

The second hurdle to overcome in comparative study is the matter of translation. Let me first deal very briefly with several controversial renderings. A little earlier I referred to *li* and *ch'i*. Needham understands *li* as order or pattern, but I prefer to interpret it as principle. Actually whether one translates it as "principle," "reason," "law," "order," or "pattern" is a matter of personal choice. None of these is really satisfactory, for no English philosophical term corresponds exactly to a Chinese philosophical term. No matter which term is chosen, some

[31] Ibid., 86.7a–9a.

[32] Chu Hsi, *Chu Tzu yü-lei* 107.27 (p. 4246).

[33] Wang Mao-hung, *Chu Tzu nien-p'u* (Taipei: World Book Company, 1962), p. 228.

element of the Chinese term is left out and some element of the English term is brought in. This is the price we have to pay in translation. It is true that in the Han Dynasty (206 B.C.–A.D. 220), commentators of the Confucian classics interpreted *li* in the sense of order or pattern, like grains in a piece of jade; but in Chu Hsi it certainly means more than an arrangement or an organization. He definitely said that before the existence of heaven and earth there is *li*.[34] The main thing is to distinguish its two basic meanings and apply the translation carefully to its pertinent period in history.

The translation of *ch'i* requires a more careful consideration. Originally *ch'i* means breath. As such it is essentially a movement based on some physical stuff. Whatever the translation, this operational aspect must be indicated. This is the reason for my translation of "material force." "Matter-energy" will do, except that the hyphenated compound is clumsy. Generally I try to avoid hyphenated translations. Not only do they impede smooth reading; they actually introduce an ambiguity because the reader is not sure which part of the compound is meant in a particular context. "Ether" suggests air. It may be considered operational but it is too physical. Because of the dynamic character of *ch'i*, renderings like "matter" and "stuff" will not do because they are too static. *Ch'i* is also psychological, as in the case of *hao-jan chih ch'i* described by Mencius.[35] My translation of "strong, moving power" may be inadequate,[36] but I have not found a better translation. "Vital force" or "vital power" may do in such cases.

This dynamic quality is at the heart of the translation of *wu-hsing*, metal, wood, water, fire, and earth.[37] According to the commentary of Cheng Hsüan (127–200) on the "Hung-fan" (Grand Plan) chapter of the *Book of History*, where the phrase originated, *hsing* is "material force operating according to na-

[34] Chu Hsi, *Chu Tzu yü-lei* 1.1 (p. 1).

[35] *Book of Mencius*, 2A.2.

[36] Wing-tsit Chan, *A Source Book in Chinese Philosophy* (Princeton: Princeton University Press, 1963), p. 63.

[37] The order of the five varies in different works and periods.

ture."[38] The term has been variously rendered as "Five Elements," "Five Aspects," "Five Phases," "Five Powers," and more. It can readily be seen that "Five Elements" and "Five Aspects" are too static for this dynamic concept. "Five Powers" is misleading because it is too easily associated with the Three Powers (*san-ts'ai*), that is, heaven, earth, and man. "Five Phases" is now popular among many scholars. As long as the term denotes five stages or the succession of five dynasties, it is appropriate. But *wu-hsing* is not merely a theory of history. Each of the five represents a quality, like liquidity and hotness for fire and liquidity and coolness for water. As it is said in the "Hung-fan," "Water means whatever is moist and descending and fire means whatever is heated and ascending."[39] This being the case, the character of each of the five has an influence on other things. It is for this reason that water is equated with wisdom, for example, because a wise person benefits everything, adjusts to varying conditions, and is humble. Thus the five correspond to the Five Constant Virtues in the order of righteousness, humanity, wisdom, propriety, and faithfulness.[40] Basically, *hsing* means to act. Metal, for example, acts on something and causes it to acquire a certain quality, very much like a chemical agent causing a substance to change. For this reason I have translated the term as "Five Agents." It is admittedly unsatisfactory, but none of the alternatives is really better.

In the case of *ching*, there is a double meaning. In ancient classics, it definitely means "reverence." It is often paired with *kung*, to respect. Both imply an object, whether a person, a deity, or a thing. It is an external expression. In Neoconfucianism, however, it has acquired a new dimension, for it now denotes a state of mind and does not direct the mind outward. As defined by Ch'eng I (1033–1107), it is "concentrating on one

[38] Cheng Hsüan's commentary is found in the *Shih-san-ching chu-shu* [Commentaries and Subcommentaries of the Thirteen Classics].

[39] *Book of History*, "Hung-Fan," sect. 5.

[40] Cheng Hsüan's commentary on the first sentence of the *Doctrine of the Mean*.

thing and not deviating from it."[41] His pupil Yin Tun (1071–1142) interpreted it in terms of "the mind being so collected that not even the smallest thing can creep in."[42] Another pupil, Hsieh Liang-tso (1050–ca. 1120), understood it as "being alert at all times."[43] Thus Ch'eng I and his school raised the concept of *ching* to a new level. Chu Hsi elaborated on Ch'eng I's doctrine and made it a cardinal idea in his philosophy. Because there is no better translation, I have followed J. P. Bruce and used "seriousness." Most scholars, however, still use "reverence," or as a compromise, "reverent seriousness." One of the most famous examples of *ching* is that when Ch'eng Hao (1012–1085), Ch'eng I's elder brother, wrote Chinese characters, he was very *ching*.[44] It can be argued that calligraphy was the object of his reverence, but I do not think he became *ching* only after the finished writing. His mind was *ching* before he started and continued to be so throughout the process, for *ching* must not be interrupted. Graham's "composure" comes very close to it, except that it may easily lead the reader to think of another Chinese character, also pronounced **ching*, which means tranquility. I do not object to "reverence" because of its religious connotation. After all, Chu Hsi was very religious. I simply want his philosophy clearly understood.

The historical evolution is even clearer in the case of the concept *jen*. From the original meanings of weakness and benevolence in the ancient classics, to "benevolence" and "universal virtue" in Confucius, to "man's heart" in Mencius,[45] to "love" in the Confucians in the Han dynasty, to "universal love" in

[41] Ch'eng I, *I-shu* [Surviving Works], 15.1a, compiled by Chu Hsi, in the *Erh-Ch'eng ch'üan-shu* [Complete Works of the Two Ch'engs] (Shanghai: Chung-hua shu-chü, 1927–1935).

[42] Yin Tun, *Yin Ho-ching chi* [Collected Works of Yin Tun] (*Cheng-i-t'ang ch'üan-shu* [Complete Series of the Hall of Rectifying Principle] ed., Fuchou: Cheng-i Press, 1866), p. 20b.

[43] Hsieh Liang-tso, *Shang-ts'ai yü-lu* 2.13a, in *Chin-shih Han-chi ts'ung k'an* (Taipei: Kuang-wen), vol. 8.

[44] Ch'eng I, *I-shu*, 3.2a.

[45] *Book of Mencius*, 6A.11.

Han Yü (768–824),[46] to "impartiality" in Chou-Tun-i,[47] it went through a long process of evolution. But in the Ch'eng brothers there was a radical development. On the one hand, a man of *jen* forms one body with heaven and earth;[48] and on the other, *jen*, the same character in another sense, is seed,[49] the moral quality that produces all other virtues. The development culminated in Chu Hsi, who defined it as "the character of love and the principle of the mind."[50] He began his *Treatise on Jen* with the sentence, "The mind of heaven and earth is to produce things."[51] Obviously no single translation can cover all these ideas. "Benevolence" or "humaneness" may do for *jen* as a particular virtue. "Human-heartedness" is popular but is limited only to Mencius's interpretation. I have chosen "humanity" simply to preserve the same translation as is used for it in the Four Beginnings. As Ch'eng I has said, spoken of separately, *jen* is one virtue—namely benevolence—but spoken of collectively, it embraces all the four constant virtues.[52] He could have said all virtues, for it is the universal virtue that makes all virtues possible. I also want to preserve the homonym of *jen* meaning man. In the *Doctrine of the Mean*, it is said that "*Jen* (humanity) is **jen* (man),"[53] that is, *jen* is that which makes a man a man and not a beast. Often one has to transliterate, but I am satisfied to use "benevolence" where *jen* is a particular virtue and "humanity" where it is a universal virtue. For the same linguistic reason I have translated *T'ai-chi* as "Great Ultimate" because the word *t'ai* comes from the word

[46] Han Yü, *Han Ch'ang-li ch'üan-chi* [Collected Works of Han Yü] (Shanghai: Chung-hua shu-chü, 1927–1935), 11.1a, "Yüan Tao" [An Inquiry on the Way].

[47] Chou Tun-i, *T'ung-shu* [Penetrating the *Book of Changes*], chap. 37.

[48] Ch'eng I, *I-shu*, 2A.2a, 3a.

[49] Ibid., 18.2a.

[50] Chu Hsi, *Lun-yü chi-chu* [Collected Commentaries on the Analects], comment on the *Analects* 1.2.

[51] Chu Hsi, *Chu Tzu wen-chi* 67.20a.

[52] Ch'eng I, *I-chuan* [Commentary on the *Book of Changes*] 1.2b, in the *Erh-Ch'eng ch'üan-shu*.

[53] *Doctrine of the Mean*, chap. 20.

ta, both meaning great. "Supreme Ultimate" is probably better English, but I think there is merit in preserving the homonym. Besides, "supreme" suggests a hierarchy, while *T'ai-chi* is beyond comparison.

The foregoing may still be considered as a matter of preference. The common translation of the next is definitely a mistake. I mean the phrase *huo-jan kuan-t'ung*, a concept central to Chu Hsi's doctrine of the investigation of things. In his commentary on the *Great Learning*, he emended, to use his own word, a section that he thought was lost. By way of explanation, he said, "If one wishes to extend his knowledge to the utmost, he must investigate the principles of all things he comes into contact with. . . . He must proceed from what knowledge he has of their principles, and investigate further until he reaches the limit. After exerting himself in this way for a long time, he will one day achieve a wide and far-reaching penetration."[54] There is no problem about *kuan-t'ung*, which means penetration, or even *huo-jan*, which means wide and far-reaching. Since the character *huo* has as a component *ku* meaning a valley, its meaning should be obvious. But most scholars would add the word "sudden" to mean a sudden penetration. This tendency may be due to James Legge's translation of *i-tan* as sudden, but Legge was wrong, for *i-tan* simply means some time later or someday. Possibly these translators may have been misled by Chu Hsi himself, for when he discussed this concept with his students, he used the term *t'o-jan*, which means to get rid of,[55] as if *huo-jan* and *t'o-jan* were interchangeable. This has misled some to interpret *huo-jan kuan-t'ung* as a mystical experience of sudden release, a liberation, a leap, a breakthrough. A consultation with any dictionary will reveal that *t'o-jan* does not mean liberation but freedom from obstacles such as misconceptions and old theories. There is no suggestion of a sudden leap, as typical of mysticism. The penetra-

[54] Chu Hsi, *Ta-hsüeh chang-chu* [Commentary on the *Great Learning*], chap. 5.

[55] Chu Hsi, *Chi Tzu yü-lei*, 18.7, 9, 15 (pp. 627–628, 632).

tion is an intellectual one, without the slightest trace of mystical experience. I am not denying the mystical element in Chu Hsi's philosophy: there is plenty of it, but it is of a different type. In Chu Hsi's theory of knowledge, one must follow certain steps and proceed gradually. Some scholars have compared Chu Hsi's penetration with the gradual enlightenment of Meditation Buddhism, but adding the word "sudden" would make Chu Hsi's system sudden enlightenment instead.

Now let me offer some guidelines for translation. As a translator over several decades, I have adopted them myself. The first is that I must translate. Many oriental scholars are prone to transliterate, as indeed the Chinese did, when they imported Buddhism from India. We still have *seng* for *sangha* (monks), *p'u-t'i* for *bodhi* (wisdom), and many others. By the third century, however, they had to match Buddhist concepts with Chinese concepts, or *ko-i*, like equating *tathatā* (suchness) with the Taoist *pen-wu* (original nonbeing or pure being). The result was not only to make Buddhist ideas more readily understandable to the Chinese but also to enable Buddhism to be more readily accepted. The Buddhist experience should be our guide in translation, either from Chinese to English or vice versa.

Recently I came across an interesting case of cross-fertilization in translation among Confucianism, Taoism, and Buddhism, namely, the case of *ching-she*. The term came from the *Kuan Tzu* and means a place for refinement by achieving calmness in the mind.[56] In the first century, a number of Confucian scholars called their huts or cottages *ching-she*, where they lectured and taught while enjoying a private life. Before long the Taoists called their places *ching-she* also but used them for spiritual cultivation, especially for the refinement of the mind or vital force. By the fourth century, the Buddhists used the term to translate *vihāra*, a Buddhist retreat. The Buddhists built so many *ching-she* in the ensuing centuries that the term was

[56] *Kuan Tzu* (*Ssu-pu ts'ung-k'an* [The Four Libraries series] ed., Shanghai: Commercial Press, 1920–1922), 16.2a.

understood to be Buddhist exclusively. When the pupils of Lu Hsiang-shan (Lu Chiu-yüan, 1139–1193) built him a cottage in 1187, he had to explain that the name was acceptable because it was originally Confucian.[57] When Chu Hsi built a cottage on the Han-ch'üan Mountain by the side of his mother's grave in 1170, the Wu-i Study on Wu-i Mountain in 1183, and the Chu-lin Study in Chien-yang County in 1194 for study and teaching, he called those places *ching-she*. For a strong defender of Confucianism against Buddhism to use a term generally believed to be Buddhist, the attempt must have been desperate. My theory is that Chu Hsi purposely reasserted the Confucian heritage in order to recapture the institution from the Buddhists. This is a clear indication that a translation can have far-reaching consequences.

My second guideline is to interpret as little as possible. There are times at which an interpretation will serve a better purpose. In my recent translation of Ch'en Ch'un's (1159–1223) *Pei-hsi tzu-i* (Neoconfucian Terms Explained), for example, I had a great deal of trouble in trying to find a good English expression for the Chinese phrase *ch'in-ch'ieh*. It has all the elements of being intimate, touching, relevant to life, to the point, and so on. After many attempts, I reached the conclusion the only way out was to interpret differently in different contexts. Interpretation, however, should not replace translation as a general practice.

My third guideline is not to alter the text. I do not mean to be strictly literal, but I do not think a translator should rewrite the text. There is a growing tendency to change the courtesy name, literary name, or posthumous title to a private name. For example, when the text says "Hui-an" or "Wen Kung," the translator would change it to "Chu Hsi." In one excellent translation all the several hundred people mentioned are called by their private names, even though virtually no private name

[57] Lu Hsiang-shan, *Hsiang-shan ch'üan-chi* [Complete Collection of Literary Works of Lu Chiu-yüan] (Shanghai: Chung-hua shu-chü, 1927–1935), 2.5a and 36.15b.

is used in the original text. I suppose the reason for this rewriting is for the sake of uniformity, as if uniformity as such were a virtue, or for the convenience of the reader. The use of the computer or word processor will probably strengthen this tendency. But to render a name differently from the way it appears in the text takes away the personal touch the text provides. In their letters to Chu Hsi or in their records of his conversations, friends and pupils never used his personal name but always addressed him as "Master Chu," or by his literary name "Hui-an" or posthumous title "Wen Kung." In the *Analects* we read "The Master said so-and-so." I shudder to think that a translator should change it to read, "K'ung Ch'iu said so-and-so." All the respect intended is gone.

My fourth guideline is to consult as many commentaries as possible. To understand the meaning of a term in different periods, it is necessary to inquire into the interpretations of different periods. Take the opening sentence of the *Analects*, "Is it not a pleasure to learn and to *hsi* from time to time what has been learned?" James Legge, following Chu Hsi, translated *hsi* as "practice."[58] In revolt against Legge, Arthur Waley chose to rely on Han commentators and rendered the term "to repeat," that is, to recite.[59]

Legge and Waley reflected the commentaries of the *Analects* in two different periods. They probably did not realize that in the nineteenth century both extremes were rejected.[60] Liu Pao-nan (1791–1855), for example, understood *hsi* as both to practice and to recite, taking recitation as but one element of the practice.[61]

My fifth guideline is to avoid confusion with other terms.

[58] James Legge, trans., *The Chinese Classics* (New York: Hurd and Houghton, 1870), the *Analects*.

[59] Arthur Waley, trans., *The Analects of Confucius* (London: Allen & Unwin, 1938).

[60] Commentary on the *Analects* 1.1, by Ho Yen (190–249) in the *Shih-san-ching chu-shu*.

[61] Liu Pao-nan (1791–1855) *Lun-yü cheng-i* [Correct Meanings of the *Analects*] (Shanghai: Chung-hua shu-chü, 1927–1935).

"Love" for *jen*, for example, may be good for the Han period, but "love" immediately reminds one of *ai*, not *jen*. As far as possible, the translator should lead the reader back to the Chinese original.

My sixth guideline is to use a translation that is applicable not only to the work at hand but to other works of other schools, and other periods as well. In the case of *t'i-yung*, for example, whether one translates *t'i* as reality, substance, or essence and *yung* as operation or function, one should use the same translation for Wang Pi (226–249) in the third century, for Chu Hsi in the twelfth, and for Chang Chih-tung (1837–1909) in the nineteenth. Whatever the choice, it should remain consistent. Except for the few cases for which various translations or interpretations are required, a translation should remain consistent for the entire history of Chinese thought so the reader may know that the same concept is being discussed and that it has a continuity.

My seventh guideline has already been suggested, and it is to use different translations for the same term in different contexts. I have referred to *jen* and *ching*. One more example will suffice, the case of *kuei-shen*. Until the advent of Neoconfucianism in the eleventh century, *kuei-shen* had meant spiritual beings and should be rendered as such. But in Chang Tsai (1020–1077) it has come to connote "natural ability of *yin* and *yang*"[62] or negative and positive cosmic forces. For Ch'eng I, *kuei-shen* are "the trace of creation."[63] In such a case, the translator has to recognize the radical difference from the traditional understanding. To Chu Hsi as to other Neoconfucians, *kuei-shen* may mean spiritual beings or *yin* and *yang*. It would be a disaster to render *kuei-shen* in all cases as spiritual beings.

As has been said, Han commentators understood *li* as pattern. But even in Wang Pi, it already denoted a general principle, an unchanging, unalterable truth. This meaning was

[62] Chang Tsai, *Cheng-meng* [Correcting Youthful Ignorance] (Shanghai: Chung-hua shu-chü, 1927–1935), 1.10.

[63] *I-chuan*, 1.7b.

elaborated and refined by Ch'eng I and Chu Hsi. When Tai Chen (1723–1777) invoked the authority of Han scholars to attack Chu Hsi, insisting that originally *li* meant order and that "what the ancients called *li* was never what the latter-day Confucianists called it,"[64] he was turning history upside down. But he could not get away from *li* as universal truth. Again and again he had to say that *li* represented "feelings that do not err."[65] That is exactly how Ch'eng I and Chu Hsi explained the *Doctrine of the Mean*, which says, "When the feelings are aroused and each and all attain due measure and degree, it is called harmony."[66] For scholars to say that the *li* of Ch'eng I and Chu Hsi is the philosophy of order or pattern—as many European scholars do—is to understand Sung Neoconfucianism in terms of Han Confucianism, and that is anachronism, to say the least. I do not deny that the element of pattern is present in *li* in Chu Hsi's system, but it is only an element.

My eighth guideline goes beyond translation. To me, a translation must inform as much as possible. Following this guideline, all terms must be explained, all sets like the Five Constant Virtues must be itemized, all persons and places must be identified or accounted for, the sources of all quotations and allusions must be traced, and all titles of books and treatises must be translated. The last requirement is hardly fulfilled today, but there is a promising new development in this direction. The title of an essay or a book is sometimes extremely difficult to understand. Often one has to read the preface of the work or the biography of the author to find out what is in his mind. But the title throws a great deal of light on the author's personality and outlook and often reveals the fundamental character or purpose of the work. Take, for example, the *Chin-ssu lu*, an anthology compiled with the collaboration of Lü Tsu-ch'ien (1137–1181). The title is derived from the *Analects* 19.6, where Confucius's pupil, Tzu-hsia (507–420

[64] Tai Chen, *Meng Tzu tzu-i shu-cheng* [Commentary on the Meanings of Terms in the *Book of Mencius*] (Taipei: Ta-hua shu-chü, repr. 1978), sect. 1.

[65] Ibid., sects. 2, 3.

[66] *Doctrine of the Mean*, chap. 1.

B.C.), says that "what one should think about should be matters near at hand (*chin-ssu*)." This shows that the focus of the collection was moral cultivation and handling world affairs, not metaphysical speculation: hence the title *Chin-ssu lu* (Records of Reflections on Things at Hand). In fact, Chu Hsi did not even want to include the first chapter on the substance of Tao. It was included only at the insistence of Lü. Even then, Chu Hsi's pupil, Huang Kan, complained that the book had now become *yüan-ssu*, that is, thinking of things far away.[67] Because the *Chin-ssu lu* is the summary statement of the Neoconfucianism of northern Sung (960–1126), we know that the whole Neoconfucian movement rests with solving practical problems and not with intellectual exercise. Only with this understanding can we appreciate Chu Hsi's system of thought.

WE may ask: what is the character of Chu Hsi's thought? Here is a man who has dominated Chinese thought for eight hundred years and has exerted a tremendous influence in other fields as well, not only in China but also in Japan and Korea, a man who wrote, compiled, or commented on more than a hundred works. How can we hope to understand him in twenty minutes? Fortunately his doctrines can neatly be summed up in four Chinese characters: *chü-ching ch'iung-li*, that is, abiding in seriousness and investigating principle to the utmost. These are his own words. In writing to a pupil, he said, "Abiding in seriousness and investigating principle to the utmost—one should not neglect either of them or incline to one side."[68] Elsewhere he said, "To hold seriousness as fundamental is an essential for the preservation of the mind, and to extend knowledge is the effort to advance in learning. The two develop each other."[69] All this is summed up in Huang Kan's "Biological Account," which says, "One should investigate

[67] See my translation, *Reflections of Things at Hand* (New York: Columbia University Press, 1967), pp. xx, 323–324.

[68] Chu Hsi, *Chu Tzu wen-chi*, 41.1b, fourth letter in reply to Feng Tso-su (Feng Yün-chung).

[69] Ibid., 38.49a, letter in reply to Hsü Yüan-min.

principle to the utmost in order to extend one's knowledge and should return to oneself in order to put into practice in a concrete way. One should abide in seriousness so as to complete the process from the beginning to the end."[70] This is easily the best summary of his teaching by an outstanding pupil who probably knew him better than any other.

Chu Hsi at first studied under Li T'ung (1093–1163), who told him to achieve tranquility in order to realize through personal experience the equilibrium before the feelings of joy, anger, sorrow, and pleasure are aroused.[71] Not quite satisfied, he looked to other Neoconfucian thinkers. As a teenager, he was attracted to the teachings of the Ch'eng brothers. In 1168, when he was thirty-nine, he compiled their recorded sayings, now known as the *I-shu* (Surviving Works). In its preface, he said, "If one can abide in seriousness so as to establish the foundation and investigate principle to the utmost so as to extend one's knowledge, one's knowledge will be clearer as the foundation is established, and the foundation will become firmer as one's knowledge is refined." Two years later, he singled out Ch'eng I's saying in the *I-shu*, which says, "Self-cultivation requires seriousness. The pursuit of learning depends on the extension of knowledge."[72] In a letter to a friend, he said that these two sentences completely cover both "substance and function and both what is fundamental and what is secondary."[73] As Wang Mao-hung has observed, since Chu Hsi adopted these two sayings as cardinal principles in 1170, for twenty-five years he never wavered from this position.[74] Wang is correct, because in 1194 Chu Hsi wrote to his pupil and said,

[70] Huang Kan, *Min-chai chi* [Collected Works of Huang Kan] (*Ssu-k'u chen-pen* [Precious Works of the Four Libraries] ed., Shanghai: Commercial Press, 1935), 36.39b.

[71] Chu Hsi, *Yen-p'ing ta-wen* [Li T'ung's Answers to Questions] (*Chu Tzu i-shu* [Surviving Works of Master Chu] ed.), p. 13b.

[72] Ch'eng I, *I-shu*, 18.5b.

[73] Chu Hsi, *Chu Tzu wen-chi*, 35.12b, second letter to Liu Tzu-ch'eng (Liu Ch'ing-chih).

[74] Wang Mao-hung, *Chu Tzu nien-p'u*, pp. 43, 250.

"These two sayings are like the two wheels of a vehicle and the two wings of a bird. No vehicle can go only on one wheel and no bird can fly with only one wing."[75]

It must be pointed out that the two sayings deal with the pursuit of learning (*wei-hsüeh*), which covers both study and moral cultivation. Parallel with this pursuit is the theoretical one, namely, what constitutes the Way (*wei-Tao*). It is the philosophical foundation of the two sayings. On the basis of them, Chu Hsi constructed a system that is virtually his own. What constitutes the Way is also summed up in Huang Kan's "Chronological Account":

> This is what constitutes the Way: As there is the Great Ultimate, *yin* and *yang* are distinguished. As there are *yin* and *yang*, the Five Agents are provided. When [man and things] have received the endowment of the material forces of *yin* and *yang* and the Five Agents and are born, the principle of the Great Ultimate is present in their midst. What heaven has endowed is one's *ming*, what man has received is his nature, what have been affected by things are feelings, and that which commands nature and feelings is the mind. Rooted in human nature are the virtues of humanity, righteousness, propriety, and wisdom, and what issue from feelings are the beginnings of commiseration, shame and dislike, deference and compliance, and right and wrong. When expressed in one's body, they are the functions of hands and feet, ears, the mouth, and the nose, and when manifested in affairs, they are the constant relations of ruler and minister, father and son, husband and wife, elder and younger brothers, and friends. Probing into man, we shall find that principle in others is no different from that in oneself. And considering the realm of things, we shall realize that the principle of things is no different from that of man. These principles penetrate the past and the present and fill space and time. They are not interrupted for any movement and are not ab-

[75] Chu Hsi, *Chu Tzu wen-chi*, 63.19a, letter in reply to Sun Ching-fu (Sun Tzu-hsiu).

sent in any spot. "All of them can be separated to the finest point without becoming disorderly, and can then be combined to the largest extent without missing anything."[76]

Nowhere else can one find such a neat and clear summary of Chu Hsi's philosophical system. The significant point, however, is that in his "Biological Account," Huang Kan put the pursuit of learning ahead of what constitutes the Way. In his understanding of the Master's teaching, there is no doubt that while logical explanations are necessary, the pursuit of learning is of paramount importance.

Modern studies of Chu Hsi in the West as well as in Asia generally begin with a discussion of his theories of the Great Ultimate, principle, and material force. At the Chu Hsi conference, Professor Yamanoi Yū startled his audience by declaring that the concept of the Great Ultimate is of no importance in Chu Hsi's philosophy. He said that the Great Ultimate "remained an alien element in Chu Hsi's theoretical system." He also said that "the word *t'ai-chi* was neither woven closely into Chu Hsi's philosophy nor given its proper place within it."[77] Professor Yamanoi offered several arguments in support of his conclusion. One was that "the word *t'ai-chi* was used nowhere in the *Ssu-shu chi-chu* (Collected Commentaries on the Four Books).[78] Another was that Chu Hsi discussed the Great Ultimate only in connection with Chou Tun-i's *Explanation of the Diagram of the Great Ultimate*.[79]

As the *Collected Commentaries on the Four Books* is the most important work of Chu Hsi, Professor Yamanoi has a point. Chu Hsi spent decades on the work and was still revising his

[76] Huang Kan, *Mien-chai chi*, 36.40a–b. The quotation is from Chu Hsi's *Ta-hsüeh huo-wen* (Questions and Answers on the *Great Learning*) (*Chin-shih Han-chi ts'ung-k'an*, vol. 5), p. 8a.

[77] Paper presented at the international conference on Chu Hsi, "Great Ultimate (*T'ai-chi*) and Heaven (*T'ien*) in Chu Hsi's Philosophy," p. 7. The conference papers have been published by the University of Hawaii Press under the title *Chu Hsi and Neo-Confucianism*, ed. Wing-tsit Chan, 1986.

[78] Ibid., p. 9.

[79] Ibid., p. 8.

commentary on the *Great Learning* three days before he died.[80] A number of his key concepts came from the *Collected Commentaries*, such as *jen* as "the character of the mind and the principle of love,"[81] and propriety or rites as "the restraint and beautiful ornament according to the principle of heaven and the form and law of human affairs."[82] But, Professor Yamanoi is correct only insofar as Chu Hsi's doctrines on learning are concerned, for the Four Books deal only with the matter of learning and not with such matters as principle and material force. To admit that he discussed the Great Ultimate in connection with Chou Tun-i's *Explanation of the Diagram of the Great Ultimate* is to admit that the concept does occupy a central position in Chu Hsi's system of thought. The Ch'eng brothers never mentioned the Great Ultimate.[83] Chu Hsi, however, felt that while Ch'eng I greatly advanced Neoconfucianism in his doctrine of principle, he had almost nothing to say about material force. To fill the gap, Chu Hsi borrowed the concept of material force from Chang Tsai. According to Chang, things are endowed with material force in different degrees of clarity.[84] To construct a coherent system, Chu Hsi had to resort to Chou Tun-i's diagram of the Great Ultimate. According to Chou, the Great Ultimate produces the two material forces of *yin* and *yang*, and they in turn interact and engender all things.[85] As Chu Hsi understood it, the Great Ultimate is the sum-total of principles. Chu Hsi has usually been considered a great synthesizer of northern Sung philosophies. But he did more than put things together; he made use of the

[80] Wang Mao-hung, *Chu Tzu nien-p'u*, p. 216.

[81] Chu Hsi, *Ssu-shu chi-chu*, commentary on the *Analects* 1.2 (Shanghai: Chung-hua shu-chü, 1927–1935).

[82] Ibid., commentary on the *Analects* 1.12.

[83] There is a preface to the *I-chuan* written by Ch'eng I himself. Following it there is another preface without the writer's name. The term *t'ai-chi* is mentioned there, but scholars are agreed that this preface is spurious.

[84] Chang-tsai, *Cheng-meng* 6.11, 22.

[85] Chou Tun-i, "T'ai-chi-t'u shuo" [Explanation of the Diagram of the Great Ultimate], in *Chou Tzu ch'üan-shu* [Complete Works of Master Chou] (Shanghai: Commercial Press, 1929–1937), chap. 1.

northern Sung philosophies to construct a system that is practically new. Therefore, the element of Chou Tun-i in his system is of the greatest importance.

But Professor Yamanoi's point is essentially sound if we understand him correctly. I believe what he meant is that for the understanding of Chu Hsi, the Great Ultimate is of secondary importance. It is for this reason that Huang Kan spoke of his Master's pursuit of learning before what the Master conceived of the Way. Another pupil of Chu Hsi, Ch'en Ch'un, whose *Neoconfucian Terms Explained* has been regarded in China and Japan as the best summary of Chu Hsi's philosophy in all aspects, had the same understanding of his Master. The work is divided into twenty-six categories with eight sections each. There is a category on the *t'ai-chi* in nine sections, but the category on *li* has only three, and there is no category on *ch'i* at all. The work begins with the category of *ming*, thus placing one's destiny or Heaven's mandate in the first position. The main point is that our nature and feelings are endowed with principle and material force by the mandate of Heaven. It is our duty to develop our nature and exercise our feelings according to it. Hence we must do what is right and leave wealth or poverty, longevity or premature death, and similar issues to Heaven.

Chu Hsi's preoccupation with morality over metaphysics can also be seen in his instructions to pupils. In the *Chu Tzu yü-lei* there are nine chapters in which these instructions are recorded.[86] Most of these came in the last decade of his life, but some went as far back as 1173, when he was forty-four years old. Very few of these conversations deal with the Great Ultimate, principle, or material force. In fact, the second conversation is on the subject of intellectual investigation and moral cultivation as the two wheels of a vehicle.[87]

The metaphors of the two wheels of a vehicle or the two wings of a bird can be applied to practically all of his doctrines.

[86] Chu Hsi, *Chu Tzu yü-lei*, chaps. 113–121.

[87] Ibid., 113.2 (p. 4359).

To him, sincerity and enlightenment, the two qualities strongly stressed in the *Doctrine of the Mean* as the way to perfect oneself and others,[88] should advance simultaneously.[89] Following the Ch'eng brothers, he loved to quote from the *Book of Changes* that "seriousness is to straighten one's internal life and righteousness is to square one's external life."[90] When asked if principle or material force come first, he did say that if one insists on investigating their origin, one must say that there is principle first.[91] For this doctrine of the priority of principle over material force, he has been taken to task in China, Korea, and Japan ever since. But as Fung Yu-lan has explained, "From a strictly logical point of view, however, 'one is forced to admit that Principle has priority,' the reason being that Principle transcends time and space and is ever unchanging, whereas the Ether [material force] exists within time and space and does undergo change."[92] We may add that Chu Hsi preceded his saying by declaring that between principle and material force there is no question of priority. Again and again he said that there has never been one without the other.[93] I feel that in this matter he has been grossly misunderstood.

Similarly he has been accused of putting "following the path of inquiry and study" ahead of "honoring the moral nature."[94] The popular theory is that in 1175 at the Goose Lake Temple he and Lu Hsiang-shan met to resolve their philosophical differences. It is true that on their way to the meeting, Lu and his brother wrote poems deriding Chu Hsi's attention to commentaries and stressing the role of the mind, but the issue

[88] *Doctrine of the Mean*, chap. 21.

[89] Chu Hsi, *Chu Tzu wen-chi*, 1.2b, "Prose-Poem on the White Deer Hollow."

[90] *Book of Changes*, commentary on the second hexagram.

[91] Chu Hsi, *Chu Tzu yü-lei* 1.11 (p. 4).

[92] Fung Yu-lan, *A History of Chinese Philosophy*, trans. Derk Bodde, 2 vols. (Princeton: Princeton University Press, 1952–1953), 2:545.

[93] Chu Hsi, *Chu Tzu yü-lei* 1.2, 9–11, 13 (pp. 2–4); 68.32 (p. 2687); 94.49 (p. 3773); etc.

[94] *Doctrine of the Mean*, chap. 27.

never came up in their discussions.[95] Because Chu Hsi went too far to attack Lu's dependence on the mind as Buddhistic, his opponents have exaggerated his differences with Lu and labeled his school as that of "following the path of inquiry and study" and Lu's school as that of "honoring the moral nature." In 1183, Chu Hsi did admit that sometimes he overemphasized study,[96] but that does not mean that he undermined "honoring the moral nature." His lifelong advocacy of seriousness ought to lay the controversy to rest. As the *Doctrine of the Mean* says, "The superior man honors the moral nature and follows the path of inquiry and study. He achieves breadth and greatness and pursues the refined and subtle to the limit. He seeks to reach the greatest height and brilliancy and follows the path of the Mean."[97] The way to achieve this Mean is to go on both wheels and flap both wings.

But the metaphors not only mean balance; they mean unity. In discussing Chou Tun-i's "Explanation of the Diagram of the Great Ultimate," he made it very clear that there is no sequence between the Ultimate of Nonbeing (*wu-chi*) and the Great Ultimate.[98] They are simply one thing, *wu-chi* in the sense of being colorless and odorless and Great Ultimate (*t'ai-chi*) in the sense of the operation of *yin* and *yang* to the limit.[99] In other words, being and nonbeing are not distinguished as two. Like all Neoconfucians, Chu Hsi liked to speak in terms of substance and function. For instance, the ear is substance while hearing is the function,[100] and nature is substance while the feelings are function.[101] Everything can be spoken of in these terms. Nevertheless, substance and function do not represent two stages; they are one. He was fond of quoting

[95] See Wing-tsit Chan, *Chu-hsüeh lun-chi* [Anthology of the Study of Chu Hsi] (Taipei: Student Book Company, 1982), pp. 231–245.

[96] Chu Hsi, *Chu Tzu wen-chi* 54.5b, letter in reply to Hsiang P'ing-fu.

[97] *Doctrine of the Mean*, chap. 27.

[98] Chu Hsi, *Chu Tzu yü-lei* 94.16 (p. 3758).

[99] See above, n. 85.

[100] Chu Hsi, *Chu Tzu yü-lei* 1.12 (p. 4).

[101] Ibid., 5.65 (p. 148).

Ch'eng I's famous adage, "Substance and function come from the same source and there is no gap between the manifest and the hidden."[102] Likewise the one and the many are not distinguished as two levels. Instead, they are one. He often quoted Ch'eng I's well-known saying that "Principle is one but its manifestations are many."[103] As to the relation between knowledge and action, he did not get to the point of the unity of knowledge and action reached three hundred years later by Wang Yang-ming, but he appears actually to have anticipated him. I hope I am not stretching the point, but in answering a question by a pupil on the sincerity of the will, he replied, "You must really see if a thing is good or evil according to principle, and if it is evil you must be wholeheartedly unwilling to do it. Only then can the will be called sincere."[104] I need not add that like all Neoconfucians, Chu Hsi taught the unity of Heaven and man.

This being the chief characteristic of the Chu Hsi philosophy, how will it fit in with world philosophy? World philosophy is still in the process of development. I suppose it will be predominantly western, but it will embrace Marxism, Islamic philosophy, Indian philosophy, Chinese philosophy, and many more. Because of its historical strength and because of its unique features, Chu Hsi's philosophy will have a role to play in this conglomerate. There are three possibilities. One is to be modernized according to a model. For mainland China the model is Marxism. The Chu Hsi philosophy will have to be reconstructed according to Marxism to serve the state. For Chu Hsi scholars in the rest of Asia, the model seems to be western philosophy. They are not saying this in so many words, but in their works they discuss Chu Hsi's philosophy in western terms. His philosophy is explained in terms of metaphysics, cosmology, epistemology, and other western systems. As a means of study and a way to analyze, this is most

[102] Ibid., 67.36 (p. 2631), for example.

[103] Ch'eng I, *I-chuan* 3.3b; Chu Hsi, *Chu Tzu yü-lei* 20.78 (p. 745), etc.

[104] Chu Hsi, *Chu Tzu yü-lei* 15.100 (p. 482).

helpful, but to fit the Chu Hsi philosophy into a western model will destroy its character. How can the Neoconfucian doctrine of the Mean be made to conform to the western separation of the subject and the object, for example? In fact, whether western categories can be applied to Chu Hsi is still an open question. The second possibility is to present Chu Hsi's philosophy as a challenge. Some Chinese scholars have asserted that the western habit of an either–or approach distorts truth. To contrast the universal and the particular, the transcendent and the immanent, and so on destroys unity. This line of approach reminds one of Indian philosophers' criticism of the West not so long ago, that Indian spiritual values will save the West from materialism. Few Chinese philosophers have followed this line and fewer still are resorting to this approach. Most prefer the third approach, namely, that Chu Hsi's philosophy may raise certain questions in the world conglomerate. Some of the questions are: is there any merit in the doctrine of the Mean? Can philosophy be detached from actual living? Is logical consistency the only criterion of truth? What is the nature of Heaven? How does the mandate of Heaven operate? What constitutes immortality? What is the mystery of cosmic forces?

The number of questions is unlimited. While Chu Hsi's philosophy may offer some answers, it will receive some from other sources. In the process, both Chu Hsi's philosophy and world philosophy will become richer.

GLOSSARY

ai	愛
Chang Chih-tung	張之洞
Chang Tsai	張載
Ch'en Ch'un	陳淳
Cheng Hsüan	鄭玄
Cheng-i-t'ang ch'üan-shu	正誼堂全書
Cheng-meng	正蒙
Ch'eng Hao	程顥

Ch'eng I	程頤
ch'i	氣
Chien-yang	建陽
Chin-shih Han-chi ts'ung-k'an	近世漢籍叢刊
Chin-ssu lu	近思錄
ch'in-ch'ieh	親切
ching (reverence, seriousness)	敬
**ching* (tranquility)	靜
ching-she	精舍
Chou Tzu ch'üan-shu	周子全書
Chou Tun-i	周敦頤
Chu Hsi	朱熹
Chu-hsüeh lun-chi	朱學論集
Chu-lin	竹林
Chu Tzu ch'üan-shu	朱子全書
Chu Tzu i-shu	朱子遺書
Chu Tzu nien-p'u	朱子年譜
Chu Tzu ta-ch'üan	朱子大全
Chu Tzu wen-chi	朱子文集
Chu Tzu yü-lei	朱子語類
chü-ching ch'iung-li	居敬窮理
Chung-kuo che-hsüeh	中國哲學
Feng Tso-su, Yün-chung	馮作肅, 允中
Han Ch'ang-li ch'üan-chi	韓昌黎全集
Han-ch'üan	寒泉
Han Yü	韓愈
hao-jan chih ch'i	浩然之氣
Ho Yen	何晏
hsi	習
Hsi-fang tui Chu Hsi ti yen-chiu	西方對朱熹的研究
Hsiang P'ing-fu	項平甫
Hsieh Liang-tso	謝良佐
hsing-chuang	行狀
Hsü Yüan-min	徐元敏
Huang Kan	黃榦
Hui-an	晦菴
hun	魂
Hung Ch'ü-wu	洪去蕪
Hung-fan	洪範
huo-jan kuan-t'ung	豁然貫通

I-chuan	易傳
I-shu	遺書
i-tan	一旦
jen	仁
**jen*	人
Ki Kobong, Taesung	奇高峯, 大升
ko-i	格義
ku	谷
Kuan Tzu	管子
Kuang-wen	廣文
kung	恭
K'ung Ch'iu	孔丘
kuei-shen	鬼神
li	理
Li Fang-tzu	李方子
Li Mo	李默
Li T'ung	李侗
Liu K'un-i	劉坤一
Liu Pao-nan	劉寶楠
Liu Tzu-ch'eng, Ch'ing-chih	劉子澄, 清之
Lu Hsiang-shan, Chiu-yüan	陸象山, 九淵
Lü Tsu-ch'ien	呂祖謙
Lun-yü cheng-i	論語正義
Lun-yü chi-chu	論語集註
Meitoku shuppansha	明德出版社
Meng Tzu tzu-i shu-cheng	孟子字義疏證
Mien-chai chi	勉齋集
ming	命
Morohashi Tetsuji	諸橋轍次
Ō-Bei no Shushigaku	歐米の朱子學
Ou-Mei chih Chu Tzu hsüeh	歐美之朱子學
Pei-hsi tzu-i	北溪字義
pen-wu	本無
p'o	魄
p'u-t'i	菩提
san-ts'ai	三才
seng	僧
Shang-ti	上帝
Shang-ts'ai yü-lu	上蔡語錄
Shih-san-ching chu-shu	十三經注疏

Shushigaku daikei	朱子學大系
Shushigaku nyūmon	朱子學入門
Ssu-k'u chen-pen	四庫珍本
Ssu-pu pei-yao	四部備要
Ssu-pu ts'ung-k'an	四部叢刊
Ssu-shu chi-chu	四書集註
Sun Ching-fu, Tzu-hsiu	孫敬甫, 自修
ta	大
Ta-hsüeh chang-chü	大學章句
Ta-hsüeh huo-wen	大學或問
t'ai-chi	太極
T'ai-chi-t'u shuo	太極圖說
Takakusu Junjirō	高楠順次郎
Takata Hiroshige	高田博成
Tao	道
Tchou Hi	朱熹
t'i-yung	體用
T'ien	天
T'ien-chu	天主
t'o-jan	脫然
Toegye Hakbo	退溪學報
Toegyehak	退溪學
T'oegye, Yi Hwang	退溪, 李滉
T'oung Pao	通報
Tu Wei-ming	杜維明
Tung Chung-shu	董仲舒
T'ung-shu	通書
Tzu-hsia	子夏
Wang Mao-hung	王懋竑
Wang Pi	王弼
Wang Yang-ming, Shou-jen	王陽明, 守仁
wei-hsüeh	爲學
wei-Tao	爲道
Wen Kung	文公
wu-chi	無極
wu-hsing	五行
Wu-i	武夷
yang	陽
Yeh Kung-hui	葉公回
Yen-p'ing ta-wen	延平答問

Yi I, Yulgop	李珥, 栗谷
yin	陰
Yin Tun	尹焞
Youn Sa-soon	尹絲淳
yüan-ssu	遠思
Yüan Tao	原道

ROGER T. AMES

Confucius and the Ontology of Knowing

INTERPRETING across boundaries is dependent, in important measure, on the art of translation.[1] Over the past century, the classical Chinese corpus has been served well by philologically trained translators with increasingly sophisticated language skills. By contrast, philosophy as a discipline has not properly entertained the Asian traditions as "philosophy." As a consequence, the major difficulty confronted by the humanist in attempting to use translated material lies not as much in the syntax as in the semantic content of core philosophical concepts that frame these texts. Of course, when a concept is assigned an English equivalent, much of the depth of the original concept tends to be lost: its word image, its allusive effectiveness, its morphological implications. At the same time, especially with philosophical vocabulary, inappropriate associations are evoked by the translated term to the extent that it is burdened by its own cultural history.

But there is a further complication. As a result of the classical Chinese preoccupation with conjunction and continuity, a characteristic of the vocabulary in which philosophical ideas are communicated is that a shared terminology is used by competing schools to articulate significantly different concepts. The consequent ambiguity necessitates a subtlety of

[1] This paper is a working draft on the Confucian concept, *chih*, written for *Thinking Through Confucius* (Albany, N.Y.: SUNY Press, 1987) a collaborative effort between David L. Hall from the University of Texas in El Paso, and myself. Many of the ideas are drawn from his earlier publications, especially *The Uncertain Phoenix* (New York: Fordham, 1982), and have been developed in discussion with him over several years. Several of the other central concepts are translated in rather novel ways—"authoritative person" for *jen*, for example. These renderings are developed and defended in *Thinking Through Confucius*.

analysis that would benefit from those skills we generally call philosophical. At this juncture in our appropriation of Chinese philosophic literature, it is imperative that we turn our attention to a conceptual reconstruction of the central philosophical terminologies that structure the texts if we are going to be able to appeal to this alternative tradition as a resource for enriching our own opportunities to philosophize. It is to exemplify this problem in translation and to take one step toward establishing a methodology for resolving it that, in this essay, I analyze one such concept in the classical Chinese vocabulary.

The dynamics of "thinking" in Confucius can be explicated as a continuing dialectic between "learning" (*hsüeh*) and "reflecting" (*ssu*), the consequence of which is "realizing" (*chih*) through "living up to one's word" (*hsin*). The "learning"–"reflecting" dialectic might be roughly construed as the functional equivalent of "reasoning" in the dominant western paradigm, "realizing" would correspond to "knowing," and "living up to one's word" would correspond to "truth." In the discussion that follows, I hope to make it clear that this "thinking" is not to be understood as a process of abstract reasoning, but is fundamentally performative in that it is a psychosomatic activity directed at and entailing the achievement of a practical result. Far from being a means for lifting one out of the world of experience, "thinking" for Confucius is fundamentally integrative, a profoundly concrete activity that seeks to maximize the potential of the existing possibilities and the contributing conditions. Thus, in place of the primarily theoretical activity that cognizes and assesses an objective set of facts and/or values, "thinking" for Confucius is "*act*ualizing" or "*real*izing" the world and making it meaningful. "Thinking" is not simply cognition or even interpretation of a particular world; it is an occupation in which the "realizer" is a constituent element in the creative enterprise of making his world.

My procedure in interpreting the dynamics of "thinking" in Confucius will be a conceptual reconstruction involving a mutually corroborative philological and philosophical analysis: an analysis of the language in which "thinking" is couched, and then a verification of the direction established by this analysis by pursuing its philosophical implications.

The focus will be on the third element in the "thinking" cluster of concepts, *chih*, commonly translated as "to know," "to understand," but in the Confucian context, perhaps better rendered "to realize" in the sense of "a making real." In the early literature, this character is used interchangeably with **chih*, "wisdom," indicating the absence of the familiar distinction between theory and praxis adumbrated in the English distinction between "knowledgeable" and "wise."[2]

[2] The *Shuo-wen* (one of the earliest classical lexicons) analyzes *chih* as deriving from "mouth" (*k'ou*) and "arrow" (*shih*), and defines it as "verbal expression" (*ts'u*). Several commentaries on the *Shuo-wen* speculate that the character, "to understand" (**shih*), should precede *ts'u* in this definition, viz. "understanding expressed orally." That the character, *chih*, is constituted with the "mouth" (*k'ou*) radical and is defined in terms of "verbal expression" (*ts'u*) and possibly "to understand," all having strong verbal associations, is highly significant. Commentators generally account for the "arrow" (*shih*) element as the phonetic, even though, according to B. Karlgren, *Grammata Serica Recensa* (Stockholm: Museum of Far Eastern Antiquities, 1957), its archaic pronunciation, *śiər/śi/shi, is significantly different from *chih*: *tiĕg/tie/chi. We might want to consider the semantic associations of "arrow": a missile cast with a bow in a chosen direction toward some predetermined target. Commentary in the *Shuo-wen chieh-tzu ku-lin* introduces an important inplicit sense of *chih*:

> [The Ch'ing commentator] Wang Nien-sun observes: "Some gloss *chih* as 'come in contact with' (*chieh*). The 'Yüeh-chi' [of the *Li-chi*] contains the phrase '*wu chih chih chih*,' which means that when phenomena occur *chih* makes contact with them." Because the ancients called making mutual contact *chih*, mutual contact with others was also called *chih*. Hence, there is the expression *chih-chiao* "intimate acquaintance." Because of this, to constitute a match (*p'i*) is also called *chih*. . . . Wang Nien-sun says that *chih* can also be glossed as "to manifest" (*hsien*), i.e., to manifest in one's contenance.

Chih would seem to denote participation in the realization of a relationship wherein the realizer and that realized are two integral aspects of a single event. One final connotation of *chih* that should be noted is the sense of "to do," "to administer," "to determine," as in the expression "one who administers and determines the government = governor" (*chih-kuo*). This usage is important in disclosing the active and creative dimensions of *chih*.

The etymological components of the character *chih* and the implications of these components are evident in the following passage from Tung Chung-shu's *Ch'un-ch'iu fan-lu*:[3]

> What is it that is called *chih*? It is to predict accurately [literally, to speak first and then for events to happen accordingly]. Any person who desires to get rid of certain conducts acts only after prescribing the situation with his *chih*. Where one's prescription is correct, he gets his way in what he does and is appropriate in his undertakings. His actions are successful and his name is illustrious. His person is therefore benefited and free of harm. His good fortune reaches to his children and grandchildren, and his beneficence spreads to all of the people. T'ang and Wu were like this.
>
> Where one's prescription is incorrect, he does not get his way in what he does and is inappropriate in his undertakings. His actions are unsuccessful and his name is disgraced. Injury befalls his person, he breaks his lineage, he brings ruin on his kind and lays waste to his ancestral temple. Nations that have perished have been thus served. Thus it is said that nothing is as urgent as *chih*.
>
> One who is *chih* can see calamity and fortune a long way off, and anticipates benefit and injury early. Phenomena move and he anticipates their transformation; affairs arise and he anticipates their outcome. He sees the beginnings and anticipates the end. When he says something, none dare dispute it; when he sets up something, it cannot be disregarded; when he takes up something it cannot be put aside.
>
> His course of action is consistent and has its proper order. He considers and then reconsiders something, and when he gets down to it, one cannot take umbrage.
>
> His words are few yet sufficient. They are brief yet instructive, simple yet explicit, terse yet comprehensive. Where they are few, they cannot be embellished, and where many, they cannot be abbreviated. His actions fit the rela-

[3] *Ch'un-ch'iu fan-lu*, Ssu-pu pei-yao ed. (Shanghai: Chung-hua, 1936), 8/10b.

tionships and his words match the task. Such a person is said to be *chih*.

There are several implications of *chih* made clear in Tung Chung-shu's discussion. First, *chih*, commonly translated as "to know," and **chih*, rendered as "wise" or "wisdom," are used interchangeably. There is no fact–value or theory–praxis distinction to separate "knowledge" from "wisdom" in this tradition. Second (and a point to emphasize), *chih* refers to a propensity for forecasting or predicting the outcome of an organic set of circumstances of which the "fore-caster" himself is a constituent and participatory element. In other words, *chih* is not simply to "pre-dict" or to prophesy—it is to "cast" a future. This definition of *chih* as an ability to anticipate, predict, and achieve a future on the basis of known conditions is common in the early literature. For example, the *Pai-hu-t'ung* says: " 'Wisdom' [**chih*] means 'to realize' (*chih*): to have no doubts about events simply on the basis of what one has seen and heard, to see a sign and realize what will ensue."[4] Similarly, in the *Chung-yung* we find this passage: "The *tao* of the highest integrity [*ch'eng*] is being able to forecast [literally, "realize in advance"]. . . . When fortune or misfortune approach, one is certain to know beforehand whether it is good or not. Thus, the highest integrity is 'godlike.' . . . Integrity is not simply completing oneself, it is the means of completing things and events. Completing oneself is 'person-making' [*jen*]; completing things and events is 'realizing' [*chih*]."[5] And there is an example of *chih* being used in this performative way in the *Analects* (15.4): "Yu [Tsu-lu], rare indeed are those who realize virtue." Many commentators interpret this passage in terms of the frequently advertised Confucian commitment to the unity of knowledge and action. Because authentication in action is a

[4] *Pai-hu-t'ung*, Harvard-Yenching Institute Sinological Index Series 2 (Taipei: Chinese Materials and Research Aids Service Center, repr. 1966), 8/30/1b.

[5] *Chung-yung* 24–25.

necessary condition of "knowing," to interpret *chih* as knowing with such a proviso is in fact to interpret it as "realizing."

There is another passage in the *Analects* (15.33) that provides a rather succinct statement of the perceived relationship that obtains among "realizing" (*chih*), "personhood" (*jen*), and "ritual action" (*li*):

> Where one realizes [*chih*] something but his personhood [*jen*] is not such that he can sustain it, even though he has it, he is certain to lose it. Where he realizes something and his personhood is such that he can sustain it but fails to handle it with proper dignity, the people will not be respectful. Where he realizes something, his personhood is such that he can sustain it, he handles it with proper dignity, yet fails to use ritual actions [*li*] to implement it, he will still not make good on it.

Without taking account of the performative force of *chih*, this passage is really quite impossible to interpret. Arthur Waley in his translation of the *Analects* despairs: "This paragraph with its highly literary, somewhat empty elaboration, and its placing ritual on a pinnacle far above Goodness [*jen*], is certainly one of the later additions to the book."[6] And the characterization of the *chün tzu*, the "exemplary person," in the passage that follows this one makes considerably more sense where *chih* is something "done" as well as "known" (15.34): "The exemplary person [*chün tzu*] cannot undertake trivial things but can be relied upon for important responsibilities. The small person, then, is the opposite."

As Waley observes, the standard renderings of this passage manipulate the grammar beyond recognition in order to force some sense out of *chih* here.[7] For an experience to be "meaningful" and thus "en-joyed," it must coordinate the senses of importance of those participating in it. Because the *chih* of the

[6] Arthur Waley, trans., *The Analects of Confucius* (London: Allen & Unwin, 1938), p. 200, n.1.

[7] Ibid., p. 200 n. 2.

exemplary person—"what he makes real"—gives rise to meaning and enjoyment, we can say that he is capable of "everyday" things, but cannot say that he is capable of "trivial" things (*hsiao chih*). Because everything he does is a fund of meaning and importance, his actions, even when "everyday," always conduce to greatness.[8]

Another suggestive passage is *Analects* 6.20: "To be fond of it is better than [just] to realize it; to enjoy it is better than [just] to be fond of it." Confucius's point here is that full realization requires a participatory "en-joyment." Three categories are introduced: realization, realization that is the consequence of considered intention, and realization that effects harmony and enjoyment. The last, for Confucius, is the richest kind of realization. To make something "real" that is neither desired nor a source of enjoyment is to have undertaken "trivial things." The fundamentally dynamic nature of this "realizing" (*chih*) and its attendant enjoyment are highlighted in the metaphorically suggestive passage 6.23: "Those who realize the world [i.e., the wise] enjoy water; those who are authoritatively human [*jen*] enjoy mountains. Those who realize the world are active; those who are authoritatively human are still. Those who realize the world enjoy; those who are authoritatively human are long-lived." This passage focuses on two fundamental and complementary dimensions of being a significant person. To the extent that one is making a world "real" with "performative" wisdom (*chih*), one is creative and dynamic, comparable to water in that it too is fluid and productive. To the extent that one is an achieved person, one is a sustainer of values and meaning, prominent and enduring like the mountain. The excellence achieved by the authoritative person is normative, changing the world with its influence to become a continuing focus of deference and a resource for emulation. The categories of "being wise" (*chih*) and "being authoritative" (*jen*) are

[8] In *Twilight of the Idols* no. 22, Nietzsche says: "Evil men have no songs." The thrust of this passage makes a similar point in reverse. Since "evil" men by definition are disintegrative, even where they might attempt music, it effects no harmony with their respondents, and falls flat as noise.

construed so as to reveal the creativity–continuity distinction present in the relationship between "reflecting" (*ssu*) and "learning" (*hsüeh*). Just as traditionally both "mountain" (*shan*) and "water" (*sui*) have been considered necessary to achieve the utmost in "natural beauty" (*shan sui*), so both the continuous and the creative are necessary constituents of the complete person.

Another passage that stresses the continuity that "wisdom" affords the world is 17.3: "Only the wisest and the most ignorant do not move." The most ignorant person, unaware of his own limitations, maintains a bovine intransigence—truly, one who "will not learn even when vexed by difficulties" (16.9). The wisest person's ostensive immobility is not quite as easy to explain, especially against the claim that sagehood is open-ended and precludes any notion of final completion.[9] It is important to remember that wisdom for Confucius is the coordination of quality relationships that are productive of meaning and enjoyment, and that the wise person can thus only be understood relationally as person-in-context. Personal cultivation, then, must be understood in relative terms. This passage does not claim that the wisest person has ceased to grow; rather, in the context of symbiotic growth, he represents the prevailing standard of constancy. He is the embodiment of meaning and value, which constitute the regularity and structure of human culture, and to the extent that there are norms, he is normative. Confucius himself, portrayed in the *Analects* as sage, says as much when he asserts, "If *t'ien* [conventionally, "heaven"] is not going to destroy this culture, what can the people of K'uang do to me?" (9.5). The metaphor in 2.1, where Confucius compares sagelike rule to the pole star, makes the same point. It is not that the pole star is utterly stationary without its own motion. Rather, the motion of the other celestial bodies is measured against it. In spite of its own motion, it is constancy. In the dynamics of interpersonal mod-

[9] See David L. Hall and Roger T. Ames, "Getting It Right: On Saving Confucius from the Confucians," *Philosophy East and West* 34.1 (1984): 3–23.

eling, the wise person is by virtue of his excellence a relatively clear "order" that can be appropriated for analogical application to situations that do not evidence the same quality of harmony.

In describing "realizing" in a holistic way that goes beyond the purely intellectual capacities of the human being, Confucius allows for the possibility of the less intellectually able to be purveyors of wisdom through realizing the world in alternative, equally valid directions. One might speculate that for Confucius, even the mentally retarded can be contributors to the tradition to the extent that they are a source of significance and value and can occasion the realization of a world over which they exercise some power of selection.

Language has an important function in realizing the world. The claim to "wisdom" (**chih*) is based on a awareness of what is going to happen and an ability to articulate this understanding in language as a communal act: "Because the exemplary person [*chün tzu*] will be deemed wise [**chih*] or not on the strength of one word, how could he be but careful about what he has to say?" (19.25). Where an objective reality is assumed, the prediction of future developments involves little more than prophecy: a claim to speak with authority on behalf of that reality. It is no more than a saying in advance of what must surely come to pass. The forecasting denoted by *chih*, as opposed to this mere saying in advance, involves three essential activities. First, *chih* is cognitive as the speculative entertainment of the outlines of possible futures informed by an awareness of contributing conditions and the implications of these conditions. Second, *chih* requires a disposition toward some of these viable possibilities to the exclusion of others. And finally, *chih* is the casting of the form of the future in such fashion and with such persuasive articulation as to invite sympathy and participation. The two aspects of forecast that go beyond any notion of the discovery of an objective "given" are the disposition toward the realization of a possible future among a number of possibilities, and the invitation to belief and to participation in the veracity of that choice. Every "pre-diction"—

oral prognostication—is personal and participatory in that it first involves the determination of one possible future from among viable futures, and then requires that that future be "cast" by personal participation and the attraction of support.[10]

The *Analects* illustrates this dimension of *chih*: "Fan Ch'ih asked about authoritative personhood [*jen*], and the Master said: 'Love others.' He asked about realization [*chih*], and the Master said, 'Realize others.' Fan Ch'ih did not understand and so the Master explained, 'If you promote the straight over the crooked you can make the crooked straight' " (12.22). Important here is that to "realize [*chih*] others" is not just a passive recognition of their relative worth, but further requires the selection and promotion of excellence. To *chih* is to contribute to and determine as well as to describe accurately.

There are several aspects of *chih* that distinguish it from "knowing" as strictly cognitive and recognitive. "Knowing" has generally been understood more in terms of correspondence and coherence, denoting that consummate level of thinking—*theoria*—attained through reasoning in which what appears to the subjective mind as idea corresponds accurately to some objective reality. It is this objective reality that stands as a basis for general agreement in the subjectivities of reasonable persons. *Chih* differs from this interpretation of "knowing" in that it is a profoundly dynamic process of articulating and determining the world rather than a passive cognizance of some predetermined reality. To *chih* is to influence the process of existence within the range of one's viable possibilities. It is social rather than individual in that it both informs and transforms one's community as a self-fulfilling prediction. It is an interpersonal activity in that the predicted and projected future is derived from a common cultural matrix and legacy, is shared in the community, and is realized by attracting popular interest and support. It suggests a direction and orchestrates an active

[10] I have developed the specifics of this definition from Hall, *Uncertain Phoenix*, pp. 37–38.

sympathy toward the realization of one's specific forecast. In that *chih* is a recommending of certain possibilities as opposed to others based on a cognitive awareness of available possibilities, it entails both fact and value. And in that it entails the *act*ualizing of a viable possibility, it is both a theoretical and a practical activity. Finally, in that it involves the person wholly in the articulation of the possibility and the subsequent casting of reality, it is a holistic activity.

In a correspondence theory of truth, there is the possibility of an absolute certainty. Knowing is thinking with certainty, and truth as the correspondence between thinking and reality is the goal of reason. Ch'en Ta-ch'i observes that the main function of *chih* is to distinguish between what is "appropriate/meaningful" (*yi*) and what is not.[11] Because what is appropriate and meaningful in any situation is relative to its specific circumstances, in order to distinguish and determine *yi*, *chih* must involve a clear perception and evaluation of the contributing conditions. In this regard, *chih* is frequently characterized as dispelling doubts (*huo*): A person with *chih* is not of two minds . . ." (9.28). Being of "two minds" refers specifically to confusion over possible alternatives. Presumably the person who does not suffer from such doubts has both selected his target and cast toward it. This is consistent with the "arrow" component of the graph, *chih*, and the directionality it suggests.

I would like to press Ch'en Ta-ch'i's insight one step further in suggesting that *chih* not only distinguishes what is appropriate and meaningful, but further involves an active role in determining it. Unlike the sort of "reasoning" that pursues the knowledge of a universal reality, *chih* is participated in by the realizer such that each realizer's reality is unique. Any understanding of the world is an understanding from some particular perspective or another. Reality is thus multiple, contingent, and relative; not universal, necessary, and absolute. Thus, to

[11] Ch'en Ta-ch'i, *K'ung Tzu hsüeh-shuo lun-chi* (Taipei: Cheng-chung, 1978), pp. 78ff.

the extent that *chih* can be an active "realizing" of viable possibilities rather than simply a cognizing of predetermined facts and values, it is to be understood in the language of aesthetic achievement rather than that of logical necessity. It is an authored achievement to be measured in quality and degree.

As I have indicated, in a correspondence theory, cognitive "knowing" involves the representation of a thing or event as it really is, where the idea is in agreement with the character of reality. "Knowing" then is a subjective state that is dependent on the absolute and necessary existence in fact (as opposed to appearance, thought, or language) of an objective reality, and the true correspondence between thought and this reality. "Knowing" thus understood requires a separate, noncontingent reality and the possibility of establishing true correspondence.

I have argued that in Confucius, with his immanental vision, "realizing" (*chih*) is significantly different from this concept of "knowing." Reality, far from being transcendent, absolute, and necessary, is immanent, relative, and contingent. It is something achieved rather than "re-cognized." Because reality is not separate from realizer, it follows that "truth" in this tradition cannot denote a relationship of correspondence. Rather, "truth" must mean a "*gen*uineness": a natural and real begetting; an "authenticity": an authored originality that possesses its own inherent authority.[12]

I have defined Confucius's concept "to realize" (*chih*) as accurate, self-fulfilling prediction. In view of the immanental presuppositions of this paradigm and the coextensive nature of "realizer" and "that realized," the final distinctions of the two-world theory are not operative. That is, not only is there no appreciable distinction between "truth" and "reality," but further, there is no distinction that obtains among the subjective

[12] See Eliot Deutsch, *On Truth: An Ontological Theory* (Honolulu: University Press of Hawaii, 1979), in which he argues that truth is a quality of any thing to be what is right for itself according to its own aim and intentionality: "The nature of truth is thus seen as a qualitative achievement. It is not a given; it is attained" (p. 98).

knower, the objective reality known, and the description of this relationship as "truth." Fundamentally, to realize (*chih*) and to be true (*ch'eng*) are two ways of saying the same thing. The character, *ch'eng*, is constituted of "to speak" (*yen*) and "to complete, to realize" (**ch'eng*): in other words, "to realize that which is spoken." Thus, it would be expected that *ch'eng*, like *chih*, would refer to an accurate, self-fulfilling prediction—and, as we have seen, it is so described in the *Chung-yung* passage cited previously.[13]

Huston Smith in a recent paper goes to some lengths in distinguishing the Chinese conception of truth. He observes that

> truth for China is personal in a dual or twofold sense. Outwardly, it takes into consideration the feelings of the persons an act or utterance will affect. . . . Meanwhile, inwardly it aligns the speaker to the self he ought to be; invoking a word dear to the correspondence theorists we can say that truth "adequates" its possessor to his normative self. The external and internal referents of the notion are tightly fused, of course, for it is primarily by identifying with the feelings of others (developing *jen*) that one becomes a *chün-tzu* (the self one should be).[14]

Smith highlights the personal nature of "truth" as a kind of "sincerity" in which one brackets his own private preferences in favor or "optimizing the feelings of all interested parties." He then goes on to define truth as something authored—a definition that is consistent with the present explication of *chih* as "to realize." Smith describes truth thus conceived as "a kind of performative": "it holds an act or utterance to be true to the extent that it 'gestalts' (composes, resolves) the ingredients of

[13] Although Confucius does not use this term, "integrity" or "sincerity" (*ch'eng*) in any way comparable to its usage in the *Chung-yung*, an argument can be made that the *Chung-yung*'s development of *ch'eng* as an ontological category is a justification for the interpersonal and social applications of "living up to one's word" (*hsin*) in the *Analects*.

[14] Huston Smith, "Western and Comparative Perspectives on Truth," *Philosophy East and West* 30.4 (1980): 425–437, at 430.

a situation in a way that furthers a desired outcome—in China's case, social harmony. Truth thus conceived is a kind of performative: it is speech or deed aimed at effecting an intended consequence."[15] Restating Smith's insight in light of my interpretation of *chih* as actually "bringing something into being," I would suggest that "truth is speech *and* deed that *effects* an intended consequence." That is, the performative force of knowing is a basis for attributing to Confucius what might be called an ontology of knowing.

GLOSSARY

ch'eng	誠
**ch'eng*	成
Ch'en Ta-ch'i	陳大齊
chieh	接
chih	知
**chih*	智
chih-chiao	知交
chih-kuo	知國
Ch'un-ch'iu fan-lu	春秋繁露
Chung-yung	中庸
chün tzu	君子
hsiao chih	小知
hsien	見
hsin	信
hsüeh	學
huo	惑
jen	仁
k'ou	口
K'ung Tzu hsüeh-shuo lun-chi	孔子學說論集
li	禮
Li-chi	禮記
Pai-hu-t'ung	白虎通
Pao-ching-t'ang ts'ung-shu	抱經堂叢書
p'i	匹

[15] Ibid., p. 432.

shan	山
shan sui	山水
shih	矢
**shih*	識
Shuo-wen chieh-tzu ku-lin	說文解字詁林
ssu	思
sui	水
tao	道
ts'u	詞
Tung Chung-shu	董仲舒
Wang Nien-sun	王念孫
wu chih chih chih	物至知知
yen	言
yi	義
Yüeh-chi	樂記

A. S. CUA

Reflections on Moral Theory and Understanding Moral Traditions

THE PHILOSOPHICAL significance of cross-cultural ethical studies depends by and large on the adoption of a viable and coherent conception of the function of moral philosophy. An inquiry into the affinity or difference between two or more moral traditions (that is to say, traditions of moral thought) and their representative thinkers may be informative and conducive to intercultural understanding. But without a broad conception of moral philosophy that can serve as a basis for cross-cultural interpretation, the results of such a valuable study are likely to be ignored by serious students of moral philosophy. This observation applies also to the cross-cultural interpretation of a single moral tradition or its representatives.

It may be said that the standard division of moral philosophy or philosophical ethics into metaethics and normative ethics, because of its currency and respectability, provides a secure basis for cross-cultural interpretation of moral traditions. Arguably, metaethics, in terms of its concern with the meaning and function of moral concepts and the nature and methodology of justification, is indispensable to cross-cultural interpretation. As a matter of fact, apart from the presence of our philosophical orientation, these concerns form the heart of much of historical and textual scholarship. In accepting the guidance of metaethics in raising important questions of conceptual clarity and analysis, it is best to avoid the contending issues between types of metaethical theories (for example, those of cognitivism and noncognitivism) in the interpretation of moral traditions.

For a philosopher interested in promoting intercultural understanding, however, the guidance of normative ethics is highly suspect and may even be obstructive to pursuing his objectives. Normative ethics is primarily concerned with arriving at rationally acceptable moral judgments or principles of conduct. To have this concern as a primary focus of interpretative inquiry may well lead us to a classification of types of theory, for example, teleological or deontological theories and their congeners, and to the arguments pro and con. In so doing, there is a danger that the integrity of a moral tradition, the wealth of its materials, will be sacrificed in favor of the prior classification along the lines of the issues that divide normative ethical theories. If such a guide is taken seriously, there is reason to believe that a cross-cultural ethical inquiry will lead to a premature and ill-informed judgment on the rationality or reasonableness of alternative moral traditions. Moreover, as a recent writer succinctly states, "the mainstream moral philosophy suffers from an ignorance of the moralities of Eastern culture"[1] and, I may add, of eastern ethical theories.

In the light of the foregoing, it seems desirable to formulate a conception of moral philosophy that is neutral between the issues of competing normative ethical theories, in other words, a conception that provides some ground rules for cross-cultural interpretation of moral traditions. More especially, we need a conception that avoids theoretical type-casting of moral traditions. In what follows, I sketch a conception of the nature of moral theory.[2] While embracing metaethical concerns, I use the term "moral theory" instead of "moral philosophy," in order to dissociate it from normative ethics. This does not mean that normative ethical questions cannot arise in

[1] David Wong, *Moral Relativism* (Berkeley: University of California Press, 1984), preface.

[2] For my earlier reflections on the nature of moral theory, see A. S. Cua, "Ethics and the Theory of Inquiry," *Ethics* 73 (1963): 214–222; idem, "Some Reflections on Methodology in Chinese Philosophy," *International Philosophical Quarterly* 11 (1971): 236–248; idem, "Uses of Dialogues and Moral Understanding," *Journal of Chinese Philosophy* 2 (1975): 131–148; and idem, "Tasks of Confucian Ethics," *Journal of Chinese Philosophy* 6 (1979): 55–67.

interpreting moral traditions. Rather, when such questions are raised, they are to be viewed as questions aiming at *understanding* rather than evaluating moral traditions. My principal aim is to offer a philosophical basis for cross-cultural interpretation (henceforth, explication). At the outset, let me remark that there is little novelty in my conception of explication. What is perhaps new is the way in which some familiar philosophical tasks are organized and the emphasis given to some aspects of these tasks. Also, it must be noted that my reflections on moral theory are largely a retrospective view of my own work on Confucian ethics, and are motivated by the desire to see more clearly, though tentatively, the direction of my future exploration.

For a preliminary elucidation, I shall follow Thomas Reid in distinguishing moral system from moral theory. According to Reid, a moral system, unlike a system of geometry, is not a species of deductive reasoning. "It resembles more a system of botany, or mineralogy, where the subsequent parts depend not for their evidence upon the preceding, and the arrangement is made to facilitate apprehension and memory, and not to give evidence."[3] In this sense, a moral system is primarily an organization of items of moral knowledge. If we regard a moral tradition as a moral system, we can properly say that it is a relatively explicit and coherent articulation of moral knowledge of the people with a common culture.[4] Distinct from moral sys-

[3] Thomas Reid, *Essays on the Active Powers of the Human Mind* (Cambridge, Mass.: M.I.T. Press, 1969), p. 376.

[4] Reid remarks that "the first writers in morals, we are acquainted with, delivered their moral instructions, not in systems, but in short unconnected sentences, or aphorisms. They saw no need for deductions of reasoning, because the truths they delivered could not but be admitted by the candid and attentive" (ibid., p. 375). It may be observed, however, that for people who share a common moral tradition, their knowledge of right and wrong, virtuous and vicious conduct, is bound to appear naturally as a corpus of self-evident truths. Whether one can generalize from this appearance, as Reid and his rationalist predecessors do, into a doctrine of ethical intuitionism is a question that belongs to metaethics. For a partial assessment, see A. S. Cua, *Reason and Virtue:*

tem is the notion of moral theory or theory of morals. Reid points out,

> By the theory of morals is meant, a just account of the structure of our moral powers; that is, of those powers of the mind by which we have our moral conceptions, and distinguish right from wrong in human actions. This, indeed, is an intricate subject, and there have been various theories and much controversy about it, in ancient and in modern times. But it has little connection with the knowledge of our duty; and those who differ most in the theory of our moral powers, agree in the practical rules of morals which they dictate.[5]

This notion of moral theory as an "account of the structure of our moral powers," however, presupposes a prior map of mental powers, in Hume's words, a "mental geography or the delineation of the distinct parts and powers of the mind."[6] In understanding a moral tradition, providing a cartography of moral experience seems essential. There are two different approaches to this task. One approach may proceed along the line of the general theory of value, by attempting to make a comprehensive survey of the basic and subordinate features of moral experience, in terms of the varieties of values and their interconnection. Alternatively, one may simply confine the inquiry to a more modest, selective cartography, focusing on certain key features of the terrain of moral experience and the manner in which these features interact in the lives and experiences of reflective agents committed to a common moral tradition. In *Dimensions of Moral Creativity*, I suggested that a selective cartography of morals may profitably employ such notions as form of life, way of life, and style of life as focal lenses or devices for understanding the different dimensions of moral experience. The notion of the form of life focuses on the

---

A Study in the Ethics of Richard Price (Athens: Ohio University Press, 1966), particularly chap. 7 and the appendix.

[5] Reid, *Essays on the Active Powers*, p. 376.

[6] David Hume, *An Inquiry Concerning Human Understanding* (Indianapolis: Bobbs-Merrill, 1955), p. 22.

consensual background of a moral tradition, which renders intelligible the uses of moral concepts. The notion of a way of life focuses on the coherence and convergent ways of behavior as congruent with a set of formulable rules of conduct; while the notion of the style of life draws attention to the diverse qualitative significance of the way of life for individual agents. As a form of philosophical inquiry, the ultimate objective of a selective cartography of morals does not lie in accurate depiction, but in presenting the possibilities for the interplay of the various features of moral experience.[7]

With respect to understanding a continuing moral tradition, a cartography of morals can be quite instructively pursued by attending to the ways in which moral notions are used, revised, and expanded throughout the history of the moral community. In the case of Confucian ethics, such notions as *jen* (humanity) and *li* (reason), as Wing-tsit Chan has insightfully shown, have a long history of conceptual evolution.[8] As for the notion of **li* or ritual propriety, we have a valuable discussion by Hu Shih in his classic study of early Chinese philosophy.[9] In light of these studies, a cartography of morals may be regarded as a form of conceptual analysis of moral notions insofar as it attends to their provenance in the moral life[10] and to their subsequent conceptual evolution. And notably, where cultural contexts differ in the emergence and development of moral notions, a cartographer of morals must be prepared to acknowledge conceptual relativity. Saying this, however, may easily give rise to the question of the adequacy of conceptual

[7] See A. S. Cua, *Dimensions of Moral Creativity: Paradigms, Principles, and Ideals* (University Park: Pennsylvania State University Press, 1978), pp. 7–10.

[8] Wing-tsit Chan, "The Evolution of the Confucian Concept Jên," *Philosophy East and West* 4.4 (1955): 295–319; idem, "Chinese and Western Interpretations of *Jen* (Humanity)," *Journal of Chinese Philosophy* 2 (1975): 107–129; and idem, "The Evolution of the Neo-Confucian Concept *Li* as Principle," *Tsing Hua Journal of Chinese Studies*, n.s. 4 (1964): 123–149.

[9] Hu Shih, *Chung-kuo che-hsüeh shih ta-kang*, vol. 1 (Peking: Commercial Press, 1919).

[10] For an incisive discussion of this theme, see Julius Kovesi, *Moral Notions* (London: Routledge and Kegan Paul, 1969).

relativism. This question, however, arises out of a misunderstanding, perhaps owing to the doctrinal orientation of the questioner. For the point at issue has no necessary connection with the claim that all moral notions are relative to cultural contexts in such wise that no comparative inquiry or evaluation is legitimate or even meaningful. Rather, an acknowledgment of conceptual relativity is an acknowledgment of the fact that moral notions are what they are, possessing operative significance as they do, because of the ways they are employed in situations or contexts embedded with a cultural background that has a continuing history. As critical terms for the assessment of human conduct, intentions, and desires, their intelligibility and significance depend on a just appreciation of this background. This does not mean that these notions, because of their background, do not have transcultural significance; rather, their significance depends on some convergent viewpoint of human concerns. In our own times, owing to greater intercultural contact among different peoples, the viewpoint may well emerge, to borrow a term from Gadamer, as a "fusion of horizons."[11] More importantly, there may exist functional equivalents of different moral notions in different cultures.[12] Illuminating comparison, not to say legitimate evaluation, may be possible, in pointing to the viability, success and failure, of the operative moral notions in coping with changing circumstances of human life in different moral communities. Thus two different moral traditions may, on first impression, be incommensurable. But a deeper investigation into the convergence of human interests may convert an issue of a cultural vision into one of humanity as a whole.

If we regard a cartography of morals as an additional task of moral theory, then with respect to a moral tradition, we can

[11] "In a tradition this process of fusion is continually going on, for there old and new continually grow together to make something of living value, without either being explicitly distinguished from the other" (Hans-Georg Gadamer, *Truth and Method* [New York: Seabury Press, 1975], p. 273).

[12] For a suggestion on functional equivalence, see Cua, *Dimensions of Moral Creativity*, pp. 76–78.

say that moral theory is in part an attempt to articulate, in a plausible and coherent way, the viability and integrity of moral tradition. For the western liberal tradition, John Rawls's theory of justice is an outstanding example of such a philosophical endeavor. In his John Dewey Lectures, Rawls remarks, "What justifies a conception of justice is not its being true to an order antecedent to and given to us, but its congruence with our deeper understanding of ourselves and our aspirations, and our realization that, given our history and the traditions embedded in our public life, it is the most reasonable doctrine for us."[13]

Along the same line, one may say more generally that a moral theory that embraces the cartography of morals as a principal task, with respect to a moral tradition, is an attempt to give a plausible explication of a moral tradition with a history. And for a reflective practitioner, it is a task in self-understanding. Much of my own work in Confucian ethics was written in this spirit.

As I have suggested, apart from the cartography of morals, moral theory is more fundamentally concerned with giving a plausible account of "the structure of our moral powers," in Reid's sense, "of those powers of the mind by which we have our moral conceptions, and distinguish right from wrong in human actions." In terms of the epistemological, psychological, and metaphysical import of these moral powers, we may divide the tasks of moral theory into three different but related enterprises. I shall label these enterprises "moral epistemology," "moral psychology," and "moral metaphysics." The first two are familiar philosophical terms. The term "moral metaphysics" has gained currency, I believe, only in connection with Neoconfucian studies.

The cartography of morals, in the diachronic inquiry into the uses of moral notions, can provide an important stage-setting for pursuing these three enterprises of moral theory, par-

[13] John Rawls, "Kantian Constructivism in Moral Theory: The John Dewey Lectures 1980," *Journal of Philosophy* 77 (1980): 519.

ticularly for moral epistemology. The central questions in moral epistemology are, in the standard sense, metaethical. Its interest in moral notions, however—unlike the cartography of morals—pertains more to synchronic than to diachronic inquiry. Equally crucial in explicating moral traditions is its concern with the function of moral discourse as a distinctive forum for explanation and/or justification of claims to moral knowledge.

In the case of explicating the Confucian moral tradition, some of these questions have been instructively discussed by recent philosophical scholars. The work of Ch'en Ta-ch'i, devoted to a comprehensive examination of the principal and secondary aretaic notions (notions of virtue), is especially illuminating.[14] Although it is confined to the *Analects* (*Lun Yü*), we have in Ch'en's work an exemplary discussion of conceptual problems in dealing, say, with the meaning and status of such terms as *jen* (humanity), **li* (ritual propriety), and *i* (rightness), and their interconnections. Nonetheless, much work remains to be done. In approaches to a systematic thinker like Hsün Tzu, for example, the problem of the unity of aretaic notions still awaits an adequate treatment.[15] When we turn to the nature of Confucian discourse as a forum of explanation and/or justification of claims to moral knowledge, there are more difficult questions.

Recently, in pursuing these questions, I have used the *Hsün Tzu* as materials for a plausible explication. Because Confucian discourse, from the epistemological point of view, is highly inexplicit in that it lacks an articulate set of canons for

[14] Ch'en Ta-ch'i, *K'ung Tzu hsüeh-shuo* (Taipei: Cheng-chung, 1976). For a different emphasis, see Cua, *Dimensions of Moral Creativity*, chaps. 3 and 4; idem, "Dimensions of *Li* (Propriety): Reflections on an Aspect of Hsün Tzu's Ethics," *Philosophy East and West* 29.4 (1979): 373–394; and idem, "*Li* and Moral Justification: A Study in the *Li Chi*," *Philosophy East and West* 33.1 (1983): 1–16.

[15] For a preliminary study, see A. S. Cua, "The Problem of Conceptual Unity in Hsün Tzu and Li Kou's Solution," *Bulletin of the Chinese Philosophical Association* 3 (1985); and idem, "Hsün Tzu and the Unity of Virtues," *Journal of Chinese Philosophy*, forthcoming.

the evaluation of explanatory and justificatory claims to moral knowledge, an approach in terms of an informal logic or the theory of argumentation seems appropriate. In *Ethical Argumentation,*[16] I offered a profile of Confucian argumentation that consists of desirable qualities of participants in argumentation, conceived as a cooperative endeavor aiming at a solution to a problem of common interest within a Confucian community. Such qualities as humaneness (*jen-hsin*), impartiality (*kung-hsin*), and receptiveness (*hsüeh-hsin*) constitute, so to speak, the style of performance. More fundamentally, there are standards of competence such as conceptual clarity, consistency, respect for linguistic practices, and accord with the requirements of rational coherence and evidence. In addition, four different phases of discourse—fixing reference of terms, matching linguistic understanding, explanation, and justification—are explicated as distinct but related types of response to difficulties that arise in the course of argumentation. This explication is followed by a discussion of the nature of ethical reasoning and the use of quasi-definitional formulas for meaning explanation and enunciation of particular standards for assessing ethical judgments. The study concludes with an examination of the sources of erroneous ethical beliefs and their exemplification in different types of linguistic confusion.

For my present purpose, the tasks of moral epistemology, in relation to explicating a moral tradition, are in a fundamental sense indispensable for cross-cultural ethical studies. Let me reiterate that the inquiry is not one of theoretical typecasting and assessment of competing metaethical theories. While such a concern may be a prime and legitimate task in recent moral philosophy, the concern is best postponed until we have a plausible explication at hand. Possibly, when such an explication is realized, the issues among metaethical theories may well ap-

[16] See A. S. Cua, *Ethical Argumentation: A Study in Hsün Tzu's Moral Epistemology* (Honolulu: University Press of Hawaii, 1985). For an application to the Confucian appeal to history in argumentation, see idem, "Ethical Uses of the Past in Early Confucianism: The Case of Hsün Tzu," *Philosophy East and West* 35.2 (1985): 133–156.

pear to be irrelevant in the sense that they cannot be intelligibly raised for certain moral traditions. Moreover, in a plausible explication of a moral tradition, new questions may well arise that have relevance for resolving the issues between metaethical theories, thus opening up new avenues for philosophical exploration.

In Reid's terms, we may say that a moral epistemology is an account of those powers which pertain to the reasoned employment of moral notions and reasoned formation of moral judgments. In moral psychology, however, we are more directly concerned with the motivational character of moral knowledge as conceived within a moral tradition. More especially, it is an inquiry into the intrinsic rather than the extrinsic motivational import of moral knowledge. In the Confucian tradition, the main question pertains to the explication of the connection between moral knowledge or learning and action. For pursuing this question, I have made use of Wang Yang-ming's discussion of his doctrine of the unity of moral knowledge and action (*chih-hsing ho-i*) as materials for a reconstruction of a Confucian moral psychology.[17] In Wang, we find an interesting attempt to establish the connection between moral knowledge and action through a display of the mediating roles of intellectual and volitional acts, along with intention, desire, and motive. Thus the problem of intrinsic motivation of moral knowledge, or what I have termed intrinsic actuation, constitutes a key aspect of Wang's Confucian moral theory. Alternatively, we can also regard the problem of intrinsic actuation as a problem of understanding the nature of Confucian commitment and achievement. In explicating Confucian moral psychology, there remain important topics to explore, for example, moral failure, the role of desires and emotions in the formation of moral judgments or beliefs, and the sense of

[17] See A. S. Cua, *The Unity of Knowledge and Action: A Study in Wang Yang-ming's Moral Psychology* (Honolulu: University Press of Hawaii, 1982), particularly chaps. 1–3.

moral shame or honor as distinct from that of guilt as a motivating factor in conduct.

As mentioned earlier, "moral metaphysics" is an unfamiliar philosophical term. As far as I know, it is a technical term coined by Mou Tsung-san to contrast a Confucian concept to that of Kant's metaphysics of morals. While I do not embrace Mou's conception, I find the term valuable in suggesting an important enterprise of moral theory. According to Mou, Kant has only a metaphysics of morals but no moral metaphysics. Kant's conception is no more than a "metaphysical exposition of morals" or "metaphysical deduction of morals." Metaphysics of morals takes morality as a subject matter. It borrows from the fruits of metaphysical inquiry in order to discover and establish the fundamental principles of morality. Moral metaphysics (inclusive of ontology and cosmology), on the contrary, which is characteristic of mainline Confucianism, considers metaphysics as a subject matter and approaches it through the human moral nature.[18] In other words, for Mou, moral practice, in the sense of authentic attainment (*ch'eng*) of sagehood, is the basis for conferring metaphysical significance on all things.

Whether Mou is right about Kant or mainline Confucianism, the distinction between moral metaphysics and metaphysics of morals seems a useful one independent of his thesis. If we regard moral theory as a relatively autonomous discipline, we can appropriate Mou's distinction for delineating an important enterprise. For my present purpose, the question, important as it is, is not whether ontological or cosmological problems can be dealt with by a moral approach—as Mou holds—but rather what sorts of questions within moral theory may be said to involve issues of metaphysical import. Put differently, moral theory may properly be concerned with metaphysical questions within its own domain of inquiry. An ac-

[18] Mou Tsung-san, *Hsin-t'i yü hsing-t'i*, 3 vols. (Taipei: Cheng-chung, 1973), 1:136–140. For an informative exposition of Mou's critique of Chu Hsi, see John H. Berthrong, "The Problem of the Mind: Mou Tsung-san's Critique of Chu Hsi," *Bulletin of the Study of Chinese Religion* (1982): 39–54.

knowledgment of the relevance of metaphysical questions within moral theory does not entail that one must espouse a moral approach to metaphysics or propose moral solutions to metaphysical questions.

I suggest that we adopt Mou's distinction by redefining the notion of moral metaphysics. For Kant, "the metaphysics of morals is meant to investigate the idea and principles of a possible pure will and not the action and conditions of the human volition as such, which are for the most part drawn from psychology."[19] The principles in question are thus a priori rather than empirical. By way of contrast, we can construe moral metaphysics as an inquiry into the metaphysical presuppositions of a moral tradition. More informatively, we have here an inquiry into the underlying conception of a moral tradition in terms of its world view or vision of the relation between the world of human affairs and the natural order. In the Confucian tradition, the notion of *tao*, as expressive of the unity and harmony of man and nature, appears to signify such a conception.[20] This vision, as I understand it, is basically a unifying perspective for responding to changing moral experiences. In Hsün Tzu's words, "The intrinsic nature of *tao* is constant and yet it is capable of exhausting all changes."[21] There remains an important and difficult problem in explicating the concrete significance of *tao*, namely, the problem of mediating the ideal

[19] Immanuel Kant, *Foundations of the Metaphysics of Morals*, trans. Lewis White Beck (Indianapolis: Bobbs-Merrill, 1959), p. 7.

[20] For my own attempt to explicate this Confucian vision, see A. S. Cua, "Confucian Vision and Experience of the World," *Philosophy East and West* 25.3 (1975): 319–333; idem, "Chinese Moral Vision, Responsive Agency, and Factual Beliefs," *Journal of Chinese Philosophy* 7 (1980): 3–26; and idem, *Unity of Knowledge and Action*, chap. 4. For a more general discussion, see idem, "Ideals and Values: A Study in Rescher's Moral Vision," in Robert Almeder, ed., *Praxis and Reason: Studies in the Philosophy of Nicholas Rescher* (Washington, D.C.: University Press of America, 1982).

[21] This is my translation of "Fu tao che, t'i-ch'ang erh chin-pien." Cf. Burton Watson, trans., *Hsün Tzu: Basic Writings* (New York: Columbia University Press, 1963), p. 126.

and the actual worlds.[22] But from the metaphysical point of view, it seems unproblematic to construe *tao* as a protometaphysical vision, as a sort of root metaphor for the development of categorical systems.[23] If this interpretation is deemed plausible, particularly for Neoconfucianism, then moral metaphysics may be properly said to be concerned with metaphysical vision, with that peculiar exercise of our mental powers in comprehending the connection between nature and humanity.

This paper gives a brief sketch, admittedly personal, of a conception of moral theory that excludes normative ethics. An alternative term for moral theory is "philosophy of morals," suggestive of parallel inquiries such as philosophy of law, philosophy of science, philosophy of religion, and the like. Moral theory is a philosophical study of morals. And in explicating moral traditions, in pursuing the tasks of cartography of morals, along with moral epistemology, moral psychology, and moral metaphysics, we hope to arrive at some insights into morality as a human phenomenon, more particularly into the polymorphous expressions of moral powers adaptable to the people of different cultures and history.[24]

GLOSSARY

ch'eng	成
chih-hsing ho-i	知行合一

[22] For a tentative attempt to make sense of this problem in the Confucian moral tradition, see A. S. Cua, "Practical Causation and Confucian Ethics," *Philosophy East and West* 35 (1975): A good discussion of competing Chinese moral visions is given in Yang Hui-chieh, *Tien-jen kuan-hsi lun* (Taipei: Ta-lin, 1981). For Taoism, see A. S. Cua, "Opposites as Complements: Reflections on the Significance of *Tao*," *Philosophy East and West* 31.2 (1981): 123–140.

[23] I believe that the Confucian vision, in the nonsystematic sense, has philosophical import apart from its categorical promise. See A. S. Cua, "Basic Metaphors and Root-Metaphors," *Journal of Mind and Behavior* 3 (1982). For the notion of root metaphor, see S. C. Pepper, *World Hypothesis* (Berkeley: University of California Press, 1948).

[24] I am indebted to Lik Kuen Tong and Eugenio Benitez for helpful suggestions in preparing the final version of this essay for publication.

fu tao che, t'i ch'ang erh chin pien	夫道者, 體常而盡變
hsüeh-hsin	學心
i	義
jen	仁
jen-hsin	仁心
kung-hsin	公心
li	理
**li*	禮
tao	道

WM. THEODORE DE BARY

Neoconfucianism as Traditional and Modern

TRADITION and modernity, though fixtures of the modern mind, are unfortunately not so well fixed in time. In Chinese Communist historiography, the "modern" period is defined as starting in 1840 and ending in 1949, yet in the most recent years of the so-called "contemporary" period, the dominant slogans of the age in China are the Four Modernizations, as if to concede that modernization had not taken place during the "modern" era but belonged to the present and future.

Similarly with tradition: the more we place it in the past the more striking is its persistence into the present, and the more we think of it as continuity the more noteworthy become the discontinuities that attend its revival. This paradox is especially true of Neoconfucianism. By attaching to it the prefix Neo-, we recognize something new in Sung Confucianism; with that newness, however, comes the idea of the constant renewal of the tradition, which may leave one wondering how many "Neo-s" can be added to keep up with its renewal in changing times.

Still, this is a problem of nomenclature, and it can be left aside now. For present purposes "Neoconfucianism" serves well enough, encapsulating as it does both continuity and change, tradition and innovation in the Sung Confucian revival. As regards modernity and modernization, however, we would do well to consider the Chinese case in the perspective of its East Asian neighbors. Japan and Korea have faced similar epochal changes and challenges, and not only in what we consider modern times. Japan in the sixth and seventh centuries, Korea just prior to that time in the Three Kingdoms period and again in the fourteenth century, and Japan again in the sixteenth and seventeenth centuries—to which, of course, comparable developments in Vietnam might be added—all of these reached new thresholds in their development when major borrowings were made from outside, seen for the most part as catching up with the latest developments in the higher culture of China. Coming abreast of the times did not mean, in these cases, westernization.

Marius Jansen has referred to the earlier episode in Japan, as well as the later Meiji development, as a "modernization appropriate to its time,"[1] relativizing the concept in a way that helps us to grasp the essence of the historical change. I would go farther and extend the comparison to East Asia as a whole, including not only Korea (and no doubt Vietnam) but China itself. After all, if the West in the nineteenth century was not catching up with any other civilization but only making the most of its own developmental possibilities, the same could have been true of China in the Sung. For reasons of time, however, I shall not take up here the whole range of factors operating in that historical situation (such as the problems presented by economic growth, technological change, and the rise of a centralized bureaucratic state strikingly modern in many of its features). Rather, I limit myself to those attitudes, ideas, and institutions most closely associated with the rise of Neoconfucianism.

First I must underscore the aforementioned idea of renewal as basic to all of Neoconfucianism. Its conception of the Way as fundamentally life-renewing (*sheng-sheng*) is well known to all students of the subject. Further, this premise underlies the Neoconfucian's optimistic belief that change could be understood as a process of ordered growth, rather than as one of delusion and destruction—a view that in turn underlay their high hopes for the reform of human society on the foundation of enduring human values. In *The Liberal Tradition in China* I

[1] Marius Jansen, "The Japanese Experience of Change," paper for the Conference on the Historical Experience of Change and Patterns of Reconstruction in Selected Axial Age Civilizations, Hebrew University of Jerusalem, December 28, 1983–January 1984.

have remarked on the frequency in the use of the term *hsin* ("new," "renew," "renovation") during the Sung period, common to Confucians of many political stripes, whether in the "New Laws" (*Hsin-fa*) and "New Interpretations" (*Hsin-i*) of the classics by Wang An-shih, or the "New Rituals" (**Hsin-i*) of Ch'eng I, Ssu-ma Kuang, and Cheng Chü-chung, or the "renewing of the people" (*hsin min*) in Ch'eng I and Chu Hsi.[2] Reinterpretation of the classics employed a new criticism by which neoclassicism was made to serve the purposes of reform, and a new, abridged and refocused canon was created as the scriptural basis for a new way of life. Even "restoration of the ancient order" found use as a slogan to sanction institutional innovations, while the "Way of the Sages" was in effect converted into a practical Way to Sagehood for every man to follow.

Does this mean that, with their proclivity to innovation and renovation, Sung Neoconfucians thought of themselves as "moderns"? In the strictest sense, it does not. Their strong regard for precedent and past authority still revealed itself in the need they felt to claim such precedents on behalf of reform. More importantly, the changes they sought, instead of being seen as progressive steps leading to an ever-improving future, were meant simply to serve present needs. Nor was there the millenarian faith, found later in revolutionary China, which called for present sacrifices to be made on the altar of revolution in order to win a glorious future.

Nevertheless, it would be erroneous to suppose, as was commonly done earlier in this century, that precedent-citing Confucians were mere conservatives or, worse, slaves to the past. Rather, the latter consciously repudiated their immediate past in the form of antecedent dynasties—the politics, institutions, scholarship, and thought of the Han and T'ang—in favor of new constructions of their own devising, sanctioned by

[2] See Wm. Theodore de Bary, *The Liberal Tradition in China* (Hong Kong and New York: Chinese University of Hong Kong Press, 1983), pp. 11–13. The term "new rituals or ceremonials" appears in the *Cheng-ho wu-li hsin-i*, compiled by Cheng Chü-chung (1059–1123) for Emperor Hui-tsung.

reaching over the heads of the great Han and T'ang rulers and scholars to invoke the more remote sages of high antiquity. What indeed is more conservative or reactionary about this than Abraham Lincoln's claiming the sanction of an ancient God on the freeing of the slaves?

It is nonetheless true that the great reform of the northern Sung period had faltered, and factional strife had tarnished the high ideals of their protagonists, by the time of the preeminent Neoconfucian, Chu Hsi (1130–1200). Lest disappointment breed despair, Chu redirected human energies toward more manageable goals, including what for him was the entirely practical aim of becoming a modern sage or worthy. Thus the new philosophy stressed self-reform and self-cultivation more than visionary social programs, attaching particular importance to individual self-development on the intellectual, moral, and spiritual planes.

The future did not loom large in Chu Hsi's mind. His more typical outlook is suggested by the title of his famous anthology of Sung Neoconfucian writings, *Reflections of Things at Hand* (or on what is near at hand: *Chin-ssu lu*).[3] "Near at hand" in this case was the possibility of becoming a sage or worthy if one set one's mind to it, and ready at hand as a guide to the practice of self-cultivation for sagehood were the writings of modern Confucians, which would help to bridge the gap between present and past. Note, however, that Chu started from the present, not antiquity. This was also true of the role models he put before students in his compilations of the biographies of leading Sung scholars and statesmen, the *I-lo yüan-yüan lu* (Fountainheads of the Ch'eng Brothers' School) and the *Chu Tzu ming-ch'en yen-hsing lu* (Anecdotes of Eminent Statesmen). Here, to inspire his own efforts, the student could find modern exemplars of Confucian wisdom and virtue whose achievements were won in circumstances much like one's own and in the bright light of the present day, not in some remote

[3] See Wing-tsit Chan, trans., *Reflections on Things at Hand* (New York: Columbia University Press, 1967).

past, glorious and golden perhaps, but refulgent only with the afterglow of the setting sun.

No less was this true of Chu Hsi's many public-service projects as a local administrator: almost invariably he would cite some close precedent, seeking to represent perennial values in the form of recent personages of local repute, whose personal example confirmed the practicability of these values in the contemporary world: the Lu family, for instance, contemporaries of the Ch'eng brothers, in respect to local community organization,[4] or Ch'en Hsiang (1017–1080) in respect to public instruction on the local level.[5] This attitude is also found in Chu Hsi's effort to devise a family ritual that the common man could observe in the present, something adapted from the classic texts but greatly simplified so as to be within the means of poor scholars like himself.[6] Here there is a strong consciousness of the difference between past and present. One must live in the present, but with an eye to whatever inspiration one can derive from the classics or whatever lessons one can learn from past experience.

(Parenthetically, it is an interesting commentary on the uses of the past to see how different Chu Hsi's handling of this question is from many of his later followers. For instance, his accounts of distinguished statesmen referred to their failings as well as to their successes and strong points, for Chu believed one had to learn from both. In later editions such failings often were excised, so that these accounts became much more idealized and platitudinous, much less realistic and practical.[7] This gives a clue of how a tradition, idealistic enough to start with,

[4] See his modification of the Lu Family Community Compact in *Hui-an hsien-sheng Chu Wen-kung wen-chi* (Kyoto: Chūbun shuppansha, 1977), 74.25a–32a: "Tseng-sun Lu-shih hsiang-yüeh."

[5] See the "Chieh-shih Ku-ling hsien-sheng ch'üan-yu wen," ibid., 100.5a (p. 7086).

[6] See Ueyama Shumpei, "Shushi no *Karei* to *Girei keiden tsūkai*," *Tōhō gakuhō* 54 (1982): 173–256, esp. 222, 235.

[7] Yves Hervouet, *A Sung Bibliography* (Hong Kong: Chinese University Press, 1978), p. 126, "Chu Tzu ming-ch'en yen-hsing lu."

got dressed up in such high moral style that it could only be worn with great discomfort—or perhaps with false pretensions—by later generations.)

More significant than these edifying anthologies and practical guides (the compiling of which Chu left largely to collaborators), were Chu's commentaries on and prefaces to key classic texts, especially the *Great Learning (Ta-hsüeh)*, to which he devoted much labor and thought in his last years. In the latter he enunciated the Three Guiding Principles (*San kang ling*), which in modern times have been given much less attention than the Three Bonds (*San-kang*) between parent and child, ruler and minister, and husband and wife, though the latter had no basis in the classics and were rarely mentioned by Chu in comparison to his great stress on the Three Guiding Principles.

The first of these principles is to "clarify or manifest bright virtue," referring to the moral nature in all men, which is inherently clear and luminous but must be cleansed of obscurations if it is to be made fully manifest. The potential is innate but must be actively developed, so the process is one of bringing out from within something that has its own life and luminosity, rather than imposing or imprinting on it something from without. This Chu calls the "learning of the great man" (*ta-jen*), which has the ordinary meaning of "adult" but here suggests the fullness of self-development and the grandeur of the moral nature brought to its perfection.

The second guiding principle is to "renew the people" (*hsin-min*), that is, to assist others to manifest their moral natures through self-cultivation. Here Chu follows Ch'eng I in substituting the word *hsin* ("renew") for *ch'in* ("to love, to befriend" the people). Chu specifically refers to this as "reforming the old," emphasizing active reform and renovation instead of expressing simple goodwill and generous sentiments. Politically the implication is that the ruler's self-cultivation necessarily involves him in helping the people to renew themselves through education.

Third among the guiding principles is "resting or abiding in the highest good," which means that by clarifying bright virtue (manifesting the moral nature) and renewing the people, one should reach the point of ultimate goodness and stay there. "Resting in the highest good," Chu explains, means both meeting the moral requirements of each situation and affair and fulfilling one's capability for moral action. At this point one can rest content. Peace of mind has been achieved, not by transcending the moral sphere, but by meeting one's responsibility and satisfying one's conscience. One is at ease doing what comes naturally to the moral man, not compulsively engaged in an unending struggle to change one's environment.

If I have discounted earlier any idea that Chu Hsi had millenarian expectations or looked to the future to redeem the present, it was partly in view of these three guiding principles. The impulse to renew and reform is there, but it is enough to achieve what is possible in one's own life situation and within one's limited capabilities. "To be humane is to accept being human" (*jen-che an jen*), as Confucius said in *Analects* 4.2. The fact, however, that Chu Hsi underscores these three principles at the outset of his commentary has impressed on many of his later followers the need for active renewal and reform, first out of respect for oneself and then out of concern for others.[8]

Another major point made by Chu Hsi, this time in his preface to the *Great Learning*, is the need for universal public schooling.[9] In the West such proposals are of relatively recent, nineteenth- or twentieth-century origin; in China they had already appeared before Chu Hsi's time and were a main issue among Sung reformers. Although the Sung (and other dynasties) failed to accomplish this goal (the same is no less true of many modern states, including the People's Republic), the fact that China had already matured to this point in the Sung Dynasty is an indication of the extent to which it already faced

[8] Chu Hsi, *Ta-hsüeh chang-chü*, Chung-kuo tzu-hsüeh ming-chu chi-ch'eng ed. (Taipei, 1979), Ta-hsüeh Ia-b (pp. 7–8).

[9] *Ta-hsüeh chang-chü*, preface, 1b, 2a (pp. 2–3).

problems of modern societies (and, in terms of numbers, on a modern scale).

I have discussed Chu Hsi's proposal, and his contributions to its achievement, at some length in a recent paper entitled "Chu Hsi's Aims as an Educator."[10] Here I wish simply to note the significance of Chu's heavy engagement with this issue. Because his main teachings, centering on the *Great Learning*, have stressed self-cultivation as the starting point of all political and social reform, there has been a tendency in much modern writing on Chu Hsi to charge him with oversimplifying social and institutional problems and reducing them essentially to moral questions for the individual.[11] This charge itself is an oversimplification of Chu's position. In the case at issue he was quite emphatic about the need, not just for self-cultivation, but for institutionalized education in the form of a school system. Indeed, in the only arena in which Chu had an opportunity to effectuate his own ideas he gave detailed attention to many practical problems in concrete form—to the organization of community compacts, to the local granary system, to agricultural methods, to military affairs and local security, to local academies and religious organizations, social customs and rituals, legal procedures, and so on. Later writers, preoccupied with problems of the court and central government, have tended to overlook Chu's practical achievements on the local level and to misjudge the relative weight he gave to ethical precept and philosophical principle as compared to practical solutions for concrete problems.[12]

Still, it is not a misconception to see Chu Hsi's whole sys-

[10] Wm. Theodore de Bary, "Chu Hsi's Aims as an Educator," paper prepared for the ACLS–SSRC Conference on Neo-Confucian Education, August 30–September 4, 1984.

[11] Ray Huang, *1587—a Year of No Significance: The Ming dynasty in Decline* (New Haven: Yale University Press, 1981). Huang often speaks of Neoconfucianism in these terms, and not without justice in some cases; but the more practical side of Neoconfucian thought receives scant attention.

[12] For the most complete overview of this aspect of Chu's thought, see Kusumoto Masatsugu, *Chūgoku tetsugaku kenkyū* (Tokyo: Bungensha, 1975), pp. 257–392.

tem and method as focusing on the self. To him, the way one viewed the self and the way one understood human nature were the keys to all other endeavors. The human potentiality, deriving from the goodness of man's heaven-bestowed nature, had to be the true measure of all institutions, laws, and practices. The way one developed one's potentiality and perfected one's nature was, if not all-important, at least a sine qua non of all other human enterprises. Accordingly, in a multitude of concrete ways, Chu devoted himself to defining that process and to providing the specific means by which education and self-cultivation could be accomplished, either in schools or outside them.

In one of his last essays, my late colleague Lionel Trilling wrote about a problem that had been much on the mind of Chu Hsi in the twelfth century.[13] From Trilling's conclusion I draw the following excerpts:

> If we consider the roadblocks in the path of a reestablishment of traditional humanistic education, surely none is so effectually obstructing as the tendency of our culture to regard the mere energy of impulse as being in every mental and moral way equivalent and even superior to defined intention. We may remark, as exemplary of this tendency, the fate of an idea that once was salient in Western culture: the idea of "making a life," by which was meant conceiving human existence, one's own or another's, as if it were a work of art upon which one might pass judgment, assessing it by established criteria. . . .
>
> This desire to fashion, to shape, a self and a life has all but gone from a contemporary culture whose emphasis, paradoxically enough, is so much on self. . . . Such limitation, once acceptable, now goes against the cultural grain—it is almost as if the fluidity of the contemporary world demands an analogous limitlessness in our personal perspective. Any doctrine, that of the family, religion, the school, that does

[13] Lionel Trilling, "The Uncertain Future of Humanistic Education," *American Scholar* (Winter 1974–1975): 52–67.

> not sustain this increasingly felt need for a multiplicity of options and instead offers an ideal of a shaped self, a formed life, has the sign on it of a retrograde and depriving authority, which, it is felt, must be resisted.
>
> For anyone concerned with contemporary education at whatever level, the assimilation that contemporary culture has made between social idealism, even political liberalism, and personal fluidity—a self without the old confinements—is as momentous as it is recalcitrant to correction. Among the factors in the contemporary world which militate against the formulation of an educational ideal related to the humanistic traditions of the past, this seems to me to be the most decisive.[14]

It was precisely to deal with this question in his own time that Chu Hsi developed his philosophy of human nature and "Learning for one's own sake." Modern scholars have tended to view that philosophy as primarily a system of metaphysics, admiring Chu for his impressive synthesis of Confucian, Buddhist, and Taoist concepts—certainly an achievement, which even Chu's contemporaries recognized. But for Chu the problem was more particularly how to define the self and do it in such a way as not to enclose or entrap it but to free it through self-mastery. Already this problem of the self had been put high on the agenda for Sung thinkers by the influence of Chan (Zen) Buddhism. Chan, however, had resisted all attempts to define the self in rational or conceptual terms, bent as it was on asserting an unabridged, because unstated, self-determination—an idea not unfamiliar to the modern West. Chu Hsi, for his part, saw this as an illusory freedom. Unless defined principles could be put forward and established on a rational basis that commanded public assent, there would be no way to protect men from abuse and exploitation by power seekers and influence peddlers—under cover of a specious pragmatism or "adaptability" (Buddhist *fang pien*, Taoist *tzu-jan*) or utilitar-

[14] Ibid., pp. 66–67.

ianism (*kung-li*).[15] Self-respect and moral voluntarism, though indefinable as to their marvelous workings in the human heart, could not simply be left to the promptings of individual intuition. To "clarify" or "manifest the moral nature" did indeed involve a subtle process of, as Chu Hsi put it, "getting it oneself" (finding the Way within), but an indispensable correlate of that self-discovery was acceptance of the responsibility for "renewing the people," which could only be done through a public philosophy, or, in Trilling's terms, through "a shaped self," a "formed life," a work of art on which one might pass judgment, assessing it by established criteria.

It has not been my aim to discuss here Chu Hsi's concept of the self as such, or the public philosophy that served as its matrix. These I have sketched out in *The Liberal Tradition in China* and dealt with in some detail in other recent writings.[16] Neither do I mean to imply that Chu's answers to these questions could, in themselves, provide a solution to Trilling's problem in the mid-1970s. I do, however, wish to suggest that if the problem of the self and its divorce from any public philosophy is to be seen as the great modern dilemma, Chu's attempt at reconciliation of the two might merit consideration as almost "postmodern."

In mainland China today there is something that passes for a public philosophy, but the horrors of the Cultural Revolution showed the consequences of sacrificing individual human dignity to any political movement or ideology, however egalitarian its professions or millenarian its promises. Chu Hsi was

[15] See Hoyt Cleveland Tillman, *Utilitarian Confucianism: Ch'en Liang's Challenge to Chu Hsi* (Cambridge, Mass.: Harvard University Press, 1982), esp. chaps. 4, 5.

[16] Wm. Theodore de Bary, *Neo-Confucian Orthodoxy and the Learning of the Mind-and-Heart* (New York: Columbia University Press, 1982), part 2; Hok-lam Chan and W. T. de Bary, eds., *Yuan Thought: Chinese Religion and Thought Under the Mongols* (New York: Columbia University Press, 1982), introduction; and Wm. Theodore de Bary, "Neo-Confucian Individualism and Holism," in Donald Munro, ed., *Individualism and Holism: The Confucian and Taoist Philosophical Perspectives* (Ann Arbor: University of Michigan Press, 1985).

well aware of this danger, as he showed in his rejection of a specious humanitarianism in the form of either a shallow utilitarianism or a facile universalism.

If Chu Hsi were involved in our considerations of "interpreting across boundaries," he might make the same comments as he did on Buddhism and Taoism. He did not deny that these were lofty doctrines. The trouble was that they were too lofty (*t'ai kao*). I think he would have understood and appreciated what it meant to "interpret across boundaries"—after all, there were few of his central concepts that did not reflect his implicit, very fruitful dialogue with Buddhism and Taoism. But I think in our present situation he would probably not have talked about "crossing boundaries." On the contrary, he would say that what we need to do is to set boundaries, to forego certain opportunities and possibilities, to choose voluntarily to limit ourselves in such ways as are necessary to cope with the urgent social and environmental problems of our time.

The real problem today is not parochialism. It is the lack of any parochialism, the lack of any loyalty or sense of responsibility to a particular community, which has created the severe problems of disassociation in our time. What we need is not new worlds to conquer, star wars, and all that, but a *new parochialism of the earth*, which includes within its province Confucius, Chu Hsi, the Buddha, Gandhi, Śaṅkara, al-Ghazālī, and so forth. And we shall not get this until we have decided, like Chu Hsi, what we will not do, what choices we will voluntarily forego, what limitations we will accept out of concern for the welfare of our earth, our fellow man, and the generations to come, who will suffer for our sins of earth pollution, resource exhaustion, genetic disorders, and so on.

Of course it is always easy, by an appeal to social conscience or global consciousness, to stir up the kind of frenetic activity that short-circuits reflective thought and turns direct action into anti-intellectualism. This is why, if we bring contemporary needs and problems to the fore, we must like Chu Hsi have some perennial philosophy to guide and inform that action.

The Confucians did not think of themselves as pilgrims, but they did speak about following the Way—the Way of being truly human. In Chu Hsi's case there is a sense in which it could be thought of as "coming from anywhere" (*wu-chi*, indeterminate) but not as just going anywhere. It was coming from anyone's here and now, but always going somewhere, in a definite direction (*t'ai-chi*). As Chu Hsi's colleague Chang Shih put it: Zen is like floating on the water, drifting wherever the current takes you; Confucianism is like having a rudder in the boat to guide it in a certain direction.

Again, lest I and Chu Hsi be misunderstood, going in a definite direction did not mean having a completely defined goal or model before one. The Great Ultimate, like the North Star, could give one bearings by which to set a course, but as one traveled toward one's destination (in other words, lived out one's life and grew to genuine maturity), one's vision of it was bound to change, to open out, to expand with one's enlarged capabilities (part of the meaning of *wu-chi*, "indeterminate," "without limits"). But without a sense of direction, there is no way one could hope to become truly human.

Let me close now with one last quotation from the contemporary American poet and critic, Wendell Berry. I cite this passage from his book *Standing by Words* (the title of which is Ezra Pound's rendering of the Confucian virtue *hsin*, "being true to one's word," or trustworthiness). My reason for doing so is not Berry's concern for the integrity of language, a concern he shares with the Neoconfucians (and of course Confucius), but what he has to say about the theme of this essay: a "modernity" or "contemporaneity" appropriate to our times.

> Contemporaneity, in the sense of being "up with the times," is of no value. Wakefulness to experience—as well as to instruction and example—is another matter. But what we call the modern world is not necessarily, and not often, the real world, and there is no virtue in being up-to-date in it. It is a

> false world, based upon economies and values and desires that are fantastical—a world in which millions of people have lost any idea of the materials, the disciplines, the restraints, and the work necessary to support human life, and have thus become dangerous to their own lives and to the possibility of life. The job now is to get back to that perennial and substantial world in which we really do live, in which the foundations of our life will be visible to us, and in which we can accept our responsibilities again within the conditions of necessity and mystery. In that world all wakeful and responsible people, dead, living, and unborn, are contemporaries. And that is the only contemporaneity worth having.
>
> . . . There is much that we need that we cannot get from our contemporaries—even assuming that the work we have from them is the best that is possible: they cannot give us the sense of the longevity of human experience, the sense of the practicable, of *proven* possibility, that we get from older writing. Our past is not merely something to depart from; it is to commune with, to speak with: "Day unto day uttereth speech, and night unto night showeth knowledge." Remove this sense of continuity, and we are left with the thoughtless present tense of machines. If we fail to see that we live in the same world that Homer lived in, then we not only misunderstand Homer; we misunderstand ourselves. The past is our definition. We may strive, with good reason, to escape it, or to escape what is bad in it, but we will escape it only by adding something better to it.[17]

I think there is nothing in those lines that Chu Hsi did not say, in his own twelfth-century Chinese way, to his contemporaries. Wendell Berry may not realize it yet, but Chu Hsi's name should be added to those of Homer, Dante, Milton, and Confucius, whose work gives us what he calls "the sense of the longevity of human experience, the sense of the practicable, of

[17] Wendell Berry, *Standing by Words* (San Francisco: North Point Press, 1983), pp. 13–14.

proven possibility, that we get from older writing." He is part of our past now, which we may try "to escape, . . . or to escape what is bad in it, . . . only by adding something better to it."

GLOSSARY

Cheng Chü-chung	鄭居中
Cheng-ho wu-li hsin-i	政和五禮新儀
Ch'en Hsiang	陳襄
Chieh-shih Ku-ling hsien-sheng ch'üan-yü wen	揭示古靈先生勸諭文
ch'in	親
Chin-ssu lu	近思錄
Chu Hsi	朱熹
Chu Tzu ming-ch'en yen-hsing lu	朱子名臣言行錄
fang pien	方便
hsin	新
Hsin-fa	新法
Hsin-i	新義
**Hsin-i*	新儀
hsin min	新民
Hui-tsung	徽宗
I-lo yüan-yüan lu	伊洛淵源錄
jen-che an jen	仁者安仁
kung-li	功利
San kang	三綱
San kang ling	三綱領
sheng-sheng	生生
Ta-hsüeh	大學
Ta-hsüeh chang-chü	大學章句
t'ai-chi	太極

t'ai kao	太高
ta-jen	大人
Tseng-sun Lü-shih hsiang-yüeh	增損呂氏鄉約
tzu-jan	自然
wu-chi	無極

CONTRIBUTORS

Roger T. Ames is a professor in the Department of Philosophy, University of Hawaii at Manoa, Honolulu, Hawaii.

Wm. Theodore de Bary is a professor in the Department of East Asian Languages and Literature, Columbia University, New York City.

Wing-tsit Chan is professor emeritus of Chinese culture and philosophy, Dartmouth College, Hanover, New Hampshire.

Antonio S. Cua is a professor in the Department of Philosophy, Catholic University of America, Washington, D.C.

Eliot Deutsch is a professor in the Department of Philosophy, University of Hawaii at Manoa, Honolulu, Hawaii.

Charles Hartshorne is professor emeritus, Department of Philosophy, University of Texas, Austin.

Daya Krishna is professor emeritus, Department of Philosophy, University of Rajasthan, Jaipur, Rajasthan, India.

Gerald James Larson is a professor in the Department of Religious Studies, University of California, Santa Barbara.

Sengaku Mayeda is a professor in the Department of Indian Philosophy, Tokyo University.

Hajime Nakamura is professor emeritus, Department of Indian Philosophy, Tokyo University and Director, The Eastern Institute, Tokyo.

Raimundo Panikkar is professor emeritus, Department of Religious Studies, University of California, Santa Barbara.

Karl H. Potter is a professor in the Department of Philosophy, University of Washington, Seattle.

Henry Rosemont, Jr. is a professor in the Department of Philosophy, St. Mary's College, Maryland.

Ben-Ami Scharfstein is a professor in the Department of Philosophy, Tel Aviv University, Israel.

Ninian Smart is a professor in the Department of Religious Studies, University of California, Santa Barbara.

Frits Staal is a professor in the Department of South and Southeast Asian Studies, University of California, Berkeley.

Frederick J. Streng is a professor in the Department of Religious Studies, Southern Methodist University, Dallas, Texas.

INDEX

abortion, 65
Advaita Vedanta, 101, 184, 215. *See also* Vedanta
aesthetics: study of, 57
After Virtue, 63
Amane Nishi, 138, 147
Analects, 269-271
ānvīkṣikī ("philosophy"), 139
apauruṣeya ("authorless"; "primordial language"), 132
Archaeology of Knowledge, The, 13-14
Aristotle, 63, 111
Ātman, 196-199

Bergson, Henri, 100, 110
Berry, Wendell, 306-307
bodhisattva, 159-160, 163
Book of Rites, 225-229
Borges, José Luis, 3-4
boundaries: interpreting across, 19-20, 23, 33, 98, 131, 305; and language, 9, 12, 15, 22
Bradley, F. H., 103-105, 109
Bṛhadāraṇyaka Upaniṣad, 119, 191, 210, 214, 221
Bruce, J. P., 237
Buddha, 161
Buitenen, J.A.B. van, 168-169
Burnet, John, 148

caste, 189-191
causation, 103
Chan, Wing-tsit, 5-6
Chāndogya Upaniṣad, 215-217, 219, 221, 225
Ch'en Ta-ch'i, 275, 287
Ch'eng I, 250, 252, 255, 259, 299; on *ching*, 243; on *jen*, 244
Ch'eng brothers, 252, 255
ch'i ("strong moving power"), 240-241
chih ("to realize"), 267-278
ching ("reverence"), 242-243
Chin-ssu lu, 250-251, 297
Chomsky, Noam, 40n, 47-48, 52
Chou Tun-i, 254-255
Chu Hsi, 245-250, 252-253, 255-258, 297-308; chief characteristics of his philosophy, 251, 259; on *ching*, 243; in comparative philosophy, 230, 234-238, 254, 260; concept of God, 236-237; on education, 301-303; effect on tradition, 232-233; on *jen*, 244; religious life, 239-240
Ch'un-ch'iu fan-lu, 268-269
Chung-yung, 269. See also *Doctrine of the Mean*
Chu Tza nien-p'u, 235
comparative philosophy, 6, 11, 16, 18, 116, 129; and academic divisions, 10; analysis of the term, 118-120; antecedents, 6,117; comparative studies, 71-73; definition of, 121-123; examples of, 124, 126; possibility of, 134-135; and relativism, 38; suggestions for research, 33-35, 96-97; tasks of, 131-132
conceptual schemes, 21-23, 33, 62; among users of American English, 31-32; among users of Sanskrit, 26, 30, 32; Confucian, 62; Western, 73
conceptual structures, 78, 80-81
Confucianism: and ethics, 61, 64
Confucius, 266, 271-274, 276